JUSTICE FOR HERE AND NOW

This book conveys the breadth and interconnectedness of questions of justice – a rarity in contemporary moral and political philosophy. James P. Sterba argues that a minimal notion of rationality requires morality, and that a minimal libertarian morality requires the welfare and equal opportunity endorsed by welfare liberals and the equality endorsed by socialists, as well as a full feminist agenda. Feminist justice, racial justice, homosexual justice, and multicultural justice are also shown to be mutually supporting. The author further shows the compatibility between anthropocentric and biocentric environmental ethics, as between just war and pacifist theories. Finally, he spells out when normal politics, legal protest, civil disobedience, revolutionary action, and criminal disobedience are morally permitted by justice for here and now.

This highly original and potentially controversial book is ideal for courses in moral and political philosophy, applied ethics, women's studies, environmental studies, and peace studies.

James P. Sterba is Professor of Philosophy at the University of Notre Dame. In addition to *Justice for Here and Now*, he has published 15 books.

Cambridge Studies in Philosophy and Public Policy

GENERAL EDITOR: Douglas MacLean, *University of Maryland, Baltimore County*

Other books in series

Justice for
Here and Now

JAMES P. STERBA

CAMBRIDGE
UNIVERSITY PRESS

PUBLISHED BY THE PRESS SYNDICATE OF THE UNIVERSITY OF CAMBRIDGE
The Pitt Building, Trumpington Street, Cambridge CB2 1RP, United Kingdom

CAMBRIDGE UNIVERSITY PRESS
The Edinburgh Building, Cambridge CB2 2RU, UK   http://www.cup.cam.ac.uk
40 West 20th Street, New York, NY 10011-4211, USA   http://www.cup.org
10 Stamford Road, Oakleigh, Melbourne 3166, Australia

© James P. Sterba 1998

First published 1998

Printed in the United States of America

Typeset in Palatino 10/12 pt, in Quark XPress™ [RF]

A catalog record for this book is available from the British Library

Library of Congress Cataloging in Publication data
Sterba, James P.
Justice for here and now / James P. Sterba.
p.   cm. – (Cambridge studies in philosophy and public policy)
Includes index.
ISBN 0-521-62188-7 (hardcover). – ISBN 0-521-62739-7 (pbk.)
1. Justice (Philosophy)   2. Applied ethics.   3. Social ethics.
I. Title.   II. Series.
B105.J87S74   1998
172'.2 – DC21   97-37326
CIP

To Janet Kourany, this philosopher's philosopher,
who helped create what it means and what it meant

Contents

Contents

Acknowledgments

This is my fourth book on justice. Earlier books, *The Demands of Justice* (1980), *How to Make People Just* (1988), and *Contemporary Social and Political Philosophy* (1995) all served as important stepping stones and building blocks for *Justice for Here and Now*. Yet while books cannot be thanked for making a work possible, there are many people whose help at various stages in writing the chapters of this book I am most happy to acknowledge. In particular, I would like to thank William Aiken, Timo Airaksinen, Robin Attfield, Robert Audi, Kurt Baier, Seyla Benhabib, Deryck Beyleveld, Laurence Bove, Joseph Boyle, Dan Brock, Bruce Brower, Duane Cady, Baird Callicott, Sheldon Cohen, John Cooper, Peter Dalton, Kendall D'Andrade, Stephen Darwall, Richard DeGeorge, Michael DePaul, Thomas Donaldson, Wendy Donner, Gerald Doppelt, Jay Drydyk, David Duquette, Elaine Englehardt, Jan Ester, James Fishkin, Barry Gan, Bernard Gert, Alan Gewirth, Teresa Ghilarducci, Robert Goodland, Haim Gordon, Carol Gould, Eugene Hargrove, Sue Headlee, Virginia Held, Alan Holland, Robert Holmes, John Hospers, Alison Jaggar, Zhong Jiadong, Robert Johansen, Alasdair MacIntyre, Eric Mack, Andrew McLaughlin, Maria Maimonova, Harlon Miller, Phillip Montague, Ronald Moore, Janice Moulton, Jan Narveson, Bryan Norton, Sharon O'Brien, David O'Connor, Ernest Partridge, Rodney Peffer, Robert Phillips, Alvin Plantinga, Val Plumwood, Phillip Quinn, Douglas Rasmussen, Tom Regan, Jeffrey Reiman, Eric Reitan, Bernard Rollin, Mary Roso, Juris Rozenvalds, Ronald Santoni, Kenneth Sayre, George Schedler, Jerome Schneewind, Sally Scholz, Jonathan Schonsheck, Ofelia Schutte, Matthew Silliman, Paula Smithka, David Solomon, Brian Steverson, Paul Taylor, Rosemarie Tong, Aviezer Tucker, John Wagner, Karen Warren, Paul Weithman, Carl Wellman, Peter Wenz, Richard Werner, Laura Westra, and Xia-Long Xin for their helpful comments. I would also like to thank the editors of *Ethics*, *Social Theory and Practice*, the *Journal of Social Philosophy*, Rowman and Littlefield, and Wadsworth Publish-

Acknowledgments

ing Company for permission to draw on previously published work, and the Institute for Scholarship in the Liberal Arts at the University of Notre Dame for financial support. At Cambridge University Press, Terence Moore, Executive Humanities Editor, and Douglas MacLean, Series Editor, contributed in so many ways to make this book possible, and Janis Bolster and Barbara Folsom did an excellent job getting the book in final form.

Chapter 1

A Peacemaking Way of Doing Philosophy

Too often doing philosophy is modeled after fighting a battle or making war.[1] Arguments are attacked, shot down (like a plane) or sunk (like a ship). Theses are defended, defeated, or demolished (like the walls of a city). Ideas (like people) are killed and destroyed.[2] There are clearly problems with doing philosophy in this way. There is unfairness inherent in the practice, along with its tendency to undercut the possibility of reaching truly justified views, and, as I shall argue, there is a peacemaking alternative. Still the warmaking practice persists.

Just consider what not infrequently takes place at philosophy meetings. A young philosopher is making his first presentation.[3] His paper is in philosophy of law and his argument relies on a range of judicial decisions. His commentator's objections, which are based on a number of different judicial decisions, are handed to him just before his presentation. Not knowing the particulars of the judicial decisions to which his commentator refers, he is unable to offer a defense of his view. Usually, of course, things are not quite this desperate. Comments do tend to come in late, not infrequently just before the session at which they are to be presented, but speakers do manage some kind of a response, although not a very reflective one. The lateness of the comments, however, does put speakers at a disadvantage with respect to their commentators, and this frequently seems to be an intended result as well. Sometimes commentators do not seem to want to hear the best responses to their critical comments. Rather, what they seem to want to do is win a philosophical battle, triumph in a philosophical war, even at the expense of basic fairness to their philosophical opponents.

Consider some of the other tactics employed by philosophers in pursuit of victory at philosophy meetings. An acquaintance of mine was invited to make a forty-five-minute presentation at a meeting. In working out her thoughts, she discovered that her view could best be defended if her presentation exceeded the time limit by about fifteen minutes, which she decided to do. Her commentator, too, decided that the weaknesses in her view could best be exposed if he exceeded the time limit for commentators. And then my acquaintance chose to respond at length to all of her commentator's criticisms. Thus, in their attempt to triumph one over the other, both deprived their audience of virtually any opportunity to participate in the philosophical debate between them.

Moreover, at philosophy meetings, it is not unheard of for speakers, when they are provided with comments on their papers in advance, to change their papers before presenting them so as to render the comments irrelevant. In one case I witnessed, the speaker simply removed a crucial "not" from his paper and thereby avoided most of his commentator's criticisms. Some commentators also like to produce a sketch of their comments in advance, get their speakers' reactions if they can, and then revise their comments accordingly. Again, the goal here seems to be victory, even at the expense of basic fairness to their philosophical opponents.

Once, a friend of mine received in advance comments on a paper that she was to present at a colloquium. The comments were apparently devastating and actually quite humorous; they, in effect, invited her to laugh at her own philosophical execution. Her commentator, who happened to be a fairly well-known philosopher, went on to inform her magnanimously that to maximize audience participation he would have nothing further to say at the colloquium after presenting his comments. Yet on the day of the colloquium, when my friend was able to show that her commentator's criticism rested on fairly obvious misreadings of her work and the work of others, her commentator's hand shot up, demanding immediate recognition. Without acknowledging the cogency of her replies, he had a different objection to raise, which he was then able to make the focus of the discussion. What was particularly disappointing for my friend was that after the colloquium had ended, her commentator was no longer interested in discussing their differences any further. What this shows is how philosophical battles and wars are public affairs. They are enacted for public recognition. There is little behind-the-scenes discussion among the participants to reach agreement. In fact, the participants in philosophical battles and wars may only speak to each other in public confrontations.

I was once asked by a well-known philosopher why I talked to libertarians.[4] At the time, I was dumbstruck by the question, but now I believe that it reflects the dominant way that philosophy is being done these days, and maybe even the dominant way that philosophy has always been done. It sees philosophers as belonging to different groups within which there can be a significant degree of sympathetic understanding but between which there can be only hostile relations, a virtual state of war. If you believe this is the case, then there really is a question about whether you should talk to your philosophical enemies. You may perchance say something that indicates certain problems with your own philosophical view, which may in turn be used against you, and, as a result, you may lose an important philosophical battle and your reputation may decline accordingly.

This warmaking model of doing philosophy also differs from the adversary model of doing philosophy set forth by Janice Moulton.[5] According to Moulton's adversary model: "A position ought to be defended from, and subjected to, the criticism of the strongest opposition."[6] According to this model, the best way for you to present work in philosophy is to address it to your strongest opponents, mustering all the evidence you can to support it. Now this warmaking model for doing philosophy shares with Moulton's adversary model a commitment to fighting with one's opponents; it differs from Moulton's model, however, in that it is not particularly concerned that one face one's strongest opponents. According to this warmaking model, the ultimate goal is to win philosophical battles and triumph in philosophical wars. To achieve this goal, weak opponents will do just as well as strong ones; in fact, weak opponents may even be preferred. Of course, if a strong opponent is on the scene, you must do battle with that opponent. But this warmaking model, unlike Moulton's adversary model, does not require you to seek out and do battle with your strongest opponents. For this warmaking model, what is important is not so much whom you fight, but that you not be defeated.

Moreover, if we take our adversary model of doing philosophy from the law, we can see that it is similar in this regard to this warmaking model of doing philosophy. This is because in the law neither the defense nor the prosecution is required to face its strongest opponent; all that is required is that they both fight the case out as permitted by the law. So if we take our understanding of the adversary model from the law, then, just like this warmaking model, it simply requires that one defend one's views against opponents as they present themselves.

But what is so bad about doing philosophy this way? Why can't philosophy be seen as "the moral equivalent of war," to use an expression of William James, or "the battleplace of ideas," to alter a phrase associated with John Stuart Mill?[7] I have already indicated the unfairness that accompanies doing philosophy in this way, but an even more significant problem is that this way of doing philosophy undercuts the very possibility of reaching truly justified philosophical

3

views. If those doing philosophy are always trying to win philosophical battles and emerge as victorious, or at least not be defeated, in philosophical wars, they will not be able to achieve the sympathetic understanding of their opponents' views necessary for recognizing what is valuable in those views and what, therefore, needs to be incorporated into their own views. If your goal is always to achieve philosophical victory or to avoid at all costs philosophical defeat, then, given the complexity of philosophical views, it will almost always be possible to rearrange the elements of your views so as to deceive others, and even yourself, about the defensibility of those views, and thereby be able to claim philosophical victory, or at least avoid having to admit to philosophical defeat. For this reason, the warmaking model of doing philosophy renders it difficult to make needed improvements in your philosophical views, or even to abandon them entirely for the sake of better ones. It thereby undercuts the very possibility of your having truly justified philosophical views.

Unfortunately, the same problem afflicts Moulton's adversary model because, although it requires that you face your strongest opponents, it does not require that you do so honestly or with sympathetic understanding.[8] As with the warmaking model as I have characterized it, Moulton's adversary model aims simply at triumphing over your opponents by whatever means are at hand.

So while philosophers who are committed to the warmaking model of doing philosophy are trying to triumph over their philosophical opponents, their opponents, if they are also committed to the same model of doing philosophy, are trying in every way they can, both fair and foul, to avoid having to admit to philosophical defeat. No wonder, then, that so few clear and undeniable philosophical victories emerge from these contests.

But why should warmaking be our model of doing philosophy or engaging in any academic discussion? Why can't we have a more peaceful and cooperative model? Why can't we find points of agreement and attempt to build on the work of others, rather than trying to destroy their work and build anew? Why can't we try to put the most favorable interpretation on the work of others rather than looking for some interpretation with which we can disagree?

One summer a few years ago I visited a major university to talk to two well-known philosophers about the differences between their views. One of these philosophers had established his reputation as a critic of the other. I talked first to the philosopher whose work had been criticized by his colleague. I asked him, bearing in mind his critic's work, whether he had any objections to interpreting his view in a way that I thought avoided his colleague's criticisms, and he said that he did not. The next day I talked to the philosopher who was known for his critique of his colleague (I was told that they don't talk to each other)[9] and asked him whether he had any objections to this interpretation of his colleague's work, mentioning that his colleague had just accepted this interpretation the day before. He said that he did not. Yet, it turns out that this same philosopher was hard at work on a book in which he was criticizing yet another interpretation of his colleague's work – a book in which the more favorable interpretation of his colleague's work was never mentioned.

A friend of mine responding to a critic at a philosophy conference claimed that her work had been misinterpreted. Her critic in subsequent work refused to give up his "misinterpretation," claiming that others might make the same misinterpretation and so my friend should wait for an opportunity to respond to his critique in print in order to set the record straight. Not surprisingly, my friend preferred a different critical strategy. She wanted her critic, when faced with a possible misinterpretation of her text, to reexamine the text to see if it could plausibly be interpreted as she claims to have intended it, and if it could be so interpreted, then the critic should subsequently adopt her preferred interpretation in any critique. In addition to being fairer, this strategy is more likely to focus attention on the most important questions for evaluating a person's work.

So suppose we were to adopt a peaceful and cooperative model of doing philosophy which required that we put the most favorable interpretation on the work of others. To do this, we have to listen carefully to those with whom we disagree. Now it might be objected that we are not so much concerned with the views people actually hold but rather with the best formulations of those views. This is true. We are looking for the most favorable interpretations of particular views. Nevertheless, in order to get at the most favorable interpretations, it is usually necessary to listen carefully to those who actually hold particular views, because they are in a good position to determine what are the most favorable interpretations of those views.

We also need to reach out and try to understand those who have views of which we are ignorant. But this can be harder to do than one thinks. For example, another friend of mine recently presented a paper to the philosophy department at a major midwestern university. It was in fact the first paper to deal with feminism to be presented to that department. Her commentator, a recent Ph.D. from an Ivy League university, produced a set of comments almost as long as her paper, which focused entirely on the welfare liberal section of her paper. After the session, her commentator was asked by a female graduate student why he had not commented at all on the feminist part of her paper. He replied that he knew very little about feminism, and so he thought it best for him to focus on what he did know much more

5

about, which was the welfare liberal section of the paper. Apparently, the rest of the faculty attending the session felt the same way, since although they raised numerous questions, their questions too focused entirely on the welfare liberal section of her paper. What this shows is that it is very difficult to get philosophers to inform themselves about challenging new areas like feminism. The department to which my friend presented her paper was particularly deficient in this regard because, while its members remained generally ignorant of feminist philosophy, they also refused to appoint anyone to their fairly large department whose primary area of expertise is feminist philosophy.

So let us assume that we were to adopt a peacemaking model of doing philosophy that is committed to fair-mindedness and openness in seeking to determine which philosophical views are most justified. How would such a model be employed in practice? So far I have been talking about philosophy generally. I now want to focus on how this peacemaking model of doing philosophy would inform the selection of a conception of justice for here and now that specifies people's fundamental rights and duties. Now it is important that such a conception of justice be able to justify the rights and duties that it requires as far as possible. To do this, it must proceed from premises that are widely shared. Sometimes such premises are thought to be indisputable facts from which values can then be deduced, and so the question becomes: How can we bridge the fact/value gap or the is/ought gap?[10] Other times the premises are thought to be norms of rationality themselves, like consistency and non-question-beggingness, and then the question becomes: How can we show that justice or morality is required by rationality?[11] But the former approach can actually be subsumed under the latter, because whether facts entail values depends on whether we are rationally required to infer from particular facts to particular values. So, with respect to both approaches, the crucial question is: What do norms of rationality require us to do?

Suppose it were possible to show that norms of rationality require us to be moral. Since virtually everyone accepts norms of rationality,[12] it would follow that virtually everyone should be committed to morality as well. Of course, most contemporary philosophers do not claim that norms of rationality favor morality over self-interest[13] but contend that the justification of morality must proceed from commonly accepted moral values like liberty, fairness, equality, or the common good, and not from norms of rationality alone. Nevertheless, these philosophers still recognize that morality would be more firmly grounded if it could be shown to be required by norms of rationality alone. So I suggest that a *first step* to implementing our peacemaking model of doing philosophy is to examine carefully the possibility of grounding morality on the widely shared norms of rationality. Whatever our initial view of this possibility, it is important that we be able to put ourselves into the philosophical shoes of those who maintain different views and see things from their perspectives. This can be particularly difficult to do because a warmaking model of doing philosophy can incline us to see the weaknesses in other people's views rather than their strengths, or what possibilities they have for overcoming their weaknesses. It is also important that we be willing to radically and publicly change our views if the evidence points in that direction, which is akin to admitting philosophical defeat.

In Chapter 2, I take up the question of whether norms of rationality require morality and argue that they do require us to be moral. Specifically, I consider a number of other contemporary attempts to show that rationality requires morality and discuss why they fail. I then offer my own justification of morality and respond to a number of objections that have been raised to it.

As I indicated, however, most contemporary philosophers do not try to justify morality by appealing to norms of rationality alone. Rather, they claim that morality must be grounded in the acceptance of moral values like liberty, fairness, equality, or the common good, and the only question is what these moral values require in practice. At this juncture, some philosophers have taken a more pessimistic turn while others have taken a more optimistic one. Those who have taken the more pessimistic turn contend that because the moral values that people hold are incommensurable they lead to radically different practical requirements.[14] Those who have taken the more optimistic turn contend that, while people do hold some incommensurable values, it is still possible to achieve at least a partial agreement on practical requirements.[15]

One strategy for determining which of these views is correct is to examine moral and political perspectives that appear to have minimal practical requirements, like libertarianism, to determine what practical requirements actually do follow from them. If it turns out that the practical requirements of such moral and political perspectives can be shown to be more extensive than their advocates maintain, it may be possible to reconcile them at the practical level with other moral and political perspectives. For example, if the libertarian's ideal of liberty could be shown to have the same practical requirements as the welfare liberal's ideal of fairness and the socialist's ideal of equality, then, at least at the practical level, it would be possible to reconcile libertarianism with welfare liberalism and socialism. Since our peacemaking model of doing philosophy is committed to providing the strongest possible justification for practical requirements, a *second step* required by this model is carefully to examine the possibility of achieving a practical reconciliation of alternative moral and political perspectives.[16]

In Chapter 3, I examine the libertarian's ideal of liberty and argue that, despite what libertarians claim, their ideal actually supports the same rights to welfare and equal opportunity that are usually associated with a welfare liberal ideal. I further argue that these two rights lead to something like the equality that socialists endorse. In Chapter 4, I argue that these same rights lead to an ideal of a gender-free or androgynous society that many feminists defend, and I then consider the practical implications the ideal has for family structures, the distribution of economic power, overt violence against women, and sexual harassment.

Now in seeking to determine to what degree a practical reconciliation of moral and political perspectives is possible, as required by our peacemaking model of doing philosophy, two considerations are relevant. First, alternative moral and political ideals must be formulated to reflect the views of their advocates accurately. It would do no good, for example, to distort the libertarian's ideal of liberty simply in order to derive certain practical requirements. As a general rule, we can be sure that we have interpreted a moral and political perspective correctly only if there is no other morally defensible interpretation possible that has different practical requirements. The socialist ideal, for example, might be understood either as an ideal of equality or as an ideal of (positive) liberty, but since both interpretations have the same practical requirements, neither is morally preferable to the other. Second, in seeking to determine to what degree practical reconciliation is possible, it is also important to realize that there is a need to cast one's net broadly if one really wants to achieve truly justified views. We need to explore interconnections between different conceptions of justice and to reconcile apparent conflicts wherever possible. That is why philosophers who refuse to inform themselves so as to be able to enter into dialogue with other moral and political perspectives undercut the very possibility of their achieving truly justified views.[17]

Accordingly, in Chapter 5, I discuss the theoretical and practical connections between feminist justice with its ideal of a gender-free or androgynous society and three other forms of justice: racial justice, homosexual justice, and multicultural justice. I argue that there are both theoretical and practical reasons for pursuing all of these forms of justice together.

In Chapter 6, I turn to the much neglected topic of environmental ethics and argue that when the most morally defensible version of an anthropocentric environmental ethics and the most morally defensible version of a nonanthropocentric environmental ethics are laid out, despite their theoretical disagreement concerning whether humans are superior to members of other species, they both lead us to accept the

8

same principles of environmental justice. In this context, our peace-making model of doing philosophy will be shown to lead to peace-making of a different sort by significantly restricting the violence that humans can legitimately do to nature.

In Chapter 7, I discuss the traditional opposition between pacifism and just war theory and argue that once antiwar pacifism is recognized as the most morally defensible form of pacifism, and the stringent requirements of just war theory are clearly specified, then it becomes possible to see how the two views can be reconciled in practice. Here again, our peacemaking model of doing philosophy will be shown to lead to peacemaking of a different sort by restricting the occasions on which wars can be legitimately fought.

In Chapter 8, I discuss how all of these practical reconciliations help to determine the requirements of a conception of justice for here and now, and I consider when normal politics, legal protest, civil disobedience, revolutionary action, and criminal disobedience are morally justified to implement these requirements. In this context, I argue that our peacemaking model of doing philosophy legitimates certain limited departures from peace to achieve a greater peace with justice.

To embrace a peacemaking model of doing philosophy as I am characterizing it requires above all else a willingness to modify or abandon one's philosophical views should the weight of available evidence tell against them. It is this willingness to, if necessary, radically change one's philosophical views that above all else distinguishes this peace-making model of doing philosophy from what is objectionable in a war-making model of doing philosophy. This self-critical dimension also distinguishes our peacemaking model of doing philosophy from the adversary system found in the law which does not require that those who are guilty own up to their guilt, but in fact allows them to put forth arguments on behalf of their "innocence" and requires that their guilt be publicly ascertained on the basis of the evidence available to the prosecution. This self-critical dimension of our peacemaking way of doing philosophy is also difficult to put into practice. In my own case, I have been helped enormously by people's criticisms and comments to significantly modify my reconciliation arguments over the years. More-over, given that these reconciliation arguments cut against the grain of much of contemporary moral and political philosophy, further modifications and even abandonment remain distinct possibilities, and given my commitment to a peacemaking model of doing philosophy, I must remain open to these possibilities.

It is now possible to characterize this peacemaking way of doing philosophy more fully. It is a way of doing philosophy that, while seeking to determine what are the most justified philosophical views, is committed to:

9

1) a fair-mindedness that, among other things, puts the most favorable interpretation on the views of one's philosophical opponents;
2) an openness that reaches out to understand challenging new philosophical views;
3) a self-criticalness that requires modifying or abandoning one's philosophical views should the weight of available evidence require it.[18]

I have also argued that employing this model of doing philosophy to select a conception of justice for here and now requires:

1) examining the possibility of grounding morality on widely shared norms of rationality;
2) exploring the possibility of achieving a practical reconciliation of alternative moral and political perspectives;
3) a willingness to modify or abandon one's favored conception of justice should the weight of available evidence require it.

Now it might be objected that if the most favorable interpretation is placed upon a warmaking model of doing philosophy, it too can be seen to incorporate roughly the same desirable features as our peacemaking model of doing philosophy. This is true. Thus, we might conceive of a warmaking model of doing philosophy as committed to the pursuit of philosophical victory and the avoidance of philosophical defeat as a means of getting at the most justified philosophical views and hence requiring:

1) a fair-mindedness that, among other things, puts the most favorable interpretation on the views of one's opponents so that one's philosophical victories are won fair and square;
2) an openness that reaches out to understand challenging new views so that philosophical victories are not obtained for lack of worthy opponents;
3) a self-criticalness that requires admitting philosophical defeat should the weight of available evidence require it.

Obviously, a warmaking model of doing philosophy that is characterized in this way is practically indistinguishable from our peacemaking model of doing philosophy. What this shows is that there will be good reasons to favor our peacemaking model of doing philosophy over a warmaking model only when the latter is understood to endorse the pursuit of victory or the avoidance of philosophical defeat at the expense of fair-mindedness, openness, or self-criticalness.[19]

So why not use the label "a warmaking model of doing philosophy" to characterize the way of doing philosophy that I favor? This could be done. The problem with using this label, however, is that it is associated with just those bad instances of doing philosophy illustrated by my examples in this chapter. As a consequence, even those who seem somewhat favorable to a warmaking model of doing philosophy don't like to use this label to characterize their view.

Why, then, not use the label "an adversary model of doing philosophy" to characterize the way of doing philosophy that I favor? Again, this could be done. However, the problem here is that this label is associated with the adversary system in the law which is not committed either to fair-mindedness because it doesn't require participants to face their strongest opponents, or face them always honestly and with sympathetic understanding, nor to self-criticalness because it does not require its participants to own up to their guilt.

Of course, there is also a problem with using the label "a peacemaking model of doing philosophy" to characterize the way of doing philosophy that I favor. The problem is that this label may suggest that participants are interested in securing agreement or reconciliation at all costs, which violates fair-mindedness by requiring participants to give up or modify their views when there really is no good reason to do so. But I judge that the problem with this label is less severe than the problems with the other two, and for that reason I think that "a peacemaking model of doing philosophy" seems the most promising label to use.[20] This label also has the added advantage of suggesting just those kinds of constraints that must be incorporated into a warmaking model of doing philosophy if it is to be defensible. Analogously, in Chapter 7, I employ the label "just war pacifism" to suggest just those kinds of constraints that need to be met before going to war can be justified.

It should also be noted how difficult it is to determine when philosophers are actually committed to an objectionable form of a warmaking way of doing philosophy. For most surely they won't describe themselves as committed to this way of doing philosophy. Rather, they will only tend to reveal themselves by their actions, that is, by their failures to live up to the values of fair-mindedness, openness, and self-criticalness. Of course, even philosophers who are actually committed to our peacemaking way of doing philosophy will sometimes fail in just these ways. For example, they will sometimes be unfair to their opponents or sometimes fail to be open to challenging new philosophical perspectives. Accordingly, the only way we can reasonably determine when philosophers are actually committed to this objectionable form of a warmaking way of doing philosophy is by the frequency and severity of their failures, which, obviously, will not always be easy to evaluate. Nevertheless, we can still come to know what constitute the relevant "sins," as the examples in this chapter indicate, even when we are not so sure who the "true sinners" are, that is, who are really committed to the objectionable form of a warmaking way of philosophy.

There is also the question of what philosophers committed to a peacemaking way of doing philosophy as I have characterized it are supposed to do when confronted with philosophers who seem to be committed to this objectionable form of a warmaking way of doing philosophy. Obviously, this question is similar to the question of what peaceful nations or individuals are supposed to do when confronted with seemingly belligerent nations or individuals, and, not surprisingly, the answer in each case seems to be similar as well. Surely, peacemaking philosophers should not give up their commitment to the fair-mindedness, openness, and self-criticalness that make their way of doing philosophy defensible. At the same time, they can justifiably protect themselves against the unfairness and deceitfulness of those committed to this objectionable form of a warmaking philosophy, as well as strive in every way they can to expose the inadequacies of this way of doing philosophy as a method for attaining the most defensible philosophical views. Needless to say, in many ways, the future success of philosophy will depend on just how successful peacemaking philosophers turn out to be in these endeavors.

Now, with respect to the arguments of this book, it should be pointed out that, except for the last chapter, the arguments developed in subsequent chapters of the book do not presuppose acceptance of the arguments developed in earlier chapters. For example, one need not accept the argument of this chapter for a peacemaking way of doing philosophy in order to accept the argument from rationality to morality in Chapter 2. Nevertheless, earlier chapters do tend to provide arguments for the premises from which the arguments of later chapters begin. For example, Chapter 3 starts by assuming morality of at least a libertarian sort and seeks to determine what practical requirements follow from it, whereas Chapter 2 seeks to deduce morality from norms of rationality. So, while it possible to accept the arguments of later chapters without accepting the arguments of earlier chapters, ideally the arguments of earlier chapters will be seen to provide support for the premises that are assumed in later ones. Irrespective of the success or failure of particular arguments, however, the overall goal of the book is to show by example how to work out a defensible peacemaking model of doing philosophy.

Initially, when I introduced the contrast between warmaking and peacemaking ways of doing philosophy in the course of presenting my own work, I was surprised at the responses of my audiences. This is because on such occasions the questions and comments were uniformly friendly and constructive. I thought that somehow I must have failed to communicate well, because so few in my audiences seemed bent on simply attacking my central arguments. Even fairly critical points directed at those same arguments were frequently accompanied by suggestions as to how the criticisms might be met. Could it be, then, that by drawing attention to these two contrasting ways of doing philosophy, one could actually lead one's audience to react to one's work in a peacemaking rather than a warmaking manner as I have contrasted them? It is an intriguing possibility.

Consider further how this might apply to readers of this book. Suppose readers were to ask themselves the following questions:

1) Will you give this book the kind of attention necessary to assess its arguments and conclusions fairly?
2) Are you open to being informed by the discussion of topics in the book with which you are unfamiliar or positions with which you disagree?
3) When you find that you have objections to some of the arguments or conclusions of the book, will you try to uncover ways to respond effectively to your own objections?
4) Finally, but most importantly, will you approach the book entertaining the possibility that you might modify or abandon your previous views should the arguments appear compelling?

Obviously, only if readers could truthfully answer yes to all of these questions would they, in fact, be committed to a peacemaking way of doing philosophy as I have characterized it.

No doubt it is a bit unusual for an author to put readers on the spot like this by raising such challenging questions for them. But if the objectionable warmaking model of doing philosophy is to lose the hold it has on contemporary philosophical discussion, unusual steps will have to be taken. From this perspective, then, it seems far from inappropriate to inform one's readers what is required to apply this peacemaking way of doing philosophy to the reading of one's own book. In fact, given my commitment to a peacemaking way of doing philosophy, it is just what I should be doing.

Chapter 2

From Rationality to Morality

In a defense of a conception of justice for here and now, as we noted in Chapter 1, it would be helpful to show that morality is grounded in rationality. This requires not simply showing that morality is rationally permissible, because that would imply that egoism and immorality were rationally permissible as well. Rather, what needs to be shown is that morality is rationally required, thus excluding egoism and immorality as rationally permissible.[1] Unfortunately, the goal of showing that morality is rationally required has been abandoned by most contemporary philosophers, who seem content to show that morality is simply rationally permissible.[2] No doubt most contemporary philosophers would like to have an argument showing that morality is rationally required, but given the history of past failures to provide a convincing argument of this sort, most of them have simply given up hope of defending morality in this way.[3] In this chapter, I propose to provide just such a defense of morality. I will begin in Section I by arguing against one opponent of morality – the moral relativist. In Section II, I will consider two of the better-known contemporary attempts to defend morality as rationally required and, unfortunately, why they fail. In Section III, I will, with some trepidation, offer my own defense of morality as rationally required; and, in Section IV, I will consider a number of objections to it.

I. THE IMPLAUSIBILITY OF MORAL RELATIVISM

Many people think that morality is a matter of opinion and that what is right for you may be wrong for me, even if we are similarly situated. Such people are moral relativists, and they take their view to be amply supported by the diverse moral views held in different societies as well as by the level of moral disagreement that exists within any one society, such as my own. In my own society, there is presently radical

14

disagreement over abortion, welfare, homosexuality, and humanitarian intervention, to name but a few issues. Yet these disagreements seem to pall when my society is compared with other societies that presently condone infanticide, polygamy, and even cannibalism.

Nevertheless, in order for moral relativists to draw support for their view from this moral diversity, they must be able to show that the same act could be both right and wrong – right for one society, group, or individual, and wrong for some other society, group, or individual.[4] Frequently, however, the act that is condemned by one society, group, or individual is not the same act that is sanctioned by another society, group, or individual. For example, the voluntary euthanasia that is sanctioned by Eskimos as a transition to what they take to be a happier existence for their aged members is significantly different from the euthanasia that the AMA opposes, which does not assume a happier afterlife.[5] Likewise, when the Nuer gently lay their deformed infants in the river because they believe that such infants are baby hippos accidentally born to humans, their action is significantly different from the infanticide that most people condemn.[6] Even in the case of abortion, what some people judge to be right (permissible) and what other people judge to be wrong (impermissible) would not appear to be the same act because of the different views that people hold with respect to the moral status of the fetus. Those opposing abortion usually claim that the fetus is a full-fledged human person with the same right to life as you or I, while those favoring abortion usually deny that the fetus has this status.[7]

Yet even when the same act is being compared, in order for that act to be right for a person to perform, it must be possible for that person, following her best deliberation, to come to judge the act as right. Acts that are inaccessible to people's best judgment (like avoiding carcinogens in the Middle Ages) are not acts that could be morally right for them to do because morality requires a certain accessibility.[8] Accordingly, when we evaluate people's moral judgments in the context in which they formed them, it will sometimes be the case that we will recognize that they couldn't have arrived at the judgments that we think are morally right. If so, their judgments would not relevantly conflict with our own, even if what they think is right is not what we think is right, for example, as in the need for cleanliness in medical operations.

Of course, this is not to suggest that what we *think* is right for us to do necessarily *is* right for us to do. After all, we could be mistaken. It is only to suggest that if we are moral agents capable of moral deliberation, any discrepancy between what we think is right for us to do and what is right for us to do must be explained in terms of some kind of past or present failure on our part to follow our best deliberation with regard to the opportunities available to us. If it is going to make any sense to say that something is right for us to do, knowledge of that fact must somehow be accessible to us, so that any discrepancy between what we think is right for us to do and what is right for us to do must somehow be traceable to a failure on our part to deliberate wisely.[9] Consequently, in order for moral relativism to draw support from the existing moral diversity, there must be acts that are sufficiently accessible to people's moral deliberation such that the same act is judged right by some people using their best moral judgment and judged wrong by other people using their best moral judgment.

But even this is not enough. Moral relativism must also tell us what morality is supposed to be relative to.[10] Is it to be relative to the common beliefs of a society, to those of a smaller group, to those of just any individual, or could it be relative to any of these? If it could be relative to any of these, any act (e.g., contract killing) could be wrong from the point of view of some particular society, right from the point of view of some subgroup of that society (e.g., the Mafia), and wrong again from the point of view of some particular member of that society or subgroup. But if this is the case, individuals would not have any reasonable grounds for deciding what they ought to do, all things considered.

Yet even supposing that some particular reference group could be shown to be preferable (e.g., the reference group of one's own society), problems remain. First, in deciding what to do, should we simply ask what the members of our appropriate reference group think ought to be done? But if everyone in our reference group did that, we would all be waiting for everyone else to decide, and so no one would decide what ought to be done. Or we might construe moral relativism to be a second-order theory requiring that the members of our appropriate reference group first decide on some other grounds what is right and then take a vote. If a majority or a consensus emerges from such a vote, then that is what is right, all things considered. So interpreted, "moral relativism" would have some merit as a theory of collective decision making, but it clearly would require some yet-to-be-determined nonrelativist grounds for first-order moral judgments, and so it would not essentially be a relativist theory at all.

Second, the very claim that morality should be specified relativistically is not itself a relativistic claim. Rather, it claims to be a truth for all times and places. But how could this be possible? Shouldn't the truth of relativism itself be assertible as a relativistic claim? One might maintain that while moral judgments are relativistic, the thesis of moral relativism is not itself a moral claim and hence need not be relativistic. But if truth is not relativistic, why should we think that the good is relativistic?

In sum, moral relativism as an account of moral judgments faces a number of difficulties. First, it is difficult for moral relativists to show

that amid the existing moral diversity there are acts that are sufficiently accessible to people's moral deliberation such that the same
act is judged right by some and wrong by others when all are following their best moral deliberation. Second, it is difficult for moral
relativists to specify the appropriate reference group from which morality is to be determined. Third, even assuming the appropriate reference group can be determined, it is difficult for moral relativists to
explain why their theory is not committed to some nonrelativist account of at least first-order moral judgments. Last, it is difficult for
moral relativists to explain why they are committed to a nonrelativist
account of truth.

Yet while these difficulties obviously render moral relativism an
implausible theory, they do not completely defeat it in the absence of
a better, nonrelativistic account of moral judgments. In Section II, I
will consider two of the better-known contemporary attempts to provide such an account of moral judgments and, unfortunately, why
they fail, before setting out my own account in Section III.

II. RECENT ATTEMPTS TO GROUND MORALITY ON RATIONALITY

Beginning with *The Moral Point of View* (1958) and continuing in a
series of publications right up to the present, Kurt Baier has been
attempting to construct a justification of morality that is grounded in
rationality.[11] His general strategy has been to attempt to find certain
non-question-begging requirements of practical reason that then can
be shown to favor morality over egoism. For example, Baier has appealed to the following requirement in his defense of morality over
egoism.[12]

> *The Universalizability Requirement:* If it is rational for anyone
> to do A, it must be rational for everyone similarly situated to
> do A.

Giving this requirement its most straightforward interpretation, it simply maintains that rational actions are such that it must be rational
for everyone similarly situated to perform the same actions.[13] Unfortunately, given this interpretation, the requirement does not favor morality over egoism. This is because while the moralist maintains that
actions that are morally rational for one person to do are morally
rational for all persons similarly situated to do, the egoist likewise
maintains that actions that are self-interestedly rational for one person
to do are also self-interestedly rational for all persons similarly situated to do.[14] Thus, both the egoist and the moralist can accept the
Universalizability Requirement under this interpretation.

17

To support morality over egoism, Baier needed to give his Universalizability Requirement yet another interpretation.[15] According to this interpretation, if it is a good thing for one person to act rationally, it must be a good thing for all persons similarly situated to act rationally. Now this interpretation does succeed in distinguishing morality from egoism because whereas the moralist can maintain that it is a good thing for everyone to take moral reasons as supreme, the egoist must reject the idea that it is a good thing for everyone to take self-interested reasons as supreme. For good self-interested reasons, the egoist opposes others when they take self-interested reasons to be supreme, although she admits that such behavior is fully rational. The egoist does not want others reaping the benefits of following self-interested reasons at her expense, so she publicly endorses the following of moral reasons as strongly as anyone does. The egoist observes that most people take a similar stand, and she notes that many people with the "proper upbringing" in fact come to care strongly for others and, as a result, to follow moral reasons almost instinctively. Taking all this into account, the egoist reasonably concludes that it is improbable that circumstances would arise in which most people would follow the directives of egoism.

Given, then, that the egoist can be assured that most people will continue to follow the directives of morality even when the egoist follows those of self-interest, the egoist can reasonably expect that the overall effect on the satisfactoriness of her life from her taking self-interested reasons to be supreme will be positive, and considerably better than the overall effect on her life from her taking moral reasons to be supreme.[16]

So although Baier is correct in maintaining that the egoist would reject the idea that it must be a good thing for everyone always to act rationally, what needs to be shown is that the rejection of this idea is contrary to reason.[17] Yet why would it be contrary to reason for the egoist to claim that everyone ought to do what is in their best interest while still contending that it is *not* a good thing for everyone to do so, given the impact such behavior would have on the satisfactoriness of the egoist's own life?

Here the "oughts" found in most ordinary competitive games provide a useful analogy. Tennis players can judge that their opponents ought to put maximum spin on their serves without being committed to thinking that it is a good thing for them if their opponents serve in this way and they then counter with their best returns; for when this occurs, they could lose the game. After all, not infrequently one side is victorious in a game only because the other side fails to execute its best moves.[18]

Of course, there is an important dissimilarity between these two types of "oughts." Since competitive games are governed by moral constraints, when everyone does exactly what he or she ought to do, there is an accepted moral limit to what a person can lose. By contrast, when everyone takes self-interested reasons to be supreme, the only limit to what a person can lose is the point beyond which others would not benefit.

But this dissimilarity does not destroy the analogy. For it is still the case that when judged from the individual player's or the egoist's point of view, it need not be a good thing for everyone to be perfectly rational. It follows, therefore, that the egoist cannot be convicted of acting contrary to reason by rejecting Baier's second interpretation of his Universalizability Requirement. This interpretation of the requirement simply begs the question against rational egoism.

Baier, of course, could object that only when everyone takes moral reasons as overriding self-interested reasons in cases of conflict would everyone have as good self-interested reasons as everyone else for abiding by the requirements of morality.[19] While this is true, the egoist is not concerned to bring about a state of affairs where everyone has as good self-interested reasons as everyone else to abide by the requirements of morality. What the egoist wants is for others to abide by the requirements of morality even when she does not, and, as I previously argued, she may be able to achieve this result by, so to speak, covering her self-interested tracks very well and doing everything in her power to foster altruism in others. When this is possible, the egoist would have even better self-interested reasons to violate the requirements of morality than she would have to abide by those requirements. In such circumstances, the only thing that would seemingly lead anyone to abide by the requirements of morality is a concern with fairness. But clearly, the egoist is not interested in pursuing fairness at the expense of the satisfaction of her own interests.[20] So why, then, should an egoist be concerned to abide by the requirements of morality?

In his recent book, *The Rational and the Moral Order*, Baier attempts to overcome this gap between egoism and morality by interpreting morality as a system of reasons of mutual benefit that are appropriate for contexts in which everyone's following self-interested reasons would have suboptimal results for everyone.[21] So interpreted, moral reasons apply only when there exists an adequate enforcement system that makes acting against those reasons unprofitable. Morality so construed never requires any degree of altruism or self-sacrifice; it only requires that people act upon reasons of mutual benefit. According to Baier,

[The] Limited Good Will [of morality] is not a straightforward other-regarding or benevolent, let alone an altruistic . . . pattern. . . . Persons of limited conditional goodwill may thus be motivated primarily by concern for their own good life and their conforming with [moral] guidelines is a contribution to the concerns of others, which (since they may not care about these others) is made mainly or only because the realization of their own ends is seen to depend on the contributions made by others, and because they are prepared to recognize the reasonableness of reciprocity in this matter.[22]

Given this interpretation of morality, it is not possible for the egoist to do better by acting against morality. So construed, morality and egoism do not conflict.

Unfortunately, this does not seem to be the defense of morality for which we were hoping. It succeeds only by redefining morality in a question-begging way so that it no longer demands any degree of altruism or self-sacrifice, for example, for those who are poor and misfortunate, and in that way is rendered compatible with egoism. What we need, however, is a defense of morality that neither begs the question against egoism, as did Baier's earlier defense of morality, nor begs the question against morality, as does this most recent defense. What Baier's work provides is the long-sustained hope that just such a justification for morality can be found.[23]

In search of such a non-question-begging justification of morality, Alan Gewirth has proposed a quite different argument.[24] The central premises of his argument can be summarized as follows:

1) All agents regard their purposes as good according to whatever criteria are involved in their actions to fulfill them.
2) Therefore, all agents must affirm a right to the freedom and well-being necessary to achieve their purposes.
3) All agents must affirm such a right on the basis of simply being prospective, purposive agents.
4) Hence, all agents must affirm that every prospective, purposive agent has a right to freedom and well-being.

Gewirth claims that the universalized right affirmed in the conclusion of his argument is a moral right, that is, a right that is action-guiding for the right holder and for others as well, a right that implies at least that others ought not to interfere with the exercise of that right. Such rights are symmetrically action-guiding because they are action-guiding both for the right holder and for others as well.

Nevertheless, the success of Gewirth's argument depends on the impossibility of interpreting the universalized right in his conclusion as anything other than a moral right. Unfortunately for Gewirth's argument, another interpretation is possible. According to this interpretation, a universalized right can be deduced from the premises of his argument, but it is a prudential right, not a moral right. This interpretation is plausible because Gewirth maintains that the right referred to in premise (3) is prudential,[25] and the universalization of a prudential right can be understood to be another prudential right, albeit a universal one.[26]

Now what distinguishes a prudential right from a moral right is that a prudential right is action-guiding for the right holder only and not for others, and so it does not imply that others ought not to interfere with the exercise of that right. Such rights are asymmetrically action-guiding because they are action-guiding only for the right holder and not for others. Prudential rights are also analogous to the oughts found in most ordinary cases of competitive games – cases that we otherwise would have thought conform to the requirements of practical reason. For example, in football a defensive player may think that the opposing team's quarterback ought to pass on a third down with five yards to go, while not wanting the quarterback to do so and indeed hoping to foil any such attempt the quarterback makes. Or, to adapt an example of Jesse Kalin's, if you and I are playing chess, at a certain point in the game I may judge that you ought to move your bishop and put my king in check, but this judgment is not action-guiding for me. What I in fact should do is sit quietly and hope that you do not move as you ought. If you fail to make the appropriate move and, later in the game, I judge that I ought to put your king in check, that judgment, by contrast, would be action-guiding for me. So prudential rights are asymmetrically action-guiding in just the same way as these oughts of competitive games are asymmetrically action-guiding.

Given that the universal right to freedom and well-being in the conclusion of Gewirth's argument can thus plausibly be interpreted to be a prudential right, Gewirth's justification of morality cannot succeed, because it depends on the impossibility of interpreting the universal right in the conclusion of his argument as anything other than a moral right. Still, we can take from Gewirth's work the view that if morality is to be rationally required, it must be given a non-question-begging justification.

III. A NON-QUESTION-BEGGING JUSTIFICATION OF MORALITY

My own defense of morality employs the same general strategy as those offered by Baier and Gewirth. It differs from theirs primarily in that it introduces the perspective of altruism in constructing a non-question-begging argument to show that egoism is contrary to reason.

But I claim that this is just the missing ingredient that is needed to make the argument work.

Let us begin by imagining that each of us is capable of entertaining and acting upon both self-interested and moral reasons and that the question we are seeking to answer is what sorts of reasons for action it would be rational for us to accept.[27] This question is not about what sorts of reasons we should publicly affirm, as people will sometimes publicly affirm reasons quite different from those upon which they are prepared to act. Rather, it is a question about what reasons it would be rational for us to accept at the deepest level – in our heart of hearts.

Of course, there are people who are incapable of acting upon moral reasons. For such people, there is no question about their being required to act morally or altruistically. Yet the interesting philosophical question is not about such people but about people, like ourselves, who are capable of acting self-interestedly or morally and are seeking a rational justification for following a particular course of action.

In trying to determine how we should act, we would like to be able to construct a *good* argument favoring morality over egoism, and given that good arguments are non-question-begging, we would like to construct an argument that does not beg the question against egoism.[28] The question at issue here is what reasons each of us should take as supreme, and this question would be begged against egoism if we propose to answer it simply by assuming from the start that moral reasons are the reasons that each of us should take as supreme. But the question would be begged against morality as well if we proposed to answer the question simply by assuming from the start that self-interested reasons are the reasons that each of us should take as supreme. This means, of course, that we cannot answer the question of what reasons we should take as supreme simply by assuming the general principle of egoism:

> Each person ought to do what best serves his or her overall self-interest.

We can no more argue for egoism simply by denying the relevance of moral reasons to rational choice than we can argue for pure altruism simply by denying the relevance of self-interested reasons to rational choice and assuming the following principle of pure altruism:

> Each person ought to do what best serves the overall interest of others.[29]

Consequently, in order not to beg the question against either egoism or altruism, we have no other alternative but to grant the prima facie relevance of both self-interested and moral reasons to rational choice and then try to determine which reasons we would be rationally required to act upon, all things considered.[30]

Here it might be objected that we *do* have non-question-begging grounds for favoring self-interested reasons over moral reasons, if not egoism over altruism. From observing ourselves and others, don't we find that self-interested reasons are better motivators than are moral reasons, as evidenced by the fact that there seem to be more egoistically inclined people in the world than there are altruistically inclined people? It might be argued that because of this difference in motivational capacity, self-interested and moral reasons should not *both* be regarded as prima facie relevant to rational choice.

But is there really this difference in motivational capacity? Do human beings really have a greater capacity for self-interested behavior than for moral or altruistic behavior? If we focus for a change on the behavior of women, I think we are likely to observe considerably more altruism than egoism among women, particularly with respect to the care of their families.[31] Of course, if we look to men, given the prevailing patriarchal social structures, we may tend to find more egoism than altruism.[32] But most likely any differences that exist between men and women in this regard, irrespective of whether we consider them to be good or bad, are primarily due to the dominant patterns of socialization – nurture rather than nature.[33] In any case, it is beyond dispute that we humans are capable of both self-interested and altruistic behavior, and given that we have these capabilities, it seems reasonable to ask which ones should have priority.[34]

Our situation is that we find ourselves with some capacity to move along a spectrum from egoism to pure altruism, with someone like Mother Teresa of Calcutta representing the paradigm of pure altruism and someone like Thrasymachus of Plato's *Republic* representing the paradigm of egoism. Obviously, our ability to move along this spectrum will depend on our starting point, the strength of our habits, and the social circumstances under which we happen to be living. But at the outset, it is reasonable to abstract from these individual variations and simply focus on the general capacity virtually all of us have to act on both self-interested and moral reasons. From this, we should conclude that both sorts of reasons are relevant to rational choice and then ask the question which reasons should have priority. Later, with this question answered, we can take into account individual differences and the effects of socialization to adjust our expectations and requirements for particular individuals and groups. Initially, however, all we need to recognize is the relevance of both self-interested and altruistic reasons to rational choice.

In this regard, two kinds of cases must be considered. First are cases in which there is a conflict between the relevant self-interested and moral reasons.[35] Second are cases in which there is no such conflict. Now it seems obvious that where there is no conflict and both reasons are conclusive reasons of their kind, both reasons should be acted upon. In such contexts, we should do what is favored by both morality and self-interest.

Consider the following example. Suppose you accepted a job marketing a baby formula in underdeveloped countries where the formula was improperly used, leading to increased infant mortality.[36] Imagine that you could just as well have accepted an equally attractive and rewarding job marketing a similar formula in developed countries where the misuse does not occur, so that a rational weighing of the relevant self-interested reasons alone would not have favored your acceptance of one of these jobs over the other.[37] At the same time, there were obviously moral reasons that condemned your acceptance of the first job – reasons that you presumably are or were able to acquire. Moreover, by assumption in this case, the moral reasons did not clash with the relevant self-interested reasons; they simply made a recommendation where the relevant self-interested reasons were silent. Consequently, a rational weighing of all the relevant reasons in this case could not but favor acting in accord with the relevant moral reasons.[38]

Yet it might be objected that in cases of this sort there frequently will be other reasons significantly opposed to the relevant moral reasons – reasons that you are or were able to acquire. Such reasons will be either *malevolent* reasons seeking to bring about the suffering and death of other human beings, *benevolent* reasons concerned to promote nonhuman welfare even at the expense of human welfare, or *aesthetic* reasons concerned to preserve and promote objects of aesthetic value even if those objects will not be appreciated by any living being. But assuming that such malevolent reasons are ultimately rooted in some conception of what is good for oneself or others, these reasons would have already been taken into account, and by assumption outweighed by the other relevant reasons in this case.[39] And although benevolent reasons concerned to promote nonhuman welfare would have been taken into account, such reasons are not directly relevant to justifying morality over egoism.[40] Finally, although aesthetic reasons concerned to preserve and promote aesthetic objects, even if those objects will not be appreciated by any living being, might theoretically weigh against human interests, for all practical purposes, the value of such aesthetic objects will tend to correlate with the value of the aesthetic experiences such objects provide to humans.[41] Consequently, even with the presence of these other kinds of reasons, your acceptance of the first job can still be seen to be contrary to the relevant reasons in this case.

Needless to say, defenders of egoism cannot but be disconcerted by this result since it shows that actions that accord with egoism are contrary to reason, at least when there are two equally good ways of pursuing one's self-interest, only one of which does not conflict with the basic requirements of morality. Notice also that in cases where there are two equally good ways of fulfilling the basic requirements of morality, only one of which does not conflict with what is in a person's overall self-interest, it is not at all disconcerting for defenders of morality to admit that we are rationally required to choose the way that does not conflict with what is in our overall self-interest. Nevertheless, exposing this defect in egoism for cases where moral reasons and self-interested reasons do not conflict would be but a small victory for defenders of morality if it were not also possible to show that in cases where such reasons do conflict, moral reasons would have priority over self-interested reasons.

Now, when we rationally assess the relevant reasons in such cases of conflict, it is best to cast the conflict, not as one between self-interested and moral reasons, but as one between self-interested and altruistic reasons.[42] Viewed in this way, three solutions are possible. First, we could say that self-interested reasons always have priority over conflicting altruistic reasons. Second, we could say just the opposite, that altruistic reasons always have priority over conflicting self-interested reasons. Third, we could say that some kind of compromise is rationally required. In this compromise, sometimes self-interested reasons would have priority over altruistic ones and sometimes altruistic reasons would have priority over self-interested ones.

Once the conflict is described in this manner, the third solution can be seen to be the one that is rationally required. This is because the first and second solutions give exclusive priority to one class of relevant reasons over the other, and only a completely question-begging justification can be given for such an exclusive priority. Only by employing the third solution, and sometimes giving priority to self-interested reasons and sometimes giving priority to altruistic reasons, can we avoid a completely question-begging resolution.

Consider the following example. Suppose you are in the waste-disposal business and you have decided to dispose of toxic wastes in a manner that is cost-efficient for you but predictably causes significant harm to future generations. Imagine that there are alternative methods available for disposing of the waste that are only slightly less cost-efficient and will not cause any significant harm to future generations.[43] In this case, you are to weigh your self-interested reasons favoring the most cost-efficient disposal of the toxic wastes against the relevant altruistic reasons favoring the avoidance of significant harm to future generations. If we suppose that the projected loss of benefit to yourself was ever so slight and the projected harm to future generations ever so great, then a nonarbitrary compromise between the relevant self-interested and altruistic reasons would have to favor the altruistic reasons in this case. Hence, as judged by a non-question-begging standard of rationality, your method of waste disposal is contrary to the relevant reasons.

Notice also that this standard of rationality will not support just any compromise between the relevant self-interested and altruistic reasons. The compromise must be a nonarbitrary one, for otherwise it would beg the question with respect to the opposing egoistic and altruistic views. Such a compromise would have to respect the rankings of self-interested and altruistic reasons imposed by the egoistic and altruistic views, respectively. Since for each individual there is a separate ranking of that individual's relevant self-interested and altruistic reasons, we can represent these rankings from the most important reasons to the least important reasons as shown in Table 1.

Accordingly, any nonarbitrary compromise among such reasons in seeking not to beg the question against egoism or altruism will have to give priority to those reasons that rank highest in each category. Failure to give priority to the highest-ranking altruistic or self-interested reasons would, other things being equal, be contrary to reason.

Of course, there will be cases in which the only way to avoid being required to do what is contrary to your highest-ranking reasons is by requiring someone else to do what is contrary to her highest-ranking reasons. Some of these cases will be "lifeboat cases." But although such cases are surely difficult to resolve (maybe only a chance mechanism can offer a reasonable resolution), they do not reflect the typical conflict between the relevant self-interested and altruistic reasons that

Table 1

Individual A		Individual B	
Self-interested reasons	Altruistic reasons	Self-interested reasons	Altruistic reasons
1	1	1	1
2	2	2	2
3	3	3	3
•	•	•	•
•	•	•	•
•	•	•	•
N	N	N	N

we are or were able to acquire. Typically, one or the other of the conflicting reasons will rank significantly higher on its respective scale, thus permitting a clear resolution.[44]

Now it is important to see how morality can be viewed as just such a nonarbitrary compromise between self-interested and altruistic reasons. First, a certain amount of self-regard is morally required, or at least morally acceptable. Where this is the case, high-ranking self-interested reasons have priority over low-ranking altruistic reasons. Second, morality obviously places limits on the extent to which people should pursue their own self-interest. Where this is the case, high-ranking altruistic reasons have priority over low-ranking self-interested reasons. So typically "moral reasons" will be of the following sort:

All high-ranking self-interested reasons that require little or no sacrifice from others to fulfill	All high-ranking altruistic reasons that require little or no sacrifice of self-interest to fulfill
All high-ranking self-interested reasons that require a moderate sacrifice from others to fulfill	All high-ranking altruistic reasons that require a moderate sacrifice of self-interest to fulfill.

In this way, morality can be seen to be a nonarbitrary compromise between self-interested and altruistic reasons, and the "moral reasons" that constitute that compromise can be seen as having a priority over the self-interested or altruistic reasons that conflict with them.[45]

Now it might be objected that although the egoistic and the altruistic views are admittedly question-begging, the compromise view is equally so and hence is in no way preferable to the other views. In response, I deny that the compromise view is equally question-begging when compared with the egoistic and altruistic views, but I concede that the view is to a lesser degree question-begging nonetheless, for a completely non-question-begging view starts with assumptions that are acceptable to all sides of a dispute. However, the assumption of the compromise view that high-ranking altruistic reasons have priority over conflicting low-ranking self-interested reasons is not acceptable from an egoistic perspective. Nor is the compromise view's assumption that high-ranking self-interested reasons have priority over conflicting low-ranking altruistic reasons acceptable from an altruistic perspective. Relevantly, what altruism assumes is that:

1) All high-ranking altruistic reasons have priority over conflicting lower-ranking self-interested reasons.

2) All low-ranking altruistic reasons have priority over conflicting higher-ranking self-interested reasons.

By contrast, what egoism assumes is that:

1') All high-ranking self-interested reasons have priority over conflicting lower-ranking altruistic reasons.
2') All low-ranking self-interested reasons have priority over conflicting higher-ranking altruistic reasons.[46]

And what the compromise view assumes is (1) and (1'). So part of what the compromise view assumes about the priority of reasons, that is, (1) is not acceptable from an egoistic perspective, and another part, that is, (1') is not acceptable from an altruistic perspective; hence, to that extent, the compromise view does beg the question against each view. Nevertheless, since the whole of what egoism assumes about the priority of reasons – that is, (1) and (2) are unacceptable from an altruistic perspective – and the whole of what altruism assumes about the priority of reasons – that is, (1') and (2') are unacceptable from an egoistic perspective – each of these views begs the question against the other to a far greater extent than the compromise view does against either of them. Of course, it would be preferable to have an alternative that did not beg the question at all, but with respect to specifying the priority of self-interested and altruistic reasons, no such alternative exists. Consequently, on the basis of making the fewest question-begging assumptions, given that it shares important common ground with both the egoistic and the altruistic perspectives, the compromise view is the only nonarbitrary resolution of the conflict between egoism and altruism.

An analogy might help here. Suppose a judge is trying to decide how to distribute resources between two claimants, each with an equal prima facie claim to the use of those resources. Suppose further that the two claimants have conflicting plans for the use of the disputed resources, yet within each plan it is possible to rank their proposed uses on a scale of importance. Now if the judge is trying to decide how to distribute the resources in the way that would be most justified to *both* claimants, then surely a distribution that equally supports the high-ranking uses of both plans is required. Similarly, I claim, a compromise that favors high-ranking self-interested reasons over low-ranking altruistic reasons and high-ranking altruistic reasons over low-ranking self-interested reasons is required.

Notice, too, that this defense of morality succeeds not only against the view that egoism is rationally preferable to morality but also against the view that egoism is only rationally on a par with morality. The "weaker view" does not claim that we all ought to be egoists.

28

Rather, it claims that there is just as good reason for us to be egoists as there is for us to be pure altruists or anything in between. Kai Nielson summarizes this view: "We have not been able to show that reason requires the moral point of view or that all really rational persons not be individual egoists. Reason doesn't decide here."[47] Yet because the above defense of morality shows morality to be the only nonarbitrary resolution of the conflict between self-interested and altruistic reasons, it is not the case that there is just as good reason for us to endorse morality as there is for us to endorse egoism or altruism. Thus, the above defense of morality succeeds against the weaker as well as against the stronger interpretation of egoism.

Yet this defense of morality can be made even stronger once it is recognized that the alternatives of egoism, morality, and altruism are not, even initially, logically on a par. Egoism, because it requires aggressing against the basic interests of others (inflicting basic harm on others) for the sake of nonbasic benefit to oneself, has the burden of proof of showing that its view is more rationally defensible than morality, which prohibits such aggression. Requiring the infliction of basic harm for the sake of nonbasic benefit (doing more harm than good) must be shown to be more rationally preferable to its prohibition. However, egoism does not meet this burden of proof. To meet it requires providing non-question-begging reasons for rationally preferring egoism over morality, which obviously has not been done.[48] So morality emerges as rationally preferable not only because it is the least question-begging view but also because egoism fails to meet its burden of proof.

It might be objected that this defense of morality could be undercut if in the debate over egoism, altruism, and morality we simply give up any attempt to show that any one of these views is rationally preferable to the others. But we cannot rationally do this. For we are engaged in this debate as people who can act self-interestedly, can act altruistically, and can act morally; and we are trying to discover which of these ways of acting is rationally justified. To resolve this question rationally, we must be committed to finding out whether one of these views is more rationally defensible than the others. So as far as I can tell, there is no escaping the conclusion that morality is more rationally defensible than either egoism or altruism.

Unfortunately, this approach to defending morality has been generally neglected by previous moral theorists. The reason is that such theorists have tended to cast the basic conflict with egoism as a conflict between morality and self-interest. For example, according to Kurt Baier, "The very *raison d'être* of a morality is to yield reasons which overrule the reasons of self-interest in those cases when everyone's following self-interest would be harmful to everyone."[49] Viewed in this light, it did not seem possible for the defender of morality to support a compromise view, for how could such a defender say that, when morality and self-interest conflict, morality should sometimes be sacrificed to self-interest? But though previous theorists understood correctly that moral reasons could not be compromised in favor of self-interested ones, they failed to recognize that this is because moral reasons are already the result of a nonarbitrary compromise between self-interested and altruistic reasons. Thus, unable to see how morality can be represented as a compromise solution, previous theorists have generally failed to recognize this approach to defending morality.

This failure to recognize that morality can be represented as a compromise between self-interested and altruistic reasons also helps explain Thomas Nagel's inability to find a solution to the problem of the design of just institutions.[50] According to Nagel, to solve the problem of the design of just institutions, we need a morally acceptable resolution of the conflict between the personal and the impersonal standpoints, which he thinks is unattainable. But while Nagel may be right that a morally acceptable resolution of the conflict between these two standpoints is unattainable, the reason why this may be the case is that these two standpoints already represent different resolutions of the conflict between self and others. The personal standpoint represents the personally chosen resolution of this conflict, while the impersonal standpoint represents a completely impartial resolution of this conflict, which may not be identical with the personally chosen resolution.[51] Since each of these standpoints already represents a resolution of the conflict between oneself and others, any further resolution of the conflict between the two standpoints would seem to violate the earlier resolutions, either by favoring oneself or others too much or too little in light of the earlier resolutions.[52] It is no wonder, then, that an acceptable resolution of the two standpoints seems unattainable. By contrast, if we recast the underlying conflict between oneself and others, as I have suggested, in terms of a conflict between egoism and altruism, self-interested reasons and altruistic reasons, then happily a rationally defensible resolution can be seen to emerge.

In setting out this defense of morality, I assumed that we humans have the capacity to move along a spectrum from egoism to pure altruism. I granted that our ability to move along this spectrum will depend on our starting point, the strength of our habits, and the social circumstances under which we happen to be living. But I argued that, at the outset, it is reasonable to abstract from these individual variations and simply focus on the general capacity virtually all of us have to act on both self-interested and moral reasons. Now, however, that I have argued that both self-interested and altruistic reasons are relevant to rational choice and are assigned priorities in cases of conflict, it is appropriate to return to the question of how individual differences and the effects of socialization should adjust our expectations and requirements for particular individuals and groups.

Here two kinds of cases seem particularly relevant. In one case, certain people by nature lack, to some degree, the capacity to act on high-ranking altruistic reasons when they conflict with low-ranking self-interested reasons. In the other case, certain people, due to socialization, lack to some degree the capacity to act on high-ranking altruistic reasons when they conflict with low-ranking self-interested reasons. Obviously, people who have the capacity for altruism will have to try to work around and, if necessary, protect themselves from those who, to varying degrees, lack this capacity. In cases in which those who lack this capacity are themselves at least partially responsible for this lack, blame and censure are also appropriate.[53] Nevertheless, as long as the greater majority of people have by nature and/ or by nurture the capacity to act on high-ranking altruistic reasons when they conflict with low-ranking self-interested reasons, it should be possible to set up a social order that corresponds with the requirements of morality. Moreover, once we take into account the capacities of *both* men and women, there is good reason to think that the majority do have this capacity for altruism.[54]

Now it might be objected that we should not take into account people's capacities but simply whatever reasons they happen to have, whether these reasons are just self-interested reasons, or just altruistic reasons, or a combination of self-interested and altruistic reasons. As a matter of fact, however, we rarely limit our evaluations of other people to reasons they just happen to have. In imputing moral responsibility, for example, it is not necessary to show that people have the relevant moral reasons for acting otherwise, as we hold people morally responsible even when they lack such reasons, provided they are morally responsible for the lack. Thus, if political leaders have the capabilities and opportunities to become aware of their society's racist and sexist practices but in fact fail to do so, with the consequence that they presently lack any moral reasons to oppose such practices, we still hold them morally responsible, because their lack of moral reasons in this regard is something for which they are morally responsible. Similarly, if parents have the capacities and opportunities to become more sensitive to their children's needs but in fact fail to do so, with the consequence that they presently lack the moral reasons to respond effectively to those needs, they are still held morally responsible, because their lack of moral reasons in this regard is something for which they are morally responsible.[55] As these examples indicate, having moral reasons to act otherwise is not necessary for imputing moral responsibility. Rather, what is necessary is that people

31

are or were able to acquire the relevant moral reasons. What is not so generally recognized, however, is that the reasons a person could have acquired can also be relevant when assessing a person's conduct from a self-interest point of view.

Consider the following example. An acquaintance of mine bought a house on the last day it was being offered for sale, when it was too late to have the house inspected. The house was found to have such a termite infestation that it cost several thousands of dollars to correct the structural damage. Apparently, the previous owners did not know about the termites, and my acquaintance, having inspected the house on her own, did not think that she needed to have the house professionally inspected. My acquaintance now admits, I think rightly, that she acted unreasonably in purchasing the house without a professional inspection. I think it is plausible to say that her action was not unreasonable in terms of any reasons she had at the time of purchase, because at that time she didn't know or have reason to believe that the house had termites, and the opportunity to have the house inspected no longer existed. Rather, her action is best seen as unreasonable in terms of the reasons she could have had at the time of purchase if only she had arranged to have the house professionally inspected. What these examples show is that not just the reasons people have but also the reasons they could have acquired are relevant to a rational evaluation of their conduct. Accordingly, we do need to take into account people's capacity for both egoism and altruism when providing a rational assessment of their conduct.[56]

IV. OBJECTIONS LARGE AND SMALL

Let us call my defense of morality "Morality as Compromise." In this section, I will deal with three specific objections that have been raised to it and two general objections that could be raised to it. Let me begin with the general objections.

A Hobbesian Objection

I suppose the most general objection that could be raised to Morality as Compromise is that we simply don't need it. We don't need this justification of morality, this objection goes on to argue, because we already have a more straightforward justification for morality grounded in self-interest, namely, the justification for morality that has been developed by David Gauthier.[57]

In *Morals by Agreement*, Gauthier has constructed an elaborate argument to show that acquiring a disposition to act morally can be justified in terms of self-interest or, as he puts it, that adopting a strategy of constrained maximization can be justified in terms of the max-imization of individual utility.[58] Gauthier contends that the disposition of a rational individual to comply with a strategy of constrained max-imization is conditional upon the person's expectation that "she will benefit in comparison with the utility she could expect were no one to cooperate."[59] According to Gauthier, in order for a strategy of con-strained maximization to be justified on the basis of maximizing in-dividual utility, it must be the case that constrained maximizers can tell beforehand whether they are interacting with other constrained maximizers or with straightforward maximizers. Only in this way can they avoid being taken advantage of by straightforward maximizers. Happily, this obstacle can be overcome, Gauthier argues, provided that constrained maximizers are present in sufficient numbers and that people's dispositions to cooperate may be ascertained by others "not with certainty but as more than mere guesswork."[60]

A final condition that Gauthier maintains must be met before a strategy of constrained maximization is said to be justified on grounds of maximizing individual utility is that its adoption proceed from a noncoercive starting point.[61] The test for such a starting point is that, other things being equal, no one is made worse off by the actions of others than they would be if those others had never existed.[62] Thus, for example, it would not be enough for slaveholders simply to free their slaves; they would also have to compensate them so that they would be no worse off than they would have been had the slavehold-ers never existed. Without such a noncoercive starting point, Gauthier contends, it would not be rational for someone freely to adopt a strat-egy of constrained maximization, for "morals arise in and from the rational agreement of equals."[63]

But does Gauthier's argument actually succeed in showing that mo-rality can be justified in terms of self-interest? I think his argument clearly succeeds in showing that a limited disposition to take into account the interests of others can be justified on grounds of self-interest; or, put another way, that acting from duty – that is, from the motive of doing one's duty – can be required, at least sometimes, by self-interest. This is a significant result. However, whether it succeeds as a justification for morality or not depends upon how we go on to specify our definition of morality.

For Gauthier, morality takes into account the interests of everyone alike, but it does so only within a voluntary system of mutual benefit. Thus, on his account, attempts by American slaveholders to keep their slaves or those by South African whites to retain their privileged status, when no other course of action better served their individual utility, were not immoral. Rather, they were simply beyond the pale of morality.[64] On more standard accounts of morality, however, such instances of coercive exploitation constitute some of our clearest examples of immorality. Moreover, on Gauthier's account of morality, we cannot even morally approve of the actions of those who violently throw off the shackles of coercive exploitation to establish a more just society against the interests of their former slaveholders or rulers. But again, on more standard accounts of morality, such cases are among our clearest examples of justified moral action.

Some philosophers have also questioned Gauthier's strong assumption that for the requirements of morality to be justified, people must be "translucent" with respect to their disposition to cooperate. Stephen Darwall, for example, objects that in real life such knowledge is not likely to obtain.[65] Yet with respect to many actions whose good consequences depend on a sufficient number of other people doing likewise, such as paying one's taxes or fighting for one's country, we assume that such knowledge does obtain. This is because our obligation to perform such actions is dependent upon a sufficient number of other individuals doing likewise. In standard accounts of morality, however, we have other obligations and duties that do not depend upon other people doing likewise, such as our obligation not to torture or kill innocent people. By contrast, on Gauthier's account of morality, such obligations and duties are nonexistent.

In addition, on Gauthier's account of morality, making people worse off is not wrong in itself.[66] Rather, what is wrong, and also irrational, is for people to accept conditions in which they have been made worse off as a starting point for the voluntary agreements that, in Gauthier's view, constitute morality. But when making people worse off serves to promote individual utility more than such voluntary agreements would, Gauthier has no objection to such behavior. For him, it is simply beyond the pale of morality.

In sum, while Gauthier's justification for morality is successful within a limited domain, too much still falls outside of his account for it to be a fully adequate justification of morality in terms of self-interest. So I maintain that there is still a need for a justification of morality more broadly understood, which is provided by Morality as Compromise.

An Aristotelian Objection

A second general objection that can be raised to Morality as Compromise is that, although a justification for morality is certainly needed, it offers the wrong kind. According to this objection, the very idea of framing the justification of morality as requiring a response to the egoist presupposes a Kantian understanding of a morality of obligations rather than an Aristotelian understanding of a morality of personal flourishing or eudaimonia.

34

In response to this objection, it should be noted that dealing with the egoist has venerable Platonic roots (recall Thrasymachus), and so this concern should not be alien to an Aristotelian understanding of morality. Nevertheless, the claim that Morality as Compromise favors a Kantian conception of a morality of obligations over an Aristotelian conception of a morality of personal flourishing seems correct. Accordingly, if Morality as Compromise is going to provide an adequate defense of morality, it must be possible to recast its central argument in an Aristotelian framework. That is what I propose to do.

Of course, among Aristotelians, while morality is conceived in terms of personal flourishing, there is considerable debate over how personal flourishing is to be understood.[67] According to some views, which draw heavily on Book 10 of the *Nicomachean Ethics*, personal flourishing is understood in terms of just one activity: contemplation. According to other views, personal flourishing includes a range of different (virtuous) activities in addition to contemplation. Fortunately, I don't need to enter this debate here. What I want to argue is that, however this debate is resolved, it is possible to construct an argument within an Aristotelian framework that parallels the argument of Morality as Compromise.

Let us begin by considering all the viable Aristotelian accounts of personal flourishing.[68] Let us ask of each account the question: Should people always seek personal flourishing? For the moment, set aside those accounts for which the answer is yes and consider just those accounts for which the answer is no. Richard Kraut's Aristotelian account of personal flourishing is one such.[69] Kraut claims that people should not pursue their personal flourishing when it conflicts significantly with the good of others. He gives the example of the son of a king who would be happiest by pursuing philosophical contemplation but for the good of others should pursue a political life instead. Another example is that of a person who curtails her pursuit of philosophical contemplation to care for an ailing parent. Now I contend that the balancing of the pursuit of personal flourishing against the pursuit of the good of others that is required here parallels the balancing of self-interested and altruistic reasons in Morality as Compromise. In both cases, the goal is to pursue a reasonable balance or compromise between self and others. Moreover, this will hold true of all viable Aristotelian accounts of personal flourishing that require that its pursuit be limited when it conflicts significantly with the good of others.

Next consider all those viable Aristotelian accounts of personal flourishing that we previously set aside which answered yes to the question of whether people should always pursue their personal flourishing. Now ask of these accounts of human flourishing how we are to explain our experience of self-sacrifice. I suggest that these accounts will try to explain how pursuing personal flourishing is compatible with self-sacrifice, either by distinguishing between conflicting interests of the self, or by distinguishing between conflicting selves, or by making some comparable move. A reasonable resolution of the recognized conflict will then be defended. Personal flourishing for such accounts is thus constituted by a compromise between conflicting interests of the self (e.g., self-regarding interests and other-regarding interests) or by a compromise between a more self-regarding (lower?) self and a more other-regarding (higher?) self, or by some similar compromise. Again, the parallel with the compromise in Morality as Compromise is evident. It follows, then, that for any viable Aristotelian account of personal flourishing, it will be possible to construct a defense of morality that parallels the defense of morality offered by Morality as Compromise. This shows that the Kantian-inspired argument of Morality as Compromise can be further defended by being recast into an Aristotelian framework.

Of course, I am not denying that there will be considerable debate about what are the relevant interests or relevant selves that need to be compromised. What I am claiming is that the debate will have to take a certain form if it is to be reasonable. That form, I claim, is captured in the Kantian-inspired Morality as Compromise as a compromise between self-interested reasons and altruistic reasons, but it can also be found in Aristotelian accounts as a compromise between personal flourishing and the good of others, or as a compromise within the account of personal flourishing itself between conflicting interests of the self or between conflicting selves or something similar.[70] In this way, it is possible to respond to the second general objection by showing that Morality as Compromise can be interpreted to provide a justification of morality that is also acceptable within an Aristotelian framework.

Contemporary Objections

The specific objections that have been raised to Morality as Compromise come from Jeffrey Reiman and Eric Mack.[71] In responding to an earlier version of Morality as Compromise, Jeffrey Reiman questions whether my argument suffices to show that altruistic reasons should be regarded as prima facie relevant to rational choice. Reiman claims that to regard them as prima facie relevant, it is not enough to show that a person does not have any non-question-begging grounds for *rejecting* altruistic reasons. Before regarding them as relevant, Reiman thinks that a person who already regards self-interested reasons as obviously relevant must be given a non-question-begging reason for *accepting* altruistic reasons as prima facie relevant. Presumably, Reiman also thinks that a person who already regards altruistic reasons as obviously relevant must be given a non-question-begging reason for *accepting* self-interested reasons as well.

But why is it reasonable to demand non-question-begging grounds for accepting reasons to which I am not already committed when I don't require non-question-begging grounds for continuing to accept the reasons to which I am already committed? Why is it reasonable to demand a higher standard of acceptability of reasons that I might come to accept than I demand of reasons I have already accepted?

The situation is even worse, because by allowing ourselves to retain our old reasons on lesser grounds than we require of ourselves for accepting new reasons, we may effectively block the acquisition of new reasons that are better grounded than our old reasons simply because these new reasons happen to conflict with our old ones. Clearly a more reasonable strategy would be to evaluate both new and old reasons by the same standard. If we were to proceed in this fashion, then both self-interested and altruistic reasons would have to be regarded as prima facie relevant since we lack a non-question-begging reason to reject reasons of either kind.

It is also the case that we all find ourselves somewhere on the spectrum between egoism and altruism with some capacity and opportunity to move toward one or the other, and with a strong interest in resolving the question of how we should act in this regard in a reasonable manner.

Reiman goes on to suggest that regarding both self-interested and altruistic reasons as prima facie relevant on these grounds would be analogous to naturalists and supernaturalists splitting the difference between their views and counting supernatural reasons as valid half the time. But as I understand the debate between naturalism and supernaturalism, many naturalists claim to have non-question-begging reasons for rejecting supernaturalism, and some supernaturalists claim to have non-question-begging grounds for rejecting naturalism. So this example does not parallel the case of egoism and altruism as I envision it.

But suppose there were equally good reasons for naturalism as for supernaturalism, would we be rationally required to act on naturalism half the time and supernaturalism the other half of the time, as Reiman suggests? In this case, a far more reasonable resolution would be to continue to lead the life of a naturalist or a supernaturalist at the practical level while periodically reevaluating the relevant reasons with the hope of some day resolving this issue. This interim solution is preferable because there is no way to compromise the issue between naturalism and supernaturalism that would respect the most important elements of each view. That is why the conflict between naturalism and supernaturalism differs from the conflict between egoism and altruism, because in the latter case there is a way to compromise the issue between the two views that respects the most important elements of each – namely, by favoring high-ranking self-interested reasons over low-ranking altruistic reasons and favoring high-ranking altruistic reasons over low-ranking self-interested reasons.

This illustrates how the requirement of non-question-beggingness favors different solutions in different contexts. Thus, in contexts where action can be deferred, it favors deferring action until compelling reasons favoring one course of action can be found – for example, putting off your choice of a vacation spot until you have good reasons for going to a particular place. However, in contexts where action cannot be deferred, either it is or it is not possible to combine the best parts of the existing alternatives into a single course of action. If it is not possible to combine the best parts of the existing alternatives, as in the case of naturalism and supernaturalism, the requirement of non-question-beggingness favors arbitrarily choosing between them, while periodically reexamining the situation to determine whether compelling reasons can be found to favor one alternative over the others. If it is possible to combine existing alternatives, however, as in the case of egoism and altruism, the requirement of non-question-beggingness favors this course of action. It is on this account that I argue that Morality as Compromise is rationally preferable to either egoism or altruism.[72]

Eric Mack has raised a different objection to Morality as Compromise.[73] He questions whether a nonarbitrary weighing of all the relevant self-interested and altruistic reasons would lead to the kind of resolutions that I favor. He gives the example of a rich woman in severe conflict with a poor man, having the following self-interested and altruistic reasons:

Altruistic reasons
1) not to kill the poor man
2) not to exploit the poor man
3) not to prevent the poor man from appropriating her surplus

Self-interested reasons
1) to retain control of her body
2) to retain control of her possessions crucial for meeting basic needs
3) to retain control of her possessions
4) to retain her surplus

Given these rankings, Mack claims that the rich woman's third-place altruistic reason would triumph over her fourth-place self-interested reason. But suppose that we alter the list of altruistic reasons to include two other reasons as follows:

38

Altruistic reasons
1) not to kill the poor man
2) not to exploit the poor man
3) not to maim the poor man
4) not to deceive the poor man
5) not to prevent the poor man from appropriating her surplus

Given these rankings, Mack claims that the rich woman's fifth-place altruistic reason would no longer triumph over her fourth-place self-interested reason. Mack contends that this shows that this whole procedure for ranking reasons is arbitrary, and so cannot be used to support morality over egoism in the way I propose.

Actually, I agree with Mack that *his procedure* for determining the ranking of self-interested and altruistic reasons is arbitrary. The arbitrariness is evident in the fact that Mack's lists of self-interested and altruistic reasons are not of the same sort: His list of self-interested reasons is more generic whereas his lists of altruistic reasons are more specific. No wonder, then, that Mack derives from these lists results everyone would want to reject. But this does not show that no nonarbitrary ranking is possible.

For example, suppose we make both lists generic, as follows:

Altruistic reasons
1) to meet the basic needs of others
2) to meet the nonbasic needs of others

Self-interested reasons
1) to meet one's basic needs
2) to meet one's nonbasic needs

Here there is no problem in determining that a nonarbitrary weighing of these prima facie relevant reasons would require us to rank the first-place self-interested reason over the second-place altruistic reason, other things being equal, and rank the first-place altruistic reason over the second-place self-interested reason, other things being equal.

Of course, there will be problems in determining which particular needs are basic or nonbasic; obviously, some needs are near the borderline. But just as obviously many needs can be seen to belong to one class or the other, thereby enabling us nonarbitrarily to resolve conflicts between self-interested and altruistic reasons in the way I propose in Morality as Compromise.

The last specific objection that I wish to consider is one that was raised by Jeffrey Reiman.[74] The objection is that a justification of morality like my own does not succeed even in its own terms, that is, it does not succeed in justifying morality. According to Reiman, avoiding inconsistency (as in Gewirth's justification) or avoiding question-beggingness (as in mine) are only logical requirements, whereas the offense of being immoral is something more than a logical offense. Reiman claims that a justification of morality like my own only succeeds in showing that the egoist or immoralist is guilty of a logical mistake, and that is not enough. Reiman asks us to imagine a murderer who says, "Yes, I've been inconsistent (or begged the question) but that is *all* I've done." Reiman claims that morality requires something more; it requires that we recognize the reality of other people, and immorality denies that reality.[75]

But notice that if Reiman's view of morality were sound, egoists and immoralists, by denying the reality of other people, would be solipsists, but clearly they are not.[76] Nevertheless, there is something to Reiman's objection. Putting a defense of morality in terms of a non-question-begging compromise between relevant self-interested and altruistic reasons for action can obscure the fact that what is at stake is the prohibition of the infliction of basic harm on others for the sake of nonbasic benefit to oneself, given that the infliction of such harm is what egoism would require. Thus, what needs to be made clear is that the failure to be moral involves both a logical and a material mistake. The logical mistake is that of begging the question or acting contrary to reason. The material mistake is the infliction of basic harm for the sake of nonbasic benefit. Both of these mistakes characterize any failure to be moral, and they mutually entail each other.[77] They are simply two different aspects of the same act.

In this chapter, I have argued that a commitment to morality is not only rationally permissible but also rationally required. I began by arguing that moral relativism is an implausible theory, but that it cannot be completely defended in the absence of a nonrelativistic defense of morality. I then considered attempts by Kurt Baier and Alan Gewirth to provide such a defense of morality and found them wanting, before turning to my own defense, which I called "Morality as Compromise." Finally, I considered and replied to a number of general and specific objections to Morality as Compromise. Now if my defense of Morality as Compromise has been successful, the next step in a defense of a conception of justice for here and now, as part of a peacemaking way of doing philosophy, is to show that even when Morality as Compromise is given the minimal interpretation of a libertarian ideal of liberty, it leads, not as libertarians claim to the practical requirements of a minimal or night-watchperson state, but rather to the practical requirements of a welfare state and beyond. At least this is what I propose to establish in the next chapter.

Chapter 3

From Liberty to Equality

Libertarians like to think of themselves as defenders of liberty. F. A. Hayek, for example, sees his work as restating an ideal of liberty for our times. "We are concerned," says Hayek, "with that condition of men in which coercion of some by others is reduced as much as possible in society."[1] Similarly, John Hospers believes that libertarianism is "a philosophy of personal liberty – the liberty of each person to live according to his own choices, provided that he does not attempt to coerce others and thus prevent them from living according to their choices."[2] And Robert Nozick claims that, if a conception of justice goes beyond libertarian "side-constraints," it cannot avoid the prospect of continually interfering with people's lives.

Libertarians have interpreted their ideal of liberty in two basically different ways. Some, following Herbert Spencer, have (1) taken a right to liberty as basic and (2) derived all other rights from this right to liberty. Others, following John Locke, have (1) taken a set of rights, including typically a right to life and a right to property, as basic and (2) defined liberty as the absence of constraints in the exercise of these rights. Both groups of libertarians regard liberty as the ultimate political ideal, but they do so for different reasons. For Spencerian libertarians, liberty is the ultimate political ideal because all other rights are derived from a right to liberty. For Lockean libertarians, liberty is the ultimate political ideal because liberty is just the absence of constraints in the exercise of people's fundamental rights.

One could, of course, develop the libertarian view in directions that libertarians are happy to go. For example, one could derive a range of nonpaternalistic policies, including the legalization of drugs, from a libertarian foundation. Unfortunately, developing libertarianism in such directions would do little to reconcile the differences between libertarians and welfare liberals over the provision of welfare and equal opportunity, given that libertarians think their own ideal requires the rejection of rights to welfare and equal opportunity, while welfare liberals endorse these rights as basic requirements of their ideal. Accordingly, I propose to develop the libertarian view in a direction that libertarians have yet to recognize by showing that the ideal requires the same rights to welfare and equal opportunity that are defended by welfare liberals. In this way, I hope to ground a conception of justice for here and now on just the sort of practical reconciliation of alternative moral and political ideals that is sought by a peacemaking way of doing philosophy.

I. SPENCERIAN AND LOCKEAN LIBERTARIANS

Let us begin by considering the view of Spencerian libertarians, who take a right to liberty to be basic and define all other rights in terms of this right to liberty. According to this view, liberty is usually interpreted as being unconstrained by other persons from doing what one wants or is able to do. Interpreting liberty this way, libertarians like to limit constraints to positive acts (that is, acts of commission) that prevent people from doing what they otherwise want or are able to do. In contrast, welfare liberals and socialists interpret constraints to include, in addition, negative acts (acts of omission) that prevent people from doing what they otherwise want or are able to do. In fact, this is one way to understand the debate between defenders of "negative liberty" and defenders of "positive liberty." This is because defenders of negative liberty interpret constraints to include only positive acts of others that prevent people from doing what they otherwise want or are able to do, while defenders of positive liberty interpret constraints to include both positive and negative acts of others that prevent people from doing what they otherwise want or are able to do.

In order not to beg the question against libertarians, suppose we interpret constraints in the manner favored by libertarians to include only positive acts by others that prevent people from doing what they otherwise want or are able to do. Libertarians go on to characterize their political ideal as requiring that each person should have the greatest amount of liberty commensurate with the same liberty for all.[3] From this ideal, they claim that a number of more specific requirements, in particular a right to life, a right to freedom of speech, press, and assembly, and a right to property, can be derived.

Here it is important to observe that the libertarian's right to life is not a right to receive from others the goods and resources necessary for preserving one's life. It is not a right to welfare: It is simply a right not to be killed unjustly. Correspondingly, the libertarian's right to property is not a right to receive from others the goods and resources necessary to meet one's basic needs, but rather a right to acquire goods and resources either by initial acquisitions or by voluntary agreements.

Of course, libertarians would allow that it would be nice of the rich to share their surplus goods and resources with the poor. Nevertheless, they deny that government has a duty to provide for such needs. Some good things, such as providing of welfare to the needy, are requirements of charity rather than justice, libertarians claim. Accordingly, failure to make such provisions is neither blameworthy nor punishable. As a consequence, libertarians contend that such acts of charity should not be coercively required. For this reason, they are opposed to any coercively supported welfare program.

For a similar reason, libertarians are opposed to coercively supported opportunity programs. This is because the basic opportunities one has under a libertarian conception of justice are primarily a function of the property one controls, and since unequal property distributions are taken to be justified under a libertarian conception of justice, unequal basic opportunities are also regarded as justified.

The same opposition to coercively supported welfare and equal opportunity programs characterizes Lockean libertarians, who take a set of rights, typically including a right to life and a right to property, as basic and then interpret liberty as being unconstrained by other persons from doing what one has a right to do. According to this view, a right to life is simply a right not to be killed unjustly; it is not a right to receive welfare. Correspondingly, a right to property is a right to acquire property either by initial acquisitions or by voluntary transactions; it is not a right to receive from others whatever goods and resources one needs to maintain oneself. Understanding a right to life and a right to property in this way, libertarians reject both coercively supported welfare programs and equal opportunity programs as violations of liberty.

A Partial Defense

In support of their view, libertarians have advanced examples of the following sort. The first two are adapted from Milton Friedman, the last from Robert Nozick.[4]

In the first example, you are to suppose that you and three friends are walking along the street and you happen to notice and retrieve a hundred-dollar bill lying on the pavement. Suppose a rich fellow had passed by earlier throwing away hundred-dollar bills and you have been lucky enough to find one of them. Now, according to Friedman, it would be nice of you to share your good fortune with your friends. Nevertheless, they have no right to demand that you do so, and hence they would not be justified in forcing you to share the hundred-dollar bill with them. Similarly, Friedman would have us believe that it would be nice of us to provide welfare to the less fortunate members of our society. Nevertheless, the less fortunate members have no right to welfare, and hence they would not be justified in forcing us to provide such.

The second example, which Friedman regards as analogous to the first, involves supposing that there are four Robinson Crusoes, each marooned on four uninhabited islands in the same neighborhood. One of these Crusoes happens to land on a large and fruitful island, which enables him to live easily and well. The others happen to land on tiny and rather barren islands from which they can barely scratch a living. Suppose one day they discover the existence of each other. Now, according to Friedman, it would be nice of the fortunate Robinson Crusoe to share the resources of his island with the other three Crusoes, but the other three Crusoes have no right to demand that he share those resources, and it would be wrong for them to force him to do so. Correspondingly, Friedman thinks it would be nice of us to provide the less fortunate in our society with welfare, but the less fortunate have no right to demand that we do so, and it would be wrong for them to force us to do so.

In the third example, Robert Nozick asks us to imagine that we are in a society that has just distributed income according to some ideal pattern, possibly a pattern of equality. We are further to imagine that in such a society someone with the talents of Wilt Chamberlain or Michael Jordan offers to play basketball for us provided that he receives, let us say, one dollar from every home game ticket that is sold. Suppose we agree to these terms, and two million people attend the home games to see this new Wilt Chamberlain or Michael Jordan play, thereby securing for him an income of two million dollars. Since such an income would surely upset the initial pattern of income distribution whatever that happened to be, Nozick contends that this illustrates how an ideal of liberty upsets the patterns required by other conceptions of justice, and hence calls for their rejection.

II. SPENCERIAN LIBERTARIANS AND THE PROBLEM OF CONFLICT

To evaluate the libertarian view, let us begin with the ideal of liberty as defended by Spencerian libertarians and consider a typical conflict situation between the rich and the poor. In this situation, the rich have more than enough goods and resources to satisfy their basic needs.[5] By contrast, the poor lack the goods and resources to meet their most basic needs, even though they have tried all the means available to

44

them that Spencerian libertarians regard as legitimate for acquiring such goods and resources. Under circumstances like these, libertarians usually maintain that the rich should have the liberty to use their goods and resources to satisfy their luxury needs if they so wish. Spencerian libertarians recognize that this liberty might well be enjoyed at the expense of the satisfaction of the most basic needs of the poor; they just think that liberty always has priority over other political ideals, and since they assume that the liberty of the poor is not at stake in such conflict situations, it is easy for them to conclude that the rich should not be required to sacrifice their liberty so that the basic needs of the poor may be met.

Of course, Spencerian libertarians allow that it would be nice of the rich to share their surplus goods and resources with the poor, just as Milton Friedman would allow that it would be nice of you to share the hundred dollars you found with your friends, and nice of the rich-islanded Robinson Crusoe to share his resources with the poor-islanded Robinson Crusoes. Nevertheless, according to Spencerian libertarians, such acts of charity cannot be required, because the liberty of the poor is not thought to be at stake in such conflict situations.

In fact, however, the liberty of the poor is at stake in such conflict situations. What is at stake is the liberty of the poor not to be interfered with in taking from the surplus possessions of the rich what is necessary to satisfy their basic needs.[6] Needless to say, Spencerian libertarians would want to deny that the poor have this liberty. But how could they justify such a denial? As this liberty of the poor has been specified, it is not a positive right to receive something but a negative right of noninterference. Nor will it do for Spencerian libertarians to appeal to a right to life or a right to property to rule out such a liberty, because on the Spencerian view liberty is basic and all other rights are derived from a right to liberty. Clearly, what Spencerian libertarians must do is recognize the existence of such a liberty and then claim that it conflicts with other liberties of the rich. But when Spencerian libertarians see that this is the case, they are often genuinely surprised – one might even say rudely awakened – for they had not previously seen the conflict between the rich and the poor as a conflict of liberties.[7]

When the conflict between the rich and the poor is viewed as a conflict of liberties, either we can say that the rich should have the liberty not to be interfered with in using their surplus goods and resources for luxury purposes or we can say that the poor should have the liberty not to be interfered with in taking from the rich what they require to meet their basic needs. If we choose one liberty, we must reject the other. What needs to be determined, therefore, is which lib-

45

erty is morally preferable, the liberty of the rich or the liberty of the poor.

Two Principles

In order to see that the liberty of the poor not to be interfered with in taking from the surplus resources of the rich what is required to meet their basic needs is morally preferable to the liberty of the rich not to be interfered with in using their surplus goods and resources for luxury purposes, we need to appeal to one of the most fundamental principles of morality, one that is common to all political perspectives. This is

> *The "Ought" Implies "Can" Principle:* People are not morally required to do what they lack the power to do or what would involve so great a sacrifice that it would be unreasonable to ask them to perform such an action and/or, in the case of severe conflicts of interest, unreasonable to require them to perform such an action.[8]

For example, suppose I promised to attend a departmental meeting on Friday, but on Thursday I am involved in a serious car accident that leaves me in a coma. Surely, it is no longer the case that I ought to attend the meeting now that I lack the power to do so. Or suppose that on Thursday I develop a severe case of pneumonia for which I am hospitalized. Surely, I could legitimately claim that I cannot attend the meeting, on the grounds that the risk to my health involved in attending is a sacrifice that it would be unreasonable to ask me to bear. Or suppose the risk to my health from having pneumonia is not so great that it would be unreasonable to ask me to attend the meeting (a supererogatory request), still it might be serious enough to be unreasonable to require my attendance at the meeting (a demand that is backed up by blame or coercion).

What is distinctive about this formulation of the "Ought" Implies "Can" Principle is that it claims that the requirements of morality cannot, all things considered, be unreasonable to ask, and/or in cases of severe conflict of interest, unreasonable to require people to abide by. The principle claims that reason and morality must be linked in an appropriate way, especially if we are going to be able justifiably to use blame or coercion to get people to abide by the requirements of morality. It should be noted, however, that although major figures in the history of philosophy, and most philosophers today, including virtually all libertarian philosophers, accept this linkage between reason and morality, this linkage is not usually conceived to be part of the "Ought" Implies "Can" Principle.[9] Nevertheless, I claim that there are good reasons for associating this linkage with the principle, namely, our use of the word *can* as in the example just given, and the natural progression from logical, physical, and psychological possibility found in the traditional "Ought" Implies "Can" Principle to the notion of moral possibility found in this formulation of the principle. In any case, the acceptability of this formulation of the "Ought" Implies "Can" Principle is determined by the virtually universal acceptance of its components and not by the manner in which I have proposed to join those components together.[10]

Now applying the "Ought" Implies "Can" Principle to the case at hand, it seems clear that the poor have it within their power willingly to relinquish such an important liberty as the liberty not to be interfered with in taking from the rich what they require to meet their basic needs. Nevertheless, it would be unreasonable to ask or require them to make so great a sacrifice. In the extreme case, it would involve asking or requiring the poor to sit back and starve to death. Of course, the poor may have no real alternative to relinquishing this liberty. To do anything else may involve worse consequences for themselves and their loved ones and may invite a painful death. Accordingly, we may expect that the poor would acquiesce, albeit unwillingly, to a political system that denies them the right to welfare supported by such a liberty at the same time that we recognize that such a system imposes an unreasonable sacrifice upon the poor – a sacrifice that we cannot morally blame the poor for trying to evade.[11] Analogously, we might expect that a woman whose life was threatened would submit to a rapist's demands at the same time that we recognize the utter unreasonableness of those demands.

By contrast, it would not be unreasonable to ask and require the rich to sacrifice the liberty to meet some of their luxury needs so that the poor could have the liberty to meet their basic needs.[12] Naturally, we might expect that the rich, for reasons of self-interest and past contribution, might be disinclined to make such a sacrifice. We might even suppose that the past contribution of the rich provides a good reason for not sacrificing their liberty to use their surplus for luxury purposes. Yet, unlike the poor, the rich cannot claim that relinquishing such a liberty would involve so great a sacrifice that it would be unreasonable to ask and require them to make it; unlike the poor, the rich can be morally blameworthy for failing to make such a sacrifice.

Notice that by virtue of the "Ought" Implies "Can" Principle, this argument establishes that:

1a) Because it would be unreasonable to ask or require the poor to sacrifice the liberty not to be interfered with when taking from the surplus goods and resources of the rich what is necessary to meet their basic needs, 1b) it is not the case that the poor are morally required to make such a sacrifice.

2a) Because it would not be unreasonable to ask and require the rich to sacrifice the liberty not to be interfered with when using their surplus goods and resources for luxury purposes, 2b) it may be the case that the rich are morally required to make such a sacrifice.

What the argument does not establish is that the rich are *morally required* to sacrifice (some of) their surplus so that the basic needs of the poor can be met. To establish that conclusion clearly, we need to appeal to a principle that is, in fact, simply the contrapositive of the "Ought" Implies "Can" Principle. It is

> *The Conflict Resolution Principle:* What people are morally required to do is what is either reasonable to ask them to do or, in the case of severe conflicts of interest, reasonable to require them to do.

While the "Ought" Implies "Can" Principle claims that if any action is *not reasonable to ask or require* a person to do, all things considered, that action is *not morally required* for that person, all things considered ($-R[A \lor Re] \rightarrow -MRe$), the conflict resolution principle claims that if any action is *morally required* for a person to do, all things considered, that action is *reasonable to ask or require* that person to do, all things considered ($MRe \rightarrow R[A \lor Re]$).

This Conflict Resolution Principle accords with the generally accepted view of morality as a system of reasons for resolving interpersonal conflicts of interest. Of course, morality is not limited to such a system of reasons. Most surely it also includes reasons of self-development. All that is being claimed by the principle is that moral resolutions of interpersonal conflicts of interest cannot be contrary to reason to ask everyone affected to accept or, in the case of severe interpersonal conflicts of interest, unreasonable to require everyone affected to accept. The reason for the distinction between the two kinds of cases is that when interpersonal conflicts of interest are not severe, moral resolutions must still be reasonable to ask everyone affected to accept, but they need not be reasonable to *require* everyone affected to accept. This is because not all moral resolutions can be justifiably enforced; only moral resolutions of severe interpersonal conflicts of interest can and *should* be justifiably enforced. Furthermore, the reason why moral resolutions of severe interpersonal conflicts of interest should be enforced is that, if the parties are simply asked but not required to abide by a moral resolution in such cases of conflict, then it is likely that the stronger party will violate the resolution, and that would be unreasonable to ask or require the weaker party to accept.[13]

When we apply the conflict resolution principle to our example of severe conflict between the rich and the poor, there are three possible moral resolutions:

I) a moral resolution that would require the rich to sacrifice the liberty not to be interfered with when using their surplus goods and resources for luxury purposes so that the poor can have the liberty not to be interfered with when taking from the surplus resources of the rich what is necessary to meet their basic needs;

II) a moral resolution that would require the poor to sacrifice the liberty not to be interfered with when taking from the surplus goods and resources of the rich what is necessary to meet their basic needs so that the rich can have the liberty not to be interfered with when using their surplus resources for luxury purposes;

III) a moral resolution that would require the rich and the poor to accept the results of a power struggle in which both the rich and the poor are at liberty to appropriate and use the surplus goods and resources of the rich.

Applying our previous discussion of the "Ought" Implies "Can" Principle to these three possible moral resolutions, it is clear that 1a (it would be unreasonable to ask or require the poor . . .) rules out II, but 2a (it would not be unreasonable to ask and require the rich . . .) does not rule out I. But what about III? Some libertarians have contended that III is the proper resolution of severe conflicts of interest between the rich and the poor.[14] But a resolution, like III, that sanctions the results of a power struggle between the rich and the poor is a resolution which, by and large, favors the rich over the poor. So, all things considered, it would be no more reasonable to require the poor to accept III than it would be to require them to accept II. This means that only I satisfies the Conflict Resolution Principle by being a resolution that is reasonable to require everyone affected to accept. Consequently, if we assume that however else we specify the requirements of morality, they cannot violate the "Ought" Implies "Can" Principle or the Conflict Resolution Principle, it follows that despite what Spencerian libertarians claim, the basic right to liberty endorsed by them, as determined by a weighing of the relevant competing liberties according to these two principles, actually favors the liberty of the poor over the liberty of the rich.[15]

Yet couldn't Spencerian libertarians object to this conclusion, claiming that it would be unreasonable to require the rich to sacrifice the liberty to meet some of their luxury needs so that the poor could have the liberty to meet their basic needs? As has been pointed out, libertarians don't usually see the situation as a conflict of liberties, but suppose they did. How plausible would such an objection be? Not very plausible at all.

Consider: What are Spencerian libertarians going to say about the poor? Isn't it clearly unreasonable to require the poor to sacrifice the liberty to meet their basic needs so that the rich can have the liberty to meet their luxury needs? Isn't it clearly unreasonable to require the poor to sit back and starve to death? If it is, then there is no resolution of this conflict that it would be reasonable to require both the rich and the poor to accept. But that would mean that libertarians could not be putting forth a moral resolution because, according to the Conflict Resolution Principle in cases of severe conflict of interest, a moral resolution resolves conflicts of interest in ways that it would be reasonable to require everyone affected to accept. Therefore, as long as libertarians think of themselves as putting forth a moral resolution for cases of severe conflict of interest, they cannot allow that it would be unreasonable *both* to require the rich to sacrifice the liberty to meet some of their luxury needs in order to benefit the poor and to require the poor to sacrifice the liberty to meet their basic needs in order to benefit the rich. But I submit that if one of these requirements is to be judged reasonable, then, by any neutral assessment, it must be the requirement that the rich sacrifice the liberty to meet some of their luxury needs so that the poor can have the liberty to meet their basic needs. There is no other plausible resolution if libertarians intend to be putting forth a moral resolution.[16]

But might not libertarians hold that putting forth a moral resolution requires nothing more than being willing to universalize one's fundamental commitments? Surely we have no difficulty imagining the rich being willing to universalize their commitments to relatively strong property rights. At the same time, we have no difficulty imagining the poor and their advocates being willing to universalize their commitment to relatively weak property rights. However, if a libertarian moral resolution is interpreted in this fashion, it would not be able to provide a basis for resolving conflicts of interest between the rich and the poor in a reasonable fashion. And without such a basis for conflict resolution, how could we flourish, as libertarians claim we would, under a minimal state?[17] For societies to flourish in this fashion, the libertarian ideal must resolve severe conflicts of interest in ways that it would be reasonable to require everyone affected to accept. But as we have seen, that requirement can be satisfied only if the rich sacrifice the liberty to meet their luxury needs so that the poor can have the liberty to meet their basic needs.

Notice that it is not the mere size of the sacrifice required of the poor that is objectionable about the possibility of favoring the liberty of the rich over the liberty of the poor, because sometimes morality does require great sacrifices from us. For example, it requires us to refrain from intentionally killing innocent people, even to save our lives. Rather, what is objectionable about this possibility is the size of the sacrifice that the poor would be required to bear compared to the size of the benefit that would thereby be secured for the rich. In the case of the prohibition against intentionally killing innocent people, the sacrifice that violating this prohibition would impose on (innocent) people is normally greater than the benefit we ourselves and others would endure from violating that prohibition; hence the reasonableness of the prohibition. Correspondingly, in the conflict between the rich and the poor, the sacrifice that would be imposed on the poor by denying them the satisfaction of their basic needs is clearly greater than the benefit the rich would obtain from satisfying their nonbasic or luxury needs; hence the unreasonableness of imposing such a sacrifice on the poor. In this case, it is more reasonable to require a certain degree of altruism from the rich than to require an even greater degree of altruism from the poor. In all such cases, the goal is to avoid imposing an unreasonable sacrifice on anyone, where the reasonableness of the sacrifice is judged by comparing the alternative possibilities. Thus, once the poor's basic needs are met, it would be unreasonable to further constrain the liberty of the rich, because that would impose an unreasonable sacrifice upon them.[18]

It should also be noted that this case for restricting the liberty of the rich depends upon the willingness of the poor to take advantage of whatever opportunities are available to them to engage in mutually beneficial work, so that failure of the poor to take advantage of such opportunities would normally cancel, or at least significantly reduce, the obligation of the rich to restrict their own liberty for the benefit of the poor.[19] In addition, the poor would be required to return the equivalent of any surplus possessions they have taken from the rich once they are able to do so and still satisfy their basic needs. Nor would the poor be required to keep the liberty to which they are entitled. They could give up part of it, or all of it, or risk losing it on the chance of gaining a greater share of liberties or other social goods.[20] Consequently, the case for restricting the liberty of the rich for the benefit of the poor is neither unconditional nor inalienable.

Of course, there will be cases in which the poor fail to satisfy their basic needs, not because of any direct restriction of liberty on the part of the rich, but because the poor are in such dire need that they are unable even to attempt to take from the rich what they require to meet their basic needs. In such cases, the rich would not be performing any act of commission that would prevent the poor from taking what they require. Yet, even in such cases, the rich would normally be performing acts of commission that would prevent other persons from taking part of the rich's own surplus possessions and using it to aid the poor. And when assessed from a moral point of view, restricting the liberty of these allies or agents of the poor would not be morally justified for the very same reason that restricting the liberty of the poor to meet their own basic needs would not be morally justified: It would not be reasonable to require all of those affected to accept such a restriction of liberty.

The Benefit of the Poor

Nevertheless, Spencerian libertarians might respond that, even assuming that a right to welfare could be morally justified on the basis of the liberty of the poor not to be interfered with when taking from the rich in order to meet their basic needs and the liberty of third parties not to be interfered with when taking from the rich to provide for the basic needs of the poor, the poor still would be better off without the enforcement of such a right.[21] For example, it might be argued that when people are not forced through taxation to support a right to welfare, they are both more productive, as they are able to keep more of what they produce, and more charitable, as they tend to give more freely to those in need when they are not forced to do so. As a result, so the argument goes, the poor would benefit more from the increased charity of a libertarian society than they would from the guaranteed minimum of a welfare state.

Yet surely it is difficult to comprehend how the poor could be better off in a libertarian society, assuming, as seems likely, that they would experience a considerable loss of self-respect once they had to depend upon the uncertainties of charity for the satisfaction of their basic needs without the protection of a guaranteed minimum. It is also difficult to comprehend how people who are presently so opposed to a guaranteed minimum would turn out to be so charitable to the poor in a libertarian society.

Moreover, in a libertarian society providing for the needs of the poor would involve an impossible coordination problem. For if the duty to help the poor is at best supererogatory, as libertarians claim, then no one can legitimately force anyone who does not consent to provide help. The will of the majority on this issue could not legitimately be imposed upon dissenters.[22] Assuming, then, that providing for the needs of the poor requires coordinated action on a broad front, such coordination could not be achieved in a libertarian society, because it would first require a near unanimous agreement of all its members.[23]

Nevertheless, it might still be argued that the greater productivity of the more talented people in a libertarian society would increase employment opportunities and voluntary welfare assistance, which would benefit the poor more than a guaranteed minimum would in a welfare state. But this simply could not occur. For if the more talented members of a society were to provide sufficient employment opportunities and voluntary welfare assistance to enable the poor to meet their basic needs, then the conditions for invoking a right to a guaranteed minimum in a welfare state would not arise, since the poor are first required to take advantage of whatever employment opportunities and voluntary welfare assistance are available to them before they can legitimately invoke such a right. Consequently, when *sufficient* employment opportunities and voluntary welfare assistance obtain, there would be no practical difference in this regard between a libertarian society and a welfare state, since neither would justify invoking a right to a guaranteed minimum. Only when *insufficient* employment opportunities and voluntary welfare assistance obtain would there be a practical difference between a libertarian society and a welfare state, and then it would clearly benefit the poor to be able to invoke the right to a guaranteed minimum in a welfare state. Consequently, given the conditional nature of the right to welfare, and the practical possibility and, in most cases, the actuality of insufficient employment opportunities and voluntary welfare assistance obtaining, there is no reason to think that the poor would be better off without the enforcement of such a right.[24]

In brief, if a right to liberty is taken to be basic, then, contrary to what Spencerian libertarians claim, not only would a right to welfare be morally required but also such a right would clearly benefit the poor.

III. LOCKEAN LIBERTARIANS AND THE PROBLEM OF CONFLICT

Let us now consider whether these same conclusions can be established against Lockean libertarians, who take a set of rights, typically including a right to life and a right to property, as basic and then interpret liberty as being unconstrained by other persons from doing what one has a right to do. According to this view, a right to life is understood as a right not to be killed unjustly, and a right to property is understood as a right to acquire goods and resources either by initial acquisition or by voluntary agreement. In order to evaluate this view, we must determine what is entailed by these rights.

Presumably, a right to life understood as a right not to be killed unjustly would not be violated by defensive measures designed to protect one's person from life-threatening attacks.[25] Yet would this right be violated when the rich prevent the poor from taking what they require to satisfy their basic needs? Obviously, as a consequence of such preventive actions poor people sometimes do starve to death. Have the rich, then, in contributing to this result, killed the poor, or have they simply let them die; and, if they have killed the poor, have they done so unjustly?

Sometimes the rich, in preventing the poor from taking what they require to meet their basic needs, would not in fact be killing the poor but would only be causing them to be physically or mentally debilitated. Yet because such preventive acts involve resisting the life-preserving activities of the poor, when the poor do die as a consequence of such acts, it seems clear that the rich would be killing the poor, whether intentionally or unintentionally.[26]

Of course, libertarians would want to argue that such killing is simply a consequence of the legitimate exercise of property rights and, hence, is not unjust. But to understand why libertarians are mistaken in this regard, let us appeal again to those fundamental principles of morality, the "Ought" Implies "Can" Principle and the Conflict Resolution Principle. In this context, these principles can be used to assess two opposing accounts of property rights. According to the first account, a right to property is not conditional upon whether other persons have sufficient opportunities and resources to satisfy their basic needs. This view holds that the initial acquisition and voluntary agreement of some can leave others, through no fault of their own, dependent upon charity for the satisfaction of their most basic needs. By contrast, according to the second account, initial acquisition and voluntary agreement can confer title of property on all goods and resources except those surplus goods and resources of the rich that are required to satisfy the basic needs of those poor who, through no fault of their own, lack opportunities and resources to satisfy their own basic needs.

Recall that there were two interpretations of the basic right to liberty on which the Spencerian view is grounded. One interpretation ignores the liberty of the poor not be interfered with when taking from the surplus possessions of the rich what they require to meet their basic needs; the other gives that liberty priority over the liberty of the rich not to be interfered with when using their surplus for luxury purposes. Here, too, there are two interpretations of the right to property on which the Lockean view is grounded. One interpretation regards the right to property as *not* conditional upon the resources and opportunities available to others; the other regards the right to property as conditional upon the resources and opportunities available to others. And, just as in the case of the Spencerian view, here we need to appeal to those fundamental principles of morality, the "Ought" Implies "Can" Principle and the Conflict Resolution Principle, to decide which interpretation is morally acceptable.

It is clear that only the unconditional interpretation of property rights would generally justify the killing of the poor as a legitimate exercise of the property rights of the rich. Yet it would be unreasonable to require the poor to accept anything other than some version of the conditional interpretation of property rights. Moreover, according to the conditional interpretation, it does not matter whether the poor would actually die or are only physically or mentally debilitated as a result of such acts of prevention. Either result would preclude property rights from arising. Of course, the poor may have no real alternative to acquiescing to a political system modeled after the unconditional interpretation of property rights, even though such a system imposes an unreasonable sacrifice upon them – a sacrifice that we could not blame them for trying to evade. At the same time, although the rich may be disinclined to do so, it would not be unreasonable to require them to accept a political system modeled after the conditional interpretation of property rights – the interpretation favored by the poor. Consequently, if we assume that, however else we specify the requirements of morality, they cannot violate the "Ought" Implies "Can" Principle and the Conflict Resolution Principle, it follows that, despite what Lockean libertarians claim, the right to life and the right to property endorsed by them actually support a right to welfare.

Now it might be objected that the right to welfare which this argument establishes from libertarian premises is not the same as the right to welfare endorsed by welfare liberals and socialists. This is correct. We could mark this difference by referring to the right this argument establishes as "a negative welfare right" and by referring to the right endorsed by welfare liberals and socialists as "a positive welfare right." The significance of this difference is that a person's negative welfare right can be violated only when other people, through acts of commission, interfere with its exercise, whereas a person's positive welfare right can be violated not only by such acts of commission but by acts of omission as well. Nonetheless, this difference will have little practical import, for in recognizing the legitimacy of negative welfare rights, libertarians will come to see that virtually any use of their surplus possessions is likely to violate the negative welfare rights of the poor by preventing the poor from rightfully appropriating (some part of) their surplus goods and resources. So, in order to ensure that they will not be engaging in such wrongful actions, it will be incumbent on them to set up institutions guaranteeing adequate positive welfare rights for the poor. Only then will they be able to use legitimately any remaining surplus possessions to meet their own nonbasic needs. Furthermore, in the absence of adequate positive welfare rights, the poor, either acting by themselves or through their allies or agents, would have some discretion in determining when and how to exercise their negative welfare rights.[27] In order not to be subject to that discretion, libertarians will tend to favor the only morally legitimate way of preventing the exercise of such rights: They will set up institutions guaranteeing adequate positive welfare rights that will then take precedence over the exercise of negative welfare rights. For these reasons, recognizing the negative welfare rights of the poor will ultimately lead libertarians to endorse the same sort of welfare institutions favored by welfare liberals and socialists.[28]

IV. DISTANT PEOPLES AND FUTURE GENERATIONS

Now it is possible that libertarians, convinced to some extent by the above argument, might want to accept a right to welfare for members of their own society but deny that this right extends to distant peoples and future generations. Since it is only recently that philosophers have begun to discuss the question of what rights distant peoples and future generations might legitimately claim against us, a generally acceptable way of discussing the question has yet to be developed. Some philosophers have even attempted to "answer" the question, or at least part of it, by arguing that talk about "the rights of future generations" is conceptually incoherent and thus analogous to talk about "square circles." Thus Richard DeGeorge writes: "The argument in favor of the principle that only existing entities have rights is straightforward and simple: Nonexistent entities by definition do not exist. What does not exist cannot be subject or bearer of anything. Hence, it cannot be the subject or bearer of rights."[29] Accordingly, the key question that must be answered first is this: Can we meaningfully speak of distant peoples and future generations as having rights against us or of our having corresponding obligations to them?

Answering this question with respect to distant peoples is much easier than answering it with respect to future generations. Few philosophers have thought that the mere fact that people are at a distance from us precludes our having any obligations to them or their having any rights against us. Some philosophers, however, have argued that our ignorance of the specific membership of the class of distant peoples does rule out these moral relationships. Yet this cannot be right, given that in other contexts we recognize obligations to indeterminate classes of people, such as a police officer's obligation to help people in distress or the obligation of food producers not to harm those who consume their products.

Yet others have argued that, while there may be valid moral claims respecting the welfare of distant peoples, such claims cannot be rights, because they fail to hold against determinate individuals and groups.[30] But in what sense do such claims fail to hold against determinate individuals and groups? Surely all would agree that existing laws rarely specify the determinate individuals and groups against whom such claims hold. But morality is frequently determinate where existing laws are not. And at least there seems to be no conceptual impossibility to claiming that distant peoples have rights against us and that we have corresponding obligations to them.

Of course, before distant peoples can be said to have rights against us, we must be capable of acting across the distance that separates us. Yet as long as this condition is met – as it typically is for people living in most technologically advanced societies – it would certainly seem possible for distant peoples to have rights against us, and for ourselves to have corresponding obligations to them.

In contrast, answering the above question with respect to future generations is much more difficult and has been the subject of considerable debate among contemporary philosophers. One issue concerns the referent of the term *future generations*. Most philosophers seem to agree that the class of future generations is not "the class of all persons who simply *could* come into existence." But there is some disagreement about whether we should refer to the class of future generations as "the class of persons who will definitely come into existence, assuming that there are such" or as "the class of persons we can reasonably expect to come into existence." The first approach is more "existential," specifying the class of future generations in terms of what will exist; the second approach is more "epistemological," specifying the class of future generations in terms of our knowledge. Fortunately, there does not appear to be any practical moral significance to the choice of either approach.

Another issue relevant to whether we can meaningfully speak of future generations as having rights against us or our having obligations to them concerns whether it is logically coherent to speak of future generations as having rights now. Of course, no one who finds talk about rights to be generally meaningful should question whether we can coherently claim that future generations *will* have rights at some point in the future (specifically, when they come into existence and are no longer *future* generations). But what is questioned, since it is of considerable practical significance, is whether we can coherently claim that future generations have rights *now* when they do not yet exist.

Let us suppose, for example, that we continue to use up the earth's resources at present or even greater rates, and, as a result, it turns out that the most pessimistic forecasts for the twenty-second century are realized.[31] This means that future generations will face widespread famine, depleted resources, insufficient new technology to handle the crisis, and a drastic decline in the quality of life for nearly everyone. If this were to happen, could persons living in the twenty-second century legitimately claim that we in the twentieth century violated their rights by not restraining our consumption of the world's resources? Surely it would be odd to say that we violated their rights over one hundred years before they existed. But what exactly is the oddness?

Is it that future generations generally have no way of claiming their rights against existing generations? While this does make the recognition and enforcement of rights much more difficult (future generations would need strong advocates in the existing generations), it does not make it impossible for there to be such rights. After all, it is quite obvious that the recognition and enforcement of the rights of distant peoples is also a difficult task.

Or is it that we don't believe rights can legitimately exercise their influence over long durations of time? But if we can foresee and control at least some of the effects our actions will have on the ability of future generations to satisfy their basic needs, why should we not be responsible for those same effects? And if we are responsible for them, why should not future generations have a right that we take them into account?

Perhaps what troubles us is that future generations are not yet in existence when their rights are said to demand action. But how else could persons have a right to benefit from the effects our actions will have in the distant future if they did not exist at the time those effects would be felt? Our contemporaries cannot legitimately make the same demand, for they will not be around to experience those effects. Only future generations can have a right that the effects our actions will have in the distant future contribute to their well-being. Nor need we assume that in order for persons to have rights they must exist when their rights demand action. Thus, in saying that future generations have rights against existing generations we can simply mean that there are enforceable requirements upon existing generations that will benefit or prevent harm to future generations.

Most likely, what really bothers us is that we cannot know for sure what effects our actions will have on future generations. For example, we may at some cost to ourselves conserve resources that will be valueless to future generations, who may develop different technologies. Or, because we now regard them as useless, we may destroy or deplete resources that future generations would find to be essential to their well-being. Nevertheless, we should not allow such possibilities to blind us to the necessity for a social policy in this regard. After all, whatever we do will have its effect on future generations. The best approach, therefore, is to use the knowledge we presently have and assume that future generations will also require the basic resources we now find to be valuable. If it turns out that they require different resources to meet their basic needs, at least we will not be blamable for having acted on the basis of the knowledge we had.[32]

Notice, too, that present existence could not be a logical requirement for having rights now, for the simple reason that past people don't presently exist in our society; yet we continue to respect their rights, for example, through the enforcement of the terms of their wills. So if past people, who do not presently exist, can have rights against us, it should be possible for future people, who don't presently exist but who will exist in the future, to presently have rights against us. Hence, there is nothing logically incoherent in the possibility of future generations presently having rights against us.

Finally, we might wonder how future generations can have rights against us and we obligations to them, given that we can by our actions affect the membership and size of future generations. Consider the following example offered by Derek Parfit:

> [Suppose a woman] learns that she has an illness which would give to any child she conceives now a certain handicap. If she waits for two months, the illness would have passed, and she would then conceive a normal child. Suppose she decides not to wait – suppose that she knowingly conceives a handicapped rather than a normal child.[33]

Surely the woman in Parfit's example has determined by her actions that she will bring a handicapped child into existence. Parfit further contends, however, that the woman has not harmed the child, because if she had waited two months the child she would then have given birth to would certainly have been a different child.[34] And surely we might think that if the woman has not harmed the child, thus making the child worse off, she has not violated the child's rights either. So how could this child, before being born, have rights against the woman or anyone else who presently exists, or any of them have obligations to that child?

At the level of social choice, Parfit suggests that an analogous situation arises. Consider a developing country choosing between a laissez-faire population policy and one that restricts population growth. If the restrictive policy is followed, capital accumulation will produce general prosperity within one or two generations. If the laissez-faire policy is followed, low wages and high unemployment will continue indefinitely. Since the choice of either of these will, over time, produce different populations, those born subsequently under the laissez-faire policy could hardly claim they were harmed by the choice of that policy, because they wouldn't have been born if the restricted policies had been adopted. Again, it is difficult to see how any of those who are subsequently born could be said to have rights that are violated in this regard either. How, then, could they be said to have rights against us who presently exist or we obligations to them?

Now it is important to see that both of Parfit's examples concern the morality of procreation, or specifically, whether we can harm people or violate their rights by bringing or not bringing them into existence.[35] This is a very important question, but it is also a different question from that of whether future generations have rights against us or we obligations to them, as this latter question is usually understood. Whatever answer we give to the procreation question, the latter question, as usually understood, assumes that some sort of procreation will take place, and then asks *under that assumption* whether those who will come into existence, or those who we can reasonably expect will come into existence, have any rights against us or we obligations to them. Thus, the assumptions of the two questions are different; the latter question assumes that there will be procreation of a certain sort; the former question assumes only that there is a morality to procreation. The two questions are related in somewhat the same way that the question of whether a particular family should have another child is related to the question of whether that family should take care of whatever children it happens to have. The latter question, like the question of whether future generations have rights against us or we obligations to them, simply assumes that procreation has or will take place and is then meaningfully concerned with what rights and obligations arise under that assumption.

Once it is recognized that we can meaningfully speak of distant peoples and future generations as having rights against us and of ourselves as having corresponding obligations to them, there is no reason not to extend the argument for a right to welfare grounded on libertarian premises that I have developed in this chapter to distant peoples and future generations as well as to the members of one's own society. This is because the argument is perfectly general and applies whenever serious conflicts of liberty arise between all those who can have rights and/or corresponding obligations.

V. A RIGHT TO EQUAL OPPORTUNITY

Now it is possible that libertarians convinced to some extent by the above arguments might want to accept a right to welfare but deny that there is a right to equal opportunity. Such a stance, however, is only plausible if we unjustifiably restrict the class of morally legitimate claimants to those within a given (affluent) society, for only then would a right to equal opportunity require something different from a right not to be discriminated against in filling roles and positions in society that follows from a right to welfare.[36] To see why this is the case, consider what is required by a right to welfare when the class of morally legitimate claimants is not unjustifiably restricted but is taken to include both distant peoples and future generations.

At present there is probably a sufficient worldwide supply of goods and resources to meet the normal costs of satisfying the basic nutritional needs of all existing persons. According to former U.S. secretary of agriculture Bob Bergland, "For the past 20 years, if the available world food supply had been evenly divided and distributed, each person would have received more than the minimum number of calories."[37] Other authorities have made similar assessments of the available world food supply.[38]

Accordingly, the adoption of a policy of supporting a right to welfare for all existing persons would necessitate significant changes, especially in developed countries. For example, the large percentage of the U.S. population whose food consumption clearly exceeds even an adequately adjusted poverty index might have to alter their eating habits substantially. In particular, they might have to reduce their consumption of beef and pork in order to make more grain available for direct human consumption. (Currently, 30 percent of worldwide production of grain and 70 percent of U.S. production is fed to animals.)[39]

Of course, it might be possible simply to produce more grain to feed people in need rather than redirecting the grain already produced from animal consumption to human consumption. But in order for this to be possible we would have to have the capacity to increase grain production by around 30 percent (the amount currently fed to animals), and it is not clear that this capacity presently exists, given that the world grain harvest has grown more slowly than population since 1984 and has not grown at all since 1990.[40]

Moreover, there is reason to expect that, as China with its population of 1.2 billion continues its rapid industrialization, it will soon, like other densely populated countries that have industrialized before it (namely, Japan, South Korea, and Taiwan) become a significant importer of grain. Japan, South Korea, and Taiwan have all moved from being largely self-sufficient to importing around 70 percent of the grain they consume, and Japan has become the world's largest importer of grain. So if China develops similarly, its demand for grain will tend to absorb whatever additional capacity there is in worldwide grain production.[41]

Yet even if there were still further capacity to increase grain production, someone would have to pay to actualize it. Obviously, the malnourished cannot pay for it or they would have already done so;

61

the well-nourished would have to pay. Indeed, the well-nourished would have to divert some of the income they would have used to meet their nonbasic needs to pay for the increased grain production. And, if the nonbasic needs that the well-nourished choose not to meet include their nonbasic need for the pleasure of eating beef and pork, the resulting reduced demand for beef and pork would thereby lead to cutbacks in the amount of grain directed into beef and pork production. Of course, the well-nourished could cut back on their satisfaction of other nonbasic needs instead, and so not directly affect the production of beef and pork. But the negative impact of such cutbacks on the production of other nonbasic goods could still have a negative effect on the production of beef and pork.

Nevertheless, whatever its exact impact on the production of beef and pork, there clearly is a need for redistribution here: The satisfaction of at least some of the nonbasic needs of the more advantaged in developed countries will have to be forgone if the basic nutritional needs of all those in developing and underdeveloped countries are to be met. Of course, meeting the long-term basic nutritional needs of these societies will require other kinds of aid, including appropriate technology and training and the removal of trade barriers favoring developed societies.[42] In addition, raising the standard of living in developing and underdeveloped countries will require a substantial increase in the consumption of energy and other resources. But such an increase will have to be matched by a substantial decrease in the consumption of these goods in developed countries; otherwise, global ecological disaster will result from increased global warming, ozone depletion, and acid rain, lowering virtually everyone's standard of living.[43] For example, some type of mutually beneficial arrangement needs to be negotiated with China, which, with 50 percent of the world's coal resources, plans to double its use of coal within the next two decades yet is currently burning 85 percent of its coal without any pollution controls whatsoever.[44] Furthermore, once the basic nutritional needs of future generations are also taken into account, the satisfaction of the nonbasic needs of the more advantaged in developed countries would have to be further restricted in order to preserve the fertility of cropland and other food-related natural resources for the use of future generations. Obviously, the only assured way to guarantee the energy and resources necessary for the satisfaction of the basic needs of future generations is to set aside resources that would otherwise be used to satisfy the nonbasic needs of existing generations.

When basic needs other than nutritional ones are taken into account as well, still further restrictions will be required. For example, it has been estimated that presently a North American uses about fifty times more goods and resources than a person living in India. This means that in terms of resource consumption the North American continent's population alone consumes as much as 12.5 billion people living in India would consume.[45] So, unless we assume that basic goods and resources, such as arable land, iron, coal, oil, and so forth are in unlimited supply, this unequal consumption would have to be radically altered in order for the basic needs of distant peoples and future generations to be met.[46] Accordingly, recognizing a right to welfare applicable both to distant peoples and to future generations would lead to a state of affairs in which few resources would be available for directly meeting nonbasic needs, and this would significantly affect the right to equal opportunity that people could be guaranteed.[47]

Now the form of equal opportunity that John Rawls defends in *A Theory of Justice* requires that persons who have the same natural assets and the same willingness to use them have an equal chance to occupy roles and positions in society commensurate with their natural assets.[48] So construed, equal opportunity provides two sorts of benefits. It benefits society as a whole by helping to ensure that the most talented people will fill the most responsible roles and positions in society. It benefits individuals by ensuring that they will not be discriminated against with respect to filling the roles and positions in society for which they are qualified, thereby giving them a fair chance of securing whatever benefits attach to those roles and positions.

I have argued, however, that once it is recognized that the class of morally legitimate claimants includes distant peoples and future generations, then guaranteeing a right to welfare to all morally legitimate claimants would lead to a state of affairs in which few resources would be available for directly meeting nonbasic needs, although such needs might still be met indirectly though the satisfaction of basic needs. As a consequence, there normally would not be greater benefits attaching to certain roles and positions in society, since people could expect only to have their basic needs directly met in whatever roles and positions they happened to occupy. Of course, we would still want the most talented people to occupy the most responsible roles and positions in society, it is just that occupying those roles and positions would normally not secure greater benefits to those who occupy them. Therefore, to ensure that the most talented people occupy roles and positions commensurate with their abilities, we will need to do something like the following. First, borrowing an idea from socialist justice, we will need to make the roles and positions people occupy as intrinsically rewarding as possible. Second, we will need to convince the more talented that they have a moral responsibility to the less talented and to society as a whole to use their talents to the fullest. Consequently, the equal opportunity that will be guaranteed

to everyone in society will, for the most part, be a fair means of ensuring that everyone's basic needs are met, rather than a means of
providing differential rewards or of serving directly to meet nonbasic
needs.

Accordingly, my practical reconciliation argument fails to guarantee a right to equal opportunity that provides greater benefits to the
talented, enabling them directly to meet nonbasic as well as basic
needs. But this failure is no objection to my argument, given that
having this sort of equal opportunity is incompatible with the more
fundamental requirement of meeting everyone's basic needs. On this
account, both libertarians and welfare liberals would come to endorse
the same right to equal opportunity – an equal right not to be discriminated against in filling roles and positions in society that is compatible with a right to welfare.

One might think that a right to equal opportunity is a nonbasic
need and so is distinct from a right to welfare, which is a basic need.
But how can it be the case that a right to welfare satisfies basic needs
while a right to equal opportunity only satisfies nonbasic needs? Suppose we reflect for the moment on the U.S. constitutional system. It
should be clear that the Constitution favors its citizens with various
kinds of equal opportunity, for example, an equal right to due process
(Sixth Amendment), a right to the equal protection of the laws (Fourteenth Amendment), an equal right to vote (Fourteenth and Nineteenth Amendments). But where is a right to welfare guaranteed by
the U.S. Constitution? In the most recent U.S. Supreme Court decision
that took up this question of a constitutional right to welfare, *Wyman
v. James* (1971), the court explicitly stated that there is no constitutional
right to welfare, but only a right to welfare that is conditional upon
the particular state's willingness to provide that welfare. But how
could the U.S. Constitution guarantee that for which we have only
nonbasic needs (various equal opportunities) yet fail to guarantee that
for which we have a basic need (welfare)?

Now I would be the first to admit that the U.S. Constitution is
morally defective,[49] but I don't think the Constitution is as defective
as it would be if the various kinds of equal opportunity it guarantees
only served to meet nonbasic but not basic needs. In my view, the
U.S. Constitution is morally defective for failing to guarantee each of
its citizens a right to welfare, which is a basic need, but it is not morally defective for guaranteeing each of its citizens a certain range of
equal opportunity, because a right to equal opportunity is also a basic
need. Rather, I think that the Constitution should, in fact, guarantee
its citizens more equal opportunity than it does, not less. Accordingly,
there is no reason to draw a sharp distinction between a right to wel-

fare and a right to equal opportunity; both are required for meeting people's basic needs.

What these arguments show, therefore, is that libertarianism or a libertarian conception of justice supports the same practical requirements as welfare liberalism or a welfare liberal conception of justice: Both favor a right to welfare and a right to equal opportunity. This is not to deny, of course, that there will not be disagreements concerning how to interpret a right to welfare understood as a right to the resources necessary for meeting one's basic needs, and a right to equal opportunity understood as an equal right not to be discriminated against in filling roles and positions in society; but there is no reason to think that libertarians will disagree with welfare liberals any more than welfare liberals will disagree among themselves over the interpretation of these rights, especially over what is required for meeting people's basic needs.[50] Recall that it is generally thought that what divides welfare liberals from libertarians is that the former are committed to rights to welfare and equal opportunity whereas the latter reject both of these rights. It is quite evident that libertarians want to reject rights to welfare and equal opportunity because they think (wrongly) that to endorse these rights is to abandon their ideal of liberty. No libertarian has argued that it will do just as well to grant such rights and then disagree as to how they are to be interpreted. Thus, given my argument that both libertarians and welfare liberals are required to endorse a right to welfare understood as a right to the resources necessary for meeting one's basic needs, and a right to equal opportunity understood as an equal right not to be discriminated against in filling roles and positions in society, it is implausible for us to think that comparable differences will now emerge between libertarians and welfare liberals over the interpretation of these rights. Differences between welfare liberals and libertarians over what constitutes a basic-needs minimum are likely to be no greater than differences among welfare liberals themselves over what constitutes such a minimum. Moreover, once libertarians and welfare liberals have taken the first practical steps to implement the rights to welfare and equal opportunity for distant peoples and future generations, they will both be in an even better position to know what is required for meeting people's basic needs. This is because sincerely attempting to live out one's practical moral commitments helps one to interpret them better, just as failing to live them out makes interpreting them all the more difficult.

In brief, what I have argued is that a libertarian conception of justice supports the same rights to welfare and equal opportunity as those endorsed by a welfare liberal conception of justice.

65

VI. LIBERTARIAN OBJECTIONS

In his book *Individuals and Their Rights*, Tibor Machan criticizes the preceding argument that a libertarian ideal of liberty leads to a right to welfare, accepting its theoretical thrust but denying its practical significance.[51] He does appreciate the force of the argument enough to grant that, if the type of conflict cases that we have described between the rich and the poor actually obtained, the poor would have a right to welfare. But he denies that such cases – in which the poor have done all they legitimately can to satisfy their basic needs in a libertarian society – actually obtain. "Normally," he writes, "persons do not lack the opportunities and resources to satisfy their basic needs."[52]

This response, however, virtually concedes everything that the preceding argument intended to establish, for the poor's right to welfare is not claimed to be unconditional. Rather, it is said to be conditional principally upon the poor doing all that they legitimately can to meet their own basic needs. So it follows that only when the poor lack sufficient opportunity to satisfy their own basic needs would their right to welfare have any practical moral force. Accordingly, on libertarian grounds, Machan has conceded the legitimacy of just the kind of right to welfare that the preceding argument hoped to establish.

The only difference that remains is a practical one. Machan thinks that virtually all of the poor have sufficient opportunities and resources to satisfy their basic needs and that, therefore, a right to welfare has no practical moral force. In contrast, I think that many of the poor do not have sufficient opportunities and resources to satisfy their basic needs and that, therefore, a right to welfare has considerable practical moral force.

But isn't this practical disagreement resolvable? Who could deny that most of the 1.2 billion people who are currently living in conditions of absolute poverty "lack the opportunities and resources to satisfy their basic needs?"[53] And even within our own country, it is estimated that some thirty-two million Americans live below the official poverty index, and that one-fifth of American children are growing up in poverty.[54] Surely, it is impossible to deny that many of these Americans also "lack the opportunities and resources to satisfy their basic needs." Given the impossibility of reasonably denying these factual claims, Machan would have to concede that the right to welfare, which he grants can be theoretically established on libertarian premises, also has practical moral force.[55]

Recently, however, Machan, seeking to undercut the practical force of my argument, has contended that when we compare economic systems to determine which produce more poverty: "No one can seriously dispute that the near-libertarian systems have fared much better than those going in the opposite direction, including the welfare state."[56] Here one would think that Machan has the United States in mind as a "near-libertarian system" because earlier in the same paragraph he claims: "America is still the freest of societies, with many of its legal principles giving expression to classical liberal, near-libertarian ideas."[57] Yet apparently this is not what Machan thinks, for in a footnote to the same text he writes: "It is notable that the statistics that Sterba cites (in my above response to Machan's critique) are drawn from societies, including the United States of America, which are far from libertarian in their legal construction and are far closer to the welfare state, if not to outright socialism."[58] Obviously, then, Machan is surprisingly unclear as to whether he wants to call the United States a near-libertarian state, a welfare state, or a socialist state. Yet, whichever of these designations is most appropriate, what is clear is that the poor do less well in the United States than they do in the welfare liberal or socialist states of Western Europe such as Germany, Sweden, and Switzerland.[59] For example, 22.4 percent of children live below the poverty line in the United States as compared to 4.9 percent in Germany, 5 percent in Sweden, and 7.8 percent in Switzerland, and the United States shares with Italy the highest infant mortality rate of the major industrialized nations. The United States also ranks 67 among all nations in the percentage of national income received by the poorest 20 percent of its population, ranking the absolute lowest among industrialized nations.[60] Accordingly, the success that welfare liberal and socialist states have had, especially in Western Europe, in coming close to truly meeting the basic needs of their deserving poor should give us good reason to doubt what Machan proclaims is the superior practical effectiveness of "near-libertarian states" in dealing with poverty.

Douglas Rasmussen has developed another libertarian challenge to the previous argument that begins by conceding what Machan denied – that the poor lack the opportunity to satisfy their basic needs.[61] Rasmussen distinguishes two ways that this can occur. In one case, only a few of the poor lack the opportunity to satisfy their basic needs. Here, Rasmussen contends that libertarian property rights still apply even though the poor who are in need morally ought to take from the surplus property of the rich what they need for survival. As libertarian property rights do still apply, Rasmussen contends that the poor who do take from the legal property of the rich can be arrested and tried for their actions; but what their punishment should be, Rasmussen contends, should simply be left up to judges to decide.[62] Rasmussen also rejects the suggestion that the law should make an exception for the poor in such cases on the grounds that one can never have perfect symmetry between what is moral and what the law requires.[63]

But why should the question of punishment simply be left up to judges to decide? If the judicial proceedings determine what is assumed in this case – that the poor morally ought to take from the legal property of the rich what they need for survival – then it is difficult to see on what grounds a judge could inflict punishment. Surely, if it would be unreasonable to require the poor to do anything contrary to meeting their basic needs at minimal cost to the rich, it would be equally unreasonable to punish the poor for actually doing just that – meeting their basic needs at minimal cost to the rich.

Nor will it do to claim that we cannot expect symmetry between what morality requires and what the law requires in this case. Of course, there is no denying that sometimes the law can justifiably require us to do what is morally wrong. In such cases, opposing the law, even when what it requires is immoral, would do more harm than good. This can occur when there is a bona fide disagreement over whether what the law requires is morally wrong (for example, the *Roe v. Wade* decision), with those in favor of the law justifiably thinking that it is morally right and those against the law justifiably thinking that it is morally wrong. When this occurs, failing to obey the law, even when what it requires is immoral, could, by undermining the legal system, do more harm than good. However, in our case of severe conflict of interest between the rich and the poor, nothing of the sort obtains. In our case, it is judged that the poor morally ought to take from the legal property of the rich and that no other moral imperative favoring the rich overrides this moral imperative favoring the poor. So it is clear in this case that there are no grounds for upholding any asymmetry between what morality and the law require. Accordingly, the law in this case should be changed to favor the poor.

However, Rasmussen distinguishes another case in which many of the poor lack the opportunity to satisfy their basic needs.[64] In this case, so many of the poor lack the opportunity to satisfy their basic needs that Rasmussen claims libertarian property rights no longer apply. Here he contends that morality requires that the poor should take what they need for survival from the legal property of the rich, and that the rich should not refuse assistance. Still, he further contends that the poor have no right to assistance in this case, nor the rich presumably any corresponding obligation to help the poor, because "the situation cannot be judged in social and political terms."[65]

But why cannot the situation be judged in social and political terms? If we know what the moral directives of the rich and the poor are in this case, as Rasmussen admits we do, why would we not be justified in setting up a legal system or altering an existing legal system so that the poor would have a guaranteed right to welfare? Now it may be that Rasmussen is imagining a situation where it is not possible for the basic needs of everyone to be met. Such situations are truly lifeboat cases. But although such cases are difficult to resolve (maybe only a chance mechanism would offer a reasonable resolution), they surely do not represent the typical conflict situation between the rich and the poor. For in such situations, it is recognized that it is possible to meet everyone's basic needs, and what is at issue is whether (some of) the nonbasic or luxury needs of the rich should be sacrificed so that everyone's basic needs can be met. So when dealing with typical conflict situations between the rich and the poor, there is no justification for not securing a legal system that reflects the moral directives in these cases.

In sum, both Machan's and Rasmussen's objections to grounding a right to welfare on libertarian premises have been answered. Machan's attempt to grant the theoretical validity of a libertarian right to welfare, but then deny its practical validity, fails once we recognize that there are many poor who lack the opportunity to satisfy their basic needs. Rasmussen's attempt to grant that there are poor who lack the opportunity to meet their basic needs, then denying that the poor have any right to welfare, fails when we recognize that the moral directives he grants apply to the rich and poor in severe conflict-of-interest cases provide ample justification for a right to welfare.

More recently, different objections to my attempt to derive a right to welfare from libertarian premises have been raised by John Hospers.[66] First, Hospers contends that I am committed to distributing welfare too broadly, to the undeserving poor as well as the deserving poor. Second, he contends that the taxes on the wealthy that I defend, in effect, commit me to killing the goose that lays the golden egg, because the poor would be worse off under a tax-supported welfare system than they would be in a completely libertarian society.

In response to the first objection Hospers raises, I have in a number of places made it clear that I am defending a right to welfare only for the deserving poor – that is, the poor who have exhausted all their legitimate opportunities for meeting their basic needs. Hospers's second objection, however, questions whether even the deserving poor would be better off demanding welfare, even if they have a right to it. He cites the example of Ernst Mahler, an entrepreneurial genius who employed more than one hundred thousand people and produced newsprint and tissue products that are now used by more than two billion people. Hospers suggests that requiring Mahler to contribute to a welfare system for the deserving poor would not only "decrease his own wealth but that of countless other people."

In response to this objection, I contend that if the more talented members of a society provided sufficient employment opportunities and voluntary welfare assistance to enable the poor to meet their basic needs, then the conditions for invoking a right to welfare would not arise, since the poor are first required to take advantage of whatever employment opportunities and voluntary welfare assistance are available to them before they can legitimately invoke such a right. Consequently, if *sufficient* employment opportunities and voluntary welfare assistance obtained, there would be no practical difference in this regard between a libertarian society and a welfare or socialist state, as neither would justify invoking a right to welfare. Only when *insufficient* employment opportunities and voluntary welfare assistance obtained would there be a practical difference between a libertarian society and a welfare or socialist state, and then it would clearly benefit the poor to be able to invoke the right to welfare. Consequently, given the practical possibility, and in most cases, the actuality of insufficient employment opportunities and voluntary welfare assistance obtaining, there is no reason to think that the poor would be better off without the enforcement of such a right.

Now one might think that once the rich realized that the poor should have the liberty not to be interfered with when taking from the surplus possessions of the rich what they require to satisfy their basic needs, they would stop producing any surplus whatsoever. This appears to be what Hospers is suggesting by citing the example of Ernst Mahler. Yet it would be in the interest of the rich to stop producing a surplus only if (*a*) they did not enjoy producing a surplus, (*b*) their recognition of the rightful claims of the poor would exhaust their surplus, and (*c*) the poor would never be in a position to be obligated to repay what they appropriated from them. Fortunately for the poor, not all of these conditions are likely to obtain.[67] But suppose they all did. Wouldn't the poor be justified in appropriating, or threatening to appropriate, even the nonsurplus possessions of those who can produce more in order to get them to do so?[68] Surely this would not be an unreasonable imposition on those who can produce more, because it would not be unreasonable to require them to be a bit more productive when the alternative is requiring the poor to forgo meeting their basic needs. Surely if we have no alternative, requiring those who can produce more to be a bit more productive is less of an imposition than requiring the poor to forgo meeting their basic needs.

This is an important conclusion in our assessment of the libertarian ideal, because it shows that ultimately the right of the poor to appropriate what they require to meet their basic needs does not depend, as many have thought, upon the talented having sufficient self-interested incentives to produce a surplus. All that is necessary is that the talented be able to produce a surplus and that the (deserving) poor not be able to meet their basic needs in any other way.

It might be objected, however, that if the talented can be required to produce a surplus so that the (deserving) poor can meet their basic needs, then why can't the poor be required to sterilize themselves as a condition for receiving that surplus. What the objection rightly points to is the need for the poor, and everyone else as well, to take steps to control population growth. What the objection wrongly maintains is that the poor would have a greater obligation to limit their procreation than the rich would have to limit theirs. Surely population can be brought under control by a uniform policy that imposes the same requirements on both rich and poor. There is no need or justification for a population policy that comes down harder on the poor.

Eric Mack raises still another objection to my libertarian argument for welfare.[69] Mack allows that my appeal to the "Ought" Implies "Can" Principle does show that in severe conflict-of-interest situations the rich do not have a right to their surplus. What Mack denies, however, is that I have shown that the poor in such situations have a right to the surplus of the rich. He contends that in these conflict situations neither the rich nor the poor have a right to the surplus of the rich. Instead, he thinks that both the rich and the poor are at liberty to appropriate and use the surplus if they can. Thus, what obtains in these conflict-of-interest situations, according to Mack, is a Hobbesian state of nature, a war of all against all.

There are two problems with Mack's analysis of these conflict situations between the rich and the poor. The first problem is that his analysis denies the existence of property rights to a surplus whenever severe conflicts of interest between the rich and the poor obtain, without recognizing any alternative (welfare) rights as applicable in those circumstances. This means that property rights to a surplus would be justified only in those rare cases in which they equally served the interests of both the rich and the poor. In all other cases, no property rights to a surplus would be justified. But surely this is not the real-world justification of property rights that libertarians had promised.

The second problem with Mack's analysis is even more serious. It is that while he accepts the "Ought" Implies "Can" Principle, his own proposed moral resolution of severe conflict-of-interest situations violates that very principle, because it requires the poor to accept the results of a power struggle in which both the rich and the poor are at liberty to appropriate and use the surplus resources of the rich insofar as they are able to do so. Obviously such a resolution favors the rich over the poor. Consequently, it would be no more reasonable to require the poor to accept this resolution than it would be to require them to accept the resolution that Mack concedes fails to satisfy the "Ought" Implies "Can" Principle – the resolution that secures for the rich property rights to their surplus. This implies that for severe conflict-of-interest situations only a resolution that guarantees the poor a right to welfare would satisfy the "Ought" Implies "Can" Principle.

Moreover, this is just the sort of resolution that the contrapositive of the "Ought" Implies "Can" Principle, which I call the Conflict Resolution Principle, requires. This principle requires that moral resolutions of severe conflicts of interest must be reasonable to require everyone affected to accept them. So in the severe conflict-of-interest situation we are considering, only a moral resolution that guaranteed the poor a right to welfare would be reasonable for both the rich and the poor to accept. Thus, for such conflict situations, only a moral resolution that guarantees the poor a right to welfare would satisfy both the "Ought" Implies "Can" Principle and its contrapositive, the Conflict Resolution Principle.

If we turn to Jan Narveson's recent work on libertarianism, we find a number of points of disagreement with my preceding analysis and argument. First, Narveson starts out with a slightly different definition of liberty.[70] Second, he seems to deny that one person's liberty can come into conflict with another person's liberty.[71] Third, he rejects my use of the "Ought" Implies "Can" and the Conflict Resolution Principles in favor of a Hobbesian social contract to determine what legitimate liberty people have.[72] Fourth, he maintains that the ideals of liberty and equality are incompatible, because liberty is a negative ideal requiring that people not do certain things while equality is a positive ideal requiring that people do certain things.[73] Let me consider each of these points in turn.

In his recent work, Narveson offers a slightly different definition of liberty that further restricts it to the absence of *intentional* interference by other people.[74] Now it is true that people are clearly more responsible for actions they do intentionally, and this may be why Narveson restricts liberty in this way. Nevertheless, people can still be responsible for actions they do unintentionally, especially if they were morally negligent and should have foreseen the consequences of their actions. Given, then, that moral responsibility can extend to both intentional and unintentional interference with a person's life, it seems best to consider both types of interference as restrictions of a person's liberty.

Narveson also seems to deny that one person's liberty can come into conflict with another person's liberty. He states that "in a libertarian state, nobody's liberty 'takes precedence over' anybody else's, rich or poor, tall or short.'"[75] Thus, Narveson seems to deny that there is a conflict between the liberty of the rich and the liberty of the poor, on which my previous argument depends. However, elsewhere he does admit to conflicts of liberty of a certain sort. He writes:

> We should, of course, bear in mind that all rights restrict liberty. In saying that someone has a right to do something, what we are saying is that someone else may not do certain things, and if necessary may be compelled to refrain from them. The libertarian case is that the fundamental right is a right to liberty, but in being so it is automatically a prohibition of the liberty to do certain things: namely, acts that infringe liberty. It has been difficult, down through the years, for critics of libertarianism to understand this point, and I regret to say that it appears that Sterba likewise, despite his rather clear characterization of much of the theory, does not fully appreciate it either. [From] the fact that it is the liberty of the poor to take from the rich that is being restricted, then, it does not follow that what we have is a clash of liberties in the relevant sense: namely, a clash of liberties that the theory protects. It is, instead, a clash between a familiar kind of liberty that it is the very essence of the theory to forbid and another kind of liberty that it is the very essence of the theory to protect.[76]

Actually, it turns out that Narveson and I are really in agreement here. We agree that there is a sense in which there is, and a sense in which there is not, a conflict of liberty between the rich and the poor. We think there is a conflict because we agree that either the rich or the poor is going to be interfered with. We think there is not a conflict because we agree that only one of them has the relevant legitimate liberty. Of course, Narveson and I disagree over who it is who has the relevant legitimate liberty – he claims the rich have it, I claim the poor have it – yet we both agree that this legitimate liberty does not conflict with any other legitimate liberty.

It is also important to note that the liberty of the poor, the legitimacy of which Narveson and I are contesting, is more precisely characterized as "the liberty of the poor not to be interfered with in taking from the surplus possessions of the rich what the poor require to meet their basic needs" rather than simply as "the liberty of the poor to take from the rich." The advantage of this more precise characterization is that it makes it abundantly clear that we are trying to determine the legitimacy of a negative rather than a positive liberty of the poor.

In trying to determine what legitimate liberty people have, Narveson, at least initially, did not realize that he and I are appealing to different standards.[77] This is because he interpreted my "Ought" Implies "Can" Principle and its contrapositive, the Conflict Resolution

Principle, as equivalent to his Hobbesian social contract. To some degree this is understandable, given that Narveson has formulated his Hobbesian social contract standard in ways that resemble my two principles.[78] He says, for example, "To have the *right* to something you are using is for there to be good and sufficient reasons why everyone ought to let you do so."[79] And, in another place, he says that the "criterion of betterness is that better principles are more acceptable to people."[80] And, in still another place, he suggests that "we should expect support for our theory from the people to whom it is addressed: namely, everybody."[81] So in light of these statements, one might think Narveson is agreeing with me that the proper distribution of liberties must not be unreasonable if we are to require the rich and the poor to accept (as my "Ought" Implies "Can" Principle demands), or, put positively, that the proper distribution of basic liberties must be reasonable if we are to require both the rich and the poor to accept (as my Conflict Resolution Principle demands). The crucial difference, however, is that my two principles, as I interpret them, impose a moral constraint on what legitimate liberty people have, whereas Narveson's Hobbesian social contract imposes only a self-interested constraint on what legitimate liberty people have.[82] According to Narveson, a distribution of liberty in society passes muster only if it does not work against the self-interest of anyone, whereas my two principles, as I interpret them, approve of distributions of liberty even when they work against the self-interest of some, provided that the degree of self-sacrifice or altruism required happens to be morally acceptable.[83]

Nor is my interpretation of the "Ought" Implies "Can" Principle and its contrapositive, the Conflict Resolution Principle, in any way unusual in this regard. Most philosophers, libertarians included, do not think, as Narveson does, that morality can be founded on Hobbesian self-interest, so they would be inclined to interpret my two principles as requiring a certain degree of altruism.[84]

Moreover, even if we wanted to ground political obligation on Hobbesian self-interest, it is far from clear that we would end up with a justification for the libertarian society that Narveson envisions. Narveson is quick to point out that from his Hobbesian premises the needs of the poor may not, and usually will not, be a consideration to which the rich give any credence. But, for similar reasons, the fact that the rich got somewhere first and were first to mix their labor with something will not be considerations that, from a Hobbesian perspective, the poor must give any credence to either. From a Hobbesian perspective, everything is determined by the payoffs to each from various forms of cooperation and noncooperation. So unless the rich have invested heavily in their defense, it may turn out to be in the self-interest of the poor to take from the rich as much as they want.

From a Hobbesian perspective, everything is determined by one's relative threat advantage. So, in Narveson's view, whether the poor have a right to welfare depends on what power relations happen to obtain between the rich and the poor, and what the rich and the poor have to gain or lose from using the power they have. Thus, Narveson, commenting on an example that I used in an earlier paper, claims that D (a she that Narveson for some reason turns into a he) is lucky that A, B, and C don't run an arrow through her to eliminate any possible threat to what they claim to be their property.[85] But a similar argument could be made whenever the poor are powerful enough to threaten or dominate the rich or talented effectively. So it seems that, even in Narveson's view, a welfare state, or possibly even a socialist state, could emerge, depending on the prevailing power relations.

Fortunately, there is a way to show the preferability of the moral standard of the two principles over the Hobbesian standard that Narveson endorses. What needs to be shown is that the morality of the two principles is rationally preferable to Hobbesian self-interest. To show this, I have argued in Chapter 2 that a conception of rationality that is acceptable to rational egoists because it presupposes nothing more than non-question-beggingness requires that we strike a compromise between egoism and altruism and favor high-ranking altruistic reasons over low-ranking self-interested reasons, and high-ranking self-interested reasons over low-ranking altruistic reasons. More specifically, this conception of rationality requires the rejection of pure egoism in favor of the degree of altruism found in the two principles as I interpret them.

I should point out that Narveson's only response to this argument is to claim that we must address our justification to people where they are, and since where at least some people are is committed to pure egoism, he claims we must show that whatever rights we propose best serve the interests of these pure egoists.[86] Yet, in response, it can be argued that pure egoists are either committed to rationality or they are not committed to rationality. If they are committed to rationality, at least to the minimal rationality of non-question-beggingness, then what my argument shows is that they need to abandon their commitment to pure egoism. And if they are not committed to rationality, even to the minimal rationality of non-question-beggingness, then it is not clear how we could justify anything to them. Thus, insofar as it is possible to justify anything to pure egoists, I claim that my argument from non-question-beggingness succeeds in showing that they must abandon their pure egoism in favor of the degree of altruism found in my two principles as I interpret them.

Narveson thinks that the ideals of liberty and equality are incompatible because the ideal of liberty is a negative ideal requiring that

75

people not interfere in certain ways with one another, whereas the ideal of equality is a positive ideal requiring that people *do* certain things to bring about equality in society.[87] But even accepting for the sake of argument that it is proper to characterize liberty as a negative ideal and equality as a positive one,[88] what the argument of this chapter shows is that the two ideals can still be reconciled in practice. This is because the pattern of commissions or interferences that the ideal of equality requires is in fact justified or demanded by the pattern of omissions or noninterferences that the libertarian ideal requires. As I argued before, in recognizing the legitimacy of negative welfare rights, libertarians will come to see that virtually any use of their surplus possessions is likely to violate the negative welfare rights of the poor by preventing the poor from rightfully appropriating (some part of) their surplus goods and resources. Consequently, to ensure that they will not be engaging in such wrongful actions, it will be incumbent on them to institute adequate positive welfare rights for the poor. Only then will they be able to use legitimately any remaining surplus possessions to meet their own nonbasic needs. Likewise, in the absence of adequate positive welfare rights, the poor, either acting by themselves or through their allies or agents, would have some discretion in determining when and how to exercise their negative welfare rights. Thus, in order not to be subject to that discretion, libertarians will tend to favor the only morally legitimate way of preventing the exercise of such rights: They will set up institutions guaranteeing adequate positive welfare rights that will then take precedence over the exercise of negative welfare rights. In this way, the negative rights of the libertarian's ideal of liberty will justify or require the positive rights of a socialist ideal of equality.

In sum, what I have argued is that a libertarian conception of justice supports the practical requirements that are usually associated with a welfare liberal conception of justice, namely, a right to welfare and a right to equal opportunity. I have also attempted to show that recent work done by libertarians Tibor Machan, Douglas Rasmussen, John Hospers, Eric Mack, and Jan Narveson neither undercuts nor is incompatible with this argument for reconciling these two conceptions of justice.[89]

Now a welfare liberal conception of justice, in virtue of its right to equal opportunity, has been appealed to by contemporary feminists in support of a conception of feminist justice that accords with the ideal of a gender-free or androgynous society. In the next chapter I examine this conception of feminist justice and consider the practical applications that it requires.

Chapter 4

From Equality to Feminism

Contemporary feminists almost by definition seek to put an end to male domination and to secure women's liberation. To achieve these goals, many feminists support the political ideal of a gender-free or androgynous society.[1] According to these feminists, all assignments of rights and duties are ultimately to accord with the ideal of a gender-free or androgynous society. Since a conception of justice is usually thought to provide the ultimate grounds for the assignment of rights and duties, I refer to this ideal of a gender-free or androgynous society as "feminist justice." As we shall see, this ideal of feminist justice can be grounded in a right to equal opportunity that is endorsed by welfare liberals and, given the argument of the previous chapter, by libertarians as well. Also, this ideal can be grounded in a right to equal self-development endorsed by socialists. Unfortunately, most political philosophers who are committed to welfare liberal, libertarian, or socialist ideals have not explored the feminist implications of their ideals, despite the fact that doing so is just what is required by a peacemaking way of doing philosophy.[2]

I. THE IDEAL OF A GENDER-FREE OR ANDROGYNOUS SOCIETY

But how is this ideal of a gender-free or androgynous society to be interpreted? It is a society where basic rights and duties are not assigned on the basis of a person's biological sex. Being male or female is not the grounds for determining what basic rights and duties a person has in a gender-free society. But this is to characterize the feminist ideal only negatively. It tells us what we need to get rid of, not what we need to put in its place. A more positive characterization is provided by the ideal of androgyny. Putting the ideal of feminist

77

justice more positively in terms of the ideal of androgyny also helps to bring out why men should be attracted to feminist justice.

In a well-known article, Joyce Trebilcot distinguishes two forms of androgyny.[3] The first postulates the same ideal for everyone. According to this form of androgyny, the ideal person "combines characteristics usually attributed to men with characteristics usually attributed to women." Thus, we should expect both nurturance and mastery, openness and objectivity, compassion and competitiveness from each and every person who has the capacities for these traits.

By contrast, the second form of androgyny does not advocate the same ideal for everyone but rather a variety of options from "pure" femininity to "pure" masculinity. As Trebilcot points out, this form of androgyny shares with the first the view that biological sex should not be the basis for determining the appropriateness of gender characterization. It differs in that it holds that "all alternatives with respect to gender should be equally available to and equally approved for everyone, regardless of sex."

It would be a mistake, however, to distinguish sharply between these two forms of androgyny. Properly understood, they are simply two different facets of a single ideal. For, as Mary Ann Warren has argued, the second form of androgyny is appropriate only "with respect to feminine and masculine traits which are largely matters of personal style and preference and which have little direct moral significance."[4] However, when we consider so-called feminine and masculine virtues, it is the first form of androgyny that is required, because then, other things being equal, the same virtues are appropriate for everyone.

We can even formulate the ideal of androgyny more abstractly so that it is no longer specified in terms of so-called feminine and masculine traits. We can specify the ideal as requiring no more than that the traits that are truly desirable in society be equally open to both women and men or, in the case of virtues, equally expected of both women and men, other things being equal.

There is a problem, of course, in determining which traits of character are virtues and which are largely matters of personal style and preference. To make this determination, Trebilcot has suggested that we seek to bring about the second form of androgyny, where people have the option of acquiring the full range of so-called feminine and masculine traits.[5] But surely when we already have good grounds for thinking that such traits as courage and compassion, fairness and openness, are virtues, there is no reason to adopt a laissez-faire approach to moral education. Although, as Trebilcot rightly points out, proscribing certain options would involve a loss of freedom, nevertheless we should be able to determine, at least with respect to some character traits, when a gain in virtue is worth the loss of freedom. It may even be the case that the loss of freedom suffered by an individual now will be compensated for by a gain of freedom to that same individual in the future once the relevant virtues have been acquired.

So understood, the class of virtues will turn out to be those desirable traits which can be reasonably expected of both women and men. Admittedly, this is a restrictive use of the term "virtue." In normal usage, the term "virtue" is almost synonymous with the term "desirable trait."[6] But there is good reason to focus on those desirable traits which can be justifiably inculcated in both women and men, and for present purposes I refer to this class of desirable traits as virtues.[7]

Unfortunately, many of the challenges to the ideal of androgyny fail to appreciate how the ideal can be interpreted to combine a required set of virtues with equal choice from among other desirable traits. For example, some challenges interpret the ideal as attempting to achieve "a proper balance of moderation" among opposing feminine and masculine traits and then question whether traits like feminine gullibility or masculine brutality could ever be combined with opposing gender traits to achieve such a balance.[8] Other challenges interpret the ideal as permitting unrestricted choice of personal traits and then regard the possibility of Total Women and Hells Angels androgynes as a reductio ad absurdum of the idea.[9] But once it is recognized that the ideal of androgyny cannot only be interpreted to require of everyone a set of virtues (which need not be a mean between opposing extreme traits) but can also be interpreted to limit everyone's choice to desirable traits, then such challenges to the ideal clearly lose their force because they only work against objectionable interpretations of androgyny.

Actually, the main challenge raised by feminists to the ideal of androgyny is that the ideal is self-defeating in that it seeks to eliminate sexual stereotyping of human beings at the same time that it is formulated in terms of the very same stereotypical concepts it seeks to eliminate.[10] Or, as Warren puts it, "Is it not at least mildly paradoxical to urge people to cultivate both 'feminine' and 'masculine' virtues, while at the same time holding that virtues ought not to be sexually stereotyped?"

One response to this challenge contends that to build a better society we must begin where we are now, and where we are now people still speak of feminine and masculine character traits. Consequently, if we want to refer easily to such traits and to formulate an ideal with respect to how these traits should be distributed in society, it is plausible to refer to them in the way that people presently refer to them – that is, as feminine or masculine traits.

Another response, which attempts to avoid misunderstanding altogether, is to formulate the ideal in the more abstract way I suggested earlier, so that it no longer specifically refers to so-called feminine or masculine traits. So formulated, the ideal requires that the traits that are truly desirable in society be equally open to both women and men or, in the case of virtues, equally expected of both women and men. So characterized, the ideal of androgyny represents neither a revolt against so-called feminine virtues and traits nor their exaltation over so-called masculine virtues and traits.[11] Accordingly, the ideal of androgyny does not view women's liberation as simply the freeing of women from the confines of traditional roles, which makes it possible for them to develop in ways heretofore reserved for men. Nor does the ideal view women's liberation as simply the reevaluation and glorification of so-called feminine activities like housekeeping or mothering or so-called feminine modes of thinking as reflected in an ethic of caring. The first perspective ignores or devalues genuine virtues and desirable traits traditionally associated with women while the second ignores or devalues genuine virtues and desirable traits traditionally associated with men. In contrast, the ideal of androgyny seeks a broader-based ideal for both women and men that combines virtues and desirable traits traditionally associated with women with virtues and desirable traits traditionally associated with men. Nevertheless, the ideal of androgyny will clearly reject any so-called virtues or desirable traits traditionally associated with women or men that have been supportive of discrimination or oppression against women or men. In general, the ideal of androgyny substitutes a socialization based on natural ability, reasonable expectation, and choice for a socialization based on sexual difference.

Of course, in proposing to characterize feminist justice in terms of the ideal of a gender-free or androgynous society, I recognize that not all feminists start off endorsing this ideal. Christina Sommers, for example, has attracted attention recently by distinguishing liberal feminism, which she endorses, from androgynous feminism, which she opposes.[12] But as one gets clearer and clearer about the liberal feminism that Sommers advocates, one sees that it begins to look more and more like the androgynous feminism that she says she opposes. There is nothing surprising about this, however. We cannot have the genuine equal opportunity for men and women that Sommers wants without reforming the present distribution of gender traits. Women cannot be passive, submissive, dependent, indecisive, and weak and still enjoy the same opportunities enjoyed by men who are aggressive, dominant, independent, decisive, and strong. So I contend that liberal feminism and androgynous feminism go together because genuine equal opportunity requires the feminist ideal of a gender-free or androgynous society.

It also seems that those who claim that we cannot escape a gendered society are simply confused about what a gender-free society would be like;[13] for they seem to agree with those who favor a gender-free or androgynous society that the assignments of roles in society should be based on (natural) ability, rational expectation, and choice. But what they also maintain is that some of these assignments will be based on sex as well, because some of the natural abilities that people possess will be determined by their sex. But even assuming this is the case, it wouldn't show that society was gendered in the sense that its roles in society are based on sex rather than on (natural) ability, rational expectation, and choice. And this is the only sense of gendered society to which defenders of feminist justice would be objecting.[14] So once the notion of a gender-free society is clarified, there should be widespread agreement that the assignments of roles in society should be based on (natural) ability, rational expectation, and choice. The ideal of androgyny simply specifies this notion of a gender-free society a bit further by requiring that the traits that are truly desirable in society be equally open to (equally qualified) women and men or, in the case of virtues, equally expected of (equally capable) women and men.

Of course, insofar as natural abilities are a function of sexual difference, there will be differences in the desirable traits and virtues that women and men acquire, even in a gender-free or androgynous society. And some contend that these differences will be substantial.[15] But given that we have been slow to implement the degree of equal opportunity required by the ideal of a gender-free or androgynous society, it is difficult to know what differences in desirable traits and virtues, if any, will emerge that are both sex-based and natural ability-based. What we can be sure of is that, given the variety and types of discrimination employed against women in existing societies, a gender-free or androgynous society will look quite different from the societies that we know.

II. FROM EQUALITY TO ANDROGYNY

Most contemporary defenses of the ideal of androgyny attempt to derive it from various conceptions of equality. Some feminists have tried to derive the ideal from a welfare liberal conception of equal opportunity, and others from a socialist conception of equal self-development. Let me briefly consider each of these defenses in turn.

Obviously, a right to equal opportunity could be interpreted, minimally, as providing people only with the same legal rights of access to all advantaged positions in society for which they are qualified. But this is not the interpretation that should be given this right either by welfare liberals or by libertarians, as the argument of the Chapter 3 shows. Rather, it was argued that a right to equal opportunity should be interpreted as a right not to be discriminated against in filling the roles and positions in society, and it is this right to equal opportunity that feminists have tended to focus on in attempting to justify the ideal of androgyny.[16] The point feminists have been making is simply that failure to achieve the ideal of androgyny translates into a failure to guarantee equal opportunity to both women and men.

Now some feminists would want to pursue various possible technological transformations of human biology in order to achieve equal opportunity. For example, they would like to make it possible for women to inseminate other women and for men to lactate and even bring fertilized ova to term. But realizing such possibilities would be very costly indeed.[17] Consequently, since the means selected for achieving equal opportunity must be provided to all legitimate claimants, including distant peoples and future generations, it is unlikely that such costly means could ever be morally justified. Rather, it seems preferable to radically equalize the opportunities that are conventionally provided to women and men and wait for such changes ultimately to have their effect on human biology as well. Of course, if any "technological fixes" for achieving equal opportunity should prove to be cost-efficient, then obviously there would be every reason to utilize them.

Now the support for the ideal of androgyny provided by a socialist conception of equal self-development is as direct as that provided by a welfare liberal conception of equal opportunity.[18] Just as the ideal of androgyny can be seen to be required by a welfare liberal or libertarian right to equal opportunity, so too can it be seen to be required by a socialist right of equal self-development. In fact, once the socialist right to equal self-development is correctly understood to be an equal right to the provision of resources for self-development, it can be seen to be equivalent to the welfare liberal's right to equal opportunity.[19] What remains distinctive about the socialist defense of androgyny, however, is its claim that, in contemporary capitalist societies, the ideal of androgyny is best achieved by socializing the means of production, which is to say that a cure for capitalist exploitation will also be a cure for women's oppression.[20]

III. FEMINIST OBJECTIONS

If we turn to Alison Jaggar's work on feminist justice, one notices that in her earlier work, she seems to be defending a strong form of sexual equality that is compatible with my defense of androgyny, but in her more recent work, her commitment to sexual equality appears to be importantly qualified and she in fact explicitly criticizes my defense of androgyny. Accordingly, one might think that my own conception of feminist justice is more compatible with Jaggar's earlier view than with her more recent view. I will argue, however, that this is not the case.

In her widely anthologized article "On Sexual Equality," written over twenty years ago, Jaggar attempts to defend "the traditional conception of sexual equality as the de-institutionalization of sexual difference."[21] Here she refuses to define woman "as having a particular kind of body, having a recent history of being brought up in a patriarchal society, having an inherited history of female archetypes, having present experiences which occur because one is female, and having a future which calls for a revolution from being oppressed."[22] Rather, she favors a starker account. She writes, "For me, to be a woman is no more and no less than to be a female human being."[23] She goes on to reject special rights for women. She argues, "so long as we view the difference between the sexes as a simple physiological difference – and we have no conclusive grounds for doing more – then there is no reason to draw up a special bill of rights for women in order to ensure our equality."[24] Near the end of this article, it becomes quite clear that Jaggar is endorsing the same ideal of feminist justice that I am endorsing. She writes, "we must . . . create a new androgynous culture which incorporates the best elements of both the present male and the present female cultures."[25]

When we turn to one of Jaggar's most recent articles, however, her commitment to sexual equality and androgyny seems to be qualified by a recognition of sexual difference.[26] At first, she simply points out that there are innumerable cases where, because of differences in the social situation of men and women, "identical treatment of the sexes appears to promote women's inequality rather than their equality, at least in the short term."[27] She offers as examples no-fault divorce settlements, joint custody statutes, and an ordinance forbidding firefighters to breast-feed between calls.[28] Here Jaggar favors the strategy of recognizing certain differences in order to eliminate them. Later in this article, however, she contends that we need to recognize that there are other ways in which women are different that should not be eliminated but valorized. Here she cites approvingly both Sara Ruddick's work postulating a connection between mothering and opposition to militarism and Carol Gilligan's work, which purports to discover a different voice among many women – a voice characterized by a caring ethic. She also notes the need to recognize the differences among women, differences of race, class, sexual preference, religion, age, ethnicity, marital status, physical ability, and so on.[29] Jaggar concludes that feminists "seem caught in the dilemma of simultaneously demanding and scorning equality with men" and recommends that they abandon neither their short-term goal of achieving equality nor their long-term goal of a world where "equality [is] overshadowed by the goods of mutual care."[30]

Yet despite the fact that Jaggar's more recent work on feminist justice may appear to be a departure from her earlier work with which my own conception of feminist justice is more clearly compatible, I think it is possible to see her more recent work as simply a development and extension of her earlier work, and in no way incompatible either with it or with my conception of justice. This becomes clear once we see that in her earlier work Jaggar was primarily trying to determine what would be required by feminist justice in an ideal society. This is not a society, like one's own, plagued by a variety of different sexist practices that have left women disadvantaged in various ways. Nor is it a society, like our own, characterized by racism, classism, heterosexism, ageism, and various other institutional prejudices. Rather, it is a society where past injustices have been corrected and men and women have for some time been treated equally. So, for such a society, it makes sense for feminist justice to require that women and men continue to be treated equally.

However, in a sexist society like our own, where women have been disadvantaged through unequal treatment, simply treating women and men equally, that is, in exactly the same way, would not be just, for it would serve to perpetuate the previous injustices. For such a society, the only acceptable route to sexual equality is through a transitional stage wherein sexual inequalities of the past are corrected by compensating for them with unequal treatment. To achieve a fair outcome in a race in which some runners have been disadvantaged by being forced for some time to run with weights tied to their legs, we will need to remove the weights from these runners and provide them with some special help for an appropriate period of time. That is why in *How to Make People Just*, I not only defended a right to equal opportunity, but in addition a right to affirmative action in cases where there was denial of equal opportunity in the past.[31] So, in an unjust society, there is a need to recognize differences created by past injustices and to correct for them with unequal treatment. Moreover, this unequal treatment is required by the ideal of equality itself.

Nevertheless, differences between women and men that are due to past injustices are not the only differences that Jaggar wants to recognize. As she puts it, there are others that should not be eliminated but valorized, and here, as we already noted, Jaggar has in mind women's commitment to mothering and the caring ethic as extolled by Sara Ruddick and Carol Gilligan, respectively. But while I agree that these traits should be valorized, I think, for that very reason, steps should be taken to eliminate them as differences. For, as Ruddick rightly points out, men can be mothers too, and I think it follows from my ideal of feminist justice that if men are to be parents then they should share equally the roles of mother and father, properly understood. And the same holds true with respect to Gilligan's caring ethic. To the degree to which commitment to a caring ethic is desirable, then such a commitment should be encouraged and even inculcated in both women and men. And if this is done effectively, then, over time, these differences between women and men will in fact disappear. So I would argue that a correct interpretation of Jaggar's recent stress on the importance of sexual difference is perfectly compatible with her earlier commitment to sexual equality and the ideal of androgyny. In this respect, our views do not differ at all.

More recently, however, Jaggar has criticized the specific way I characterize feminist justice in terms of the ideal of androgyny.[32] As I define it, the ideal of androgyny requires that the traits that are truly desirable in society be equally available to both women and men or, in the case of virtues, equally expected of both women and men, other things being equal. Now Jaggar objects to this characterization, claiming that feminist justice is an ideal for reforming social structures whereas androgyny is an ideal for reforming individuals.[33] Yet the ideal of androgyny, as I define it, closely resembles the ideal of equal opportunity, and since the ideal of equal opportunity is thought to be an ideal for reforming social structures, the same should hold of the ideal of androgyny, as I define it.

Moreover, despite Jaggar's objections to the ideal of androgyny, she herself, in some of her most recent work, endorses an ideal that looks very much like the ideal of androgyny.[34] She says:

> Just as the incorporation of feminine values does not render FPD (Feminist Practical Dialogue) feminist, neither does FPD become feminist by adding masculine values to the feminine in a mix. . . . Instead I regard FPD as feminist primarily because it revises both feminine and masculine values in the light of a distinctively feminist commitment to ending women's subordination.[35]

Now compare this passage with my own account of androgyny:

> So characterized the ideal of androgyny represents neither a revolt against so-called feminine virtues and traits nor their exaltation over so-called masculine virtues and traits. Accordingly, the ideal of androgyny does not view women's liberation as simply the freeing of women from the confines of traditional roles thus making it possible for them to develop in ways heretofore reserved for men. Nor does the ideal view women's liberation as simply the revaluation and glorification of so-called feminine activities like housekeeping or mothering or so-called

feminine modes of thinking as reflected in an ethic of caring. The first perspective ignores or devalues genuine virtues and desirable traits traditionally associated with women while the second ignores or devalues genuine virtues and desirable traits traditionally associated with men. By contrast, the ideal of androgyny seeks a broader based ideal for both women and men that combines virtues and desirable traits traditionally associated with women with virtues and desirable traits traditionally associated with men. Nevertheless, the ideal of androgyny will clearly reject any so-called virtues or desirable traits traditionally associated with women or men that have been supportive of discrimination or oppression against women or men.[36]

From comparing these two passages, I conclude that there is very little separating the ideal that Jaggar endorses from the ideal of androgyny that I endorse.

IV. PRACTICAL APPLICATIONS

One locus for the radical restructuring required by the ideal of a gender-free or androgynous society is the family. Here two fundamental changes are needed. First, all children, irrespective of their sex, must be given the same type of upbringing consistent with their native capabilities. Second, normally mothers and fathers must also have the same opportunities for education and employment consistent with their native capabilities.[37]

Yet, at least in the United States, this need radically to modify traditional family structures to guarantee equal opportunity confronts a serious problem. Given that a significant proportion of the available jobs are at least nine to five, families with preschool children require day-care facilities if their adult members are to pursue their careers. Unfortunately, for many families such facilities are simply unavailable.[38] In New York City, for example, more than 144,000 children under the age of six are competing for 46,000 full-time slots in day-care centers. In Seattle, there is licensed day-care space for 8,800 of the 23,000 children who need it. In Los Angeles, there is no licensed child care available for 135,000 children who need such programs. In Miami, two children, three and four years old, were left unattended at home while their parent worked. They climbed into a clothes dryer while the timer was on, closed the door, and burned to death.[39]

Moreover, even the available day-care facilities are frequently inadequate, either because their staffs are poorly trained or because the child/adult ratio in such facilities is too high. At best, many such facilities provide little more than custodial care; at worst, they actually retard the development of those children under their care.[40] What this suggests is that, at least under present conditions, if preschool children are to be adequately cared for, frequently one of the adult members of the family has to remain at home to provide that care. But because most jobs are at least nine to five, this requires that the adult members who stay at home temporarily give up pursuing a career. However, such sacrifice appears to conflict with the equal opportunity requirement of feminist justice.

Families might try to meet this equal opportunity requirement by having one parent give up pursuing a career for a certain period of time and the other give up hers for a subsequent (equal) period of time. But there are problems here too. Some careers are difficult to interrupt for any significant period of time, while others never adequately reward latecomers. In addition, given the high rate of divorce and the inadequacies of most legally mandated child support, those who first sacrifice their careers may find themselves later faced with the impossible task of trying to begin or revive them while continuing to be the primary caretaker of their children.[41] Furthermore, there is considerable evidence that children benefit more from equal rearing from both parents.[42] So the option of having just one parent doing the child-rearing for any length of time is, other things being equal, not optimal.

It would seem therefore, that to truly share child rearing within the family what is needed are flexible (typically part-time) work schedules that allow both parents to be together with their children for a significant period every day. Some flexible work schedules have already been tried by various corporations.[43] But if equal opportunity is to be a reality in our society, the option of flexible work schedules must be guaranteed to all those with preschool children. A recent estimate shows that married full-time career women still do almost as much of the housework chores – 70 percent – as the average full-time housewife, who does 83 percent of the housework.[44] Obviously this will have to change if we are to achieve the ideal of a gender-free or androgynous society.

A second locus of change required by the ideal of a gender-free or androgynous society is the distribution of economic power in the society.

In the United States, the percentage of women in the labor force has risen steadily for three decades, from 35 percent (of those aged sixteen or more) in 1960 to 59 percent in 1995. Roughly 70 percent of women with children at home were employed in 1995, including more than 63 percent of mothers with children under the age of six and 59 percent of mothers with children under the age of one.[45]

Yet in 1995 women employed full-time still earned seventy-two cents for every dollar men earned, up from the sixty cents for every dollar that held from the 1960s through the 1980s. Earnings do increase with education for all workers, but all women, as well as men of color, earn less than white men at every level of education. For example, women with four years of college education earn less on average than men who have not completed high school.[46]

Sometimes women and men working in the same job category have different incomes. For example, while female clerical workers earned a median wage of $384 per week in 1995, the median wage for male clerical workers was $489.[47] More frequently, however, women and men tend to be employed in different job categories that are paid differently. According to one study done a few years ago in the state of Washington, women employed as clerk-typists earned less than men employed as truck drivers or warehouse workers. In another study done in Denver, women employed as nurses earned less than men employed as tree cutters. While in each of these cases the women earned about 20 percent less than the men, the women's jobs, when evaluated in terms of skill, responsibility, effort, and working conditions, were given equal or higher scores than the men's jobs with which they were compared. Clearly, denying women the opportunity to earn the same as men do for equal or comparable work is a basic injustice in our society, and it will be a very costly one to correct.[48]

It is sometimes assumed that the problem of unequal pay for comparable work will be solved once women move into male-dominated occupations.[49] Unfortunately, as women move into occupations that men are beginning to abandon, we are seeing a subsequent drop in pay for the men who remain in those occupations. For example, as the percentage of women bartenders increased by 23 points, men's pay dropped 16 percent, and as the percentage of women pharmacists increased by 12 points, men's pay fell 11 percent.[50] So the discrimination against women in the economic arena is a far more entrenched problem than is sometimes thought.

The problem assumes even greater proportions when we consider the world at large. According to a United Nations report, although women do two-thirds of the world's work, they receive only 10 percent of the salaries.[51] The same report shows that men own 99 percent of all the property in the world, and women only 1 percent. According to another report, globally, women receive 30 to 40 percent less for comparable work.[52] Clearly, we have a long way to go to achieve the equality demanded by feminist justice.

It is also important to recognize that the equality required by feminist justice cannot be achieved on men's terms. It is not an equality in which men's values prevail and women's values are lost. As an example of what should be avoided, consider the integration of Girl Scouts and Boy Scouts into the same troops in Norway.[53] Before integration, many women had been troop leaders of the Girl Scouts, but after integration, almost all troops were led by men and the former women leaders became assistant leaders. In addition, an analysis of the activities in the former Girl Scouts compared to the activities of the former Boy Scouts revealed that the activities of the girls were of a more cooperative nature than those of the boys. The boys had activities in which they competed more against each other or against other groups of boys. After integration, the competitive activities of the boys became the activities of both girls and boys, the cooperative activities of the girls being abandoned. Thus we see that the integration was made on the boys' terms.[54] But feminist justice is not a one-way street. If it is to be achieved, every person who is capable must be expected to have the virtues that are now typically associated with women (e.g., nurturance, caring, sensitivity, compassion) as well as virtues that are now typically associated with men (e.g., self-reliance, courage, decisiveness).

To remedy these inequalities suffered by women in the economic sphere will require programs of affirmative action and comparable worth.[55] Affirmative action is needed to place qualified women in positions they deserve to occupy because of past discrimination. Without affirmative action, the structural violence of past discrimination will not be rectified. Only with affirmative action can the competition for desirable jobs and positions be made fair again, given our past history of discrimination. There are even cases where affirmative action candidates are clearly the most qualified, but where those in charge of hiring, because of their prejudice, can only see the candidates as simply qualified but not as the *most* qualified candidates.[56]

Comparable worth is also needed because, without it, women will not receive the salaries they deserve. They will do work that is judged equal or comparable to the work that men are doing in male-dominated occupations, but without comparable worth they will be paid less than the men. Paying for comparable worth programs will not be easy, but it can be done. The state of Washington spent $115 million over seven years on a comparable worth program, and the state of Iowa spent almost 9 percent of its payroll over a three-year period to achieve comparable worth.[57]

A third locus of change required by the ideal of a gender-free or androgynous society is the overt violence perpetrated against women in our society. According to former Surgeon General Antonia Novello, "The home is actually a more dangerous place for the American woman than the city streets." "One-third of the women slain in the U.S.," she continues, "die at the hands of husbands and boyfriends."[58] In addition, women in the United States live in fear of rape. Twenty percent of women are raped at some time during their lives, according to one national study; 44 percent of women are subjected to either rape or attempted rape at some point during their lives, according to another study done in the San Francisco area; and almost 50 percent of male college students say they would commit rape if they were certain that they could get away with it.[59] Not infrequently, women are beaten by their own husbands and lovers (between one-quarter and one-third of women are battered in their homes by husbands and lovers).[60] One-third of all women who require emergency-room hospital treatment are there as a result of domestic violence.[61] Thirty-eight percent of little girls are sexually molested inside or outside the family.[62] Since most of these crimes are minimally prosecuted in our society, women in our society can be raped, battered, or sexually abused as children and little, if anything, will be done about it. What this shows is that the condition of women in our society is actually that of being subordinate to men by force.[63]

Moreover, this problem is not confined to the United States. S. Opdebeeck reports that 40 percent of Belgian women between thirty and forty years old experienced some form of physical and/or sexual family violence. Bert Young notes that wife assault is the leading cause of homicide in Canada.[64] Obviously, this subordination of women must end if we are to achieve the ideal of a gender-free or androgynous society.

Feminist justice demands that we put an end to the overt violence against women, which takes the distinctive form of rape, battery, and sexual abuse. This overt violence is in every way as destructive as the other forms of violence we oppose; so we cannot in consistency fail to oppose it. According to one cross-cultural study of ninety-five societies, 47 percent of them were free of rape.[65] This shows is that it is possible to eliminate, or at least drastically reduce, overt violence against women.

One way to help bring about this result is to ban hard-core pornography that celebrates and legitimizes rape, battery, and the sexual abuse of children, as the Supreme Court of Canada has recently done.[66] Catharine MacKinnon has argued that pornography of this sort goes beyond mere speech in constituting a practice of sex discrimination that is a violation of women's civil rights.[67] According to MacKinnon, men who participate in the practice learn through the pleasures of masturbation to enjoy the forceful subordination of women, and they seek to find ways to impose that same subordination on the women who come into their lives. Because of the severity of these impositions, MacKinnon and other antipornography feminists claim that the practice of hard-core pornography violates women's civil rights by denying their equal status as citizens.[68] Of course, it can be questioned whether the impositions inflicted on women by hard-core pornography are actually severe enough to justify its prohibition.

Here MacKinnon and other antipornography feminists cite studies showing that exposure to hard-core pornography increases discriminatory attitudes and behavior in men toward women that take both violent and nonviolent forms.[69] Other studies reveal that in 68 percent of 2,380 cases, the abuser beat or sexually abused the victim or someone else after looking at pornographic material, and that 58 percent of abusers show pornographic pictures or articles to their victims.[70] Although this evidence is obviously not conclusive, it does strongly favor a ban on hard-core pornography as a means of reducing overt violence against women.

Another way to decrease violence against women is to deemphasize violent sports like boxing and football. To see why this would help, all one needs to do is consider the evidence. For example, an exhaustive study of heavyweight prizefights held between 1973 and 1978 and subsequent homicide statistics revealed that homicides in the United States increased by over 12 percent directly after heavyweight championship prizefights. In fact, the increase was greatest after heavily publicized prizefights.[71] In addition, a study of twenty-four cases of campus gang rapes indicated that nine of them were committed by athletes, and in an investigation of sexual assaults on college campuses that included interviewing over 150 campus police, it turned out that football and basketball players were involved in 38 percent of the reported cases.[72] There is also a significant increase in batteries by husbands and boyfriends associated with the yearly Superbowl football game.[73] In the Chicago area, a local radio station went so far as to recommend that women "take a walk" during the game in order to avoid being assaulted in their homes.[74]

A third way to help reduce violence against women is to teach conflict resolution, child care, and the history of peacemaking in our schools. Several schools have experimented with teaching conflict resolution and child care to elementary and high school children, with impressive results, especially for boys.[75] The history of peacemaking could also provide our children with a new and better set of models than the history of warmaking has done.

We also need to recognize the connection between the forms of violence we oppose in the international arena and the overt and structural violence done to women.[76] Violence in the international arena arises when nations view each other as competitive, aggressive, and averse to cooperate, the same traits that tend to be fostered exclusively in men in a society characterized by widespread overt and structural violence against women. In contrast, the traits of openness, cooperativeness, and nurturance that promote peaceful solutions to conflicts tend to be fostered exclusively in women, who are effectively excluded from positions of power in a society characterized by widespread overt and structural violence against women. Consequently, if we want to eliminate violence in the international arena, we must also eliminate the overt and structural violence done to women.[77] Only in this way will our leaders develop the traits of openness, cooperativeness, and nurturance that will enable them to maintain peace in the international arena. Men will acquire these traits through equal sharing of child-rearing and housekeeping tasks. Women will retain these traits through an equal sharing of child-rearing and housekeeping tasks, while acquiring other traits required for personal development and leadership that have hitherto been reserved for men.

Moreover, people in general, and men in particular, first learn about violence and become skilled in its practice in their own families. They see violence, and to a greater or lesser degree accept its legitimacy, in the families in which they have been brought up, and they continue to practice it in the families they themselves form. According to one study, one-fourth of adult men and one in six adult women said that they could think of circumstances in which it would be all right for a husband to strike his wife or a wife to strike her husband. Eighty-six percent of those polled said that young people need "strong" discipline.[78] Surely, closing down violence's first school is at least as important as correcting its later manifestations among political groups.[79]

Furthermore, when those opposed to violence in the international arena champion the cause of feminist justice, they will benefit from a new surge of support from women. Adding the cause of feminist justice to one's political agenda can create new allies for one's cause within the oppressed group itself. "Women of the World Unite," or better, "Feminists of the World Unite" is not a bad rallying cry for those seeking social and political change. Or, as former Prime Minister Prunskiene of Lithuania remarked before resigning her post: "I am the only woman of rank in the government. And sometimes I look around me and think that the shape of democracy and the process of democracy might be well served if there were more women involved." Certainly the sight of the all-male U.S. Senate Judiciary Committee incapable of conducting fair hearings on Anita Hill's charge that Clarence Thomas had sexually harassed her convinced many voters in the subsequent elections that more women must occupy positions of power in the U.S government.[80]

I have argued that the achievement of feminist justice is centrally related to the pursuit of peace, so that those who oppose violence in international spheres must, in consistency, oppose violence against women as well. I have argued that one cannot consistently oppose violence in international relations while engaging in violence in personal relations. The pursuit of justice in political relations, I contend, requires the pursuit of justice in personal relations, and this requires acceptance of the feminist ideal of a gender-free or androgynous society. In brief, to pursue peace we must pursue feminist justice as well.

Another locus of change required by the ideal of a gender-free or androgynous society overlaps the previous two. It is rooted in the distribution of economic power in society, and it frequently takes the form of overt violence against women. It is the problem of sexual harassment, and, given its importance, I want to devote some time to discussing it.

Actually, sexual harassment was not recognized as an offense by U.S. trial courts until the late 1970s, and it was only affirmed by the U.S. Supreme Court as an offense in the 1980s. The term "sexual harassment" was not even coined until the 1970s. So the moral problem of sexual harassment is one that many people have only recently come to recognize. The Senate Judiciary Committee hearings on Anita Hill's charge that Clarence Thomas had sexually harassed her obviously heightened people's awareness of this problem.

According to various studies done over the last few years, sexual harassment is a widespread problem. In research conducted by psychologists, 50 percent of women questioned in the workplace said they had been sexually harassed. According to the U.S. Merit Systems Protection Board, within the federal government, 56 percent of 8,500 female workers surveyed claimed to have experienced sexual harassment. According to the *National Law Journal*, 64 percent of women in "pink-collar" jobs reported being sexually harassed, and 60 percent of 3,000 women lawyers at 250 top law firms said that they had been harassed at some point in their careers. In a recent survey by *Working Women* magazine, 60 percent of high-ranking corporate women said they have been harassed; 33 percent more knew of others who had been.[81] In a 1995 survey of 90,000 female soldiers, sailors, and fliers, 60 percent of the army women said they had been sexually harassed. Only 47 percent of the army women surveyed said that they believed their leaders were serious about putting a stop to sexual harassment.[82]

According to Ellen Bravo and Ellen Cassedy, humiliation is the term most commonly used by those who see themselves as sexually harassed when describing their experience.[83] They see themselves as demeaned and devalued, and treated as sexual playthings. Many find themselves in a double bind. If they fight back, they could lose their jobs or alienate their boss or coworkers; if they don't fight back, they could lose their self-respect. Many experience stress-related ailments: depression, sleep or eating disorders, headaches, and fatigue, and take more days off from work as a result.[84] The economic consequences for employers are also significant. A 1988 survey of 160 large manufacturing and service companies found this startling result: A typical

Fortune 500 company with 23,750 employees loses $6.7 million per year because of sexual harassment. And this loss doesn't even include lawsuits. What it does include are financial losses due to absenteeism, lower productivity, and employee turnover. Another 1988 study showed that sexual harassment cost the federal government $267 million between 1985 and 1987. It cost $37 million to replace federal workers who left their jobs, $26 million in medical leave due to stress from sexual harassment, and $204 million in lost productivity.[85]

Given the seriousness of the problem, it is important to clarify what constitutes, or should constitute, sexual harassment. In 1980, the Equal Employment Opportunity Commission (EEOC) issued guidelines finding harassment on the basis of sex to be a violation of Title VII of the Civil Rights Act of 1964 and defining sexual harassment as "unwelcome sexual advances, requests for sexual favors, and other verbal or physical conduct of a sexual nature" when such behavior occurs in any of three circumstances:

1) where submission to such conduct is made either explicitly or implicitly a term or condition of an individual's employment;
2) where submission to or rejection of such conduct by an individual is used as the basis for employment decisions affecting the individual; or
3) where such conduct has the purpose or effect of unreasonably interfering with an individual's work performance or creating an intimidating, hostile, or offensive working environment.[86]

In 1986, the U.S. Supreme Court, in *Meritor Savings Bank v. Vinson*, agreed with the EEOC, ruling that there could be two types of sexual harassment: harassment that conditions concrete employment benefits on granting sexual favors (often called the quid pro quo type), and harassment that creates a hostile or offensive work environment without affecting economic benefits (the hostile environment type).[87]

Nevertheless, the Supreme Court made it difficult for a plaintiff to establish that either of these types of sexual harassment had occurred. For example, a polite verbal no does not suffice to show that sexual advances are unwelcome; a woman's entire conduct both inside and outside the workplace is subject to appraisal in order to determine whether or not she welcomed the advances. For example, in the Vinson case, there was "voluminous testimony regarding Vinson's dress and personal fantasies," and in the Senate Judiciary Committee hearings, Anita Hill was not able to prevent intensive examination of her private life, although Clarence Thomas was able to declare key areas of his private life as off-limits, such as his practice of viewing and discussing pornographic films.

The Supreme Court also made it difficult to classify work environments as hostile to women unless the harassment is sufficiently severe or pervasive. Applying the Supreme Court's standard, a lower court, in *Christoforou v. Ryder Truck Rental*, judged a supervisor's actions of fondling a plaintiff's rear end and breasts, propositioning her, and trying to force a kiss at a Christmas party to be "too sporadic and innocuous" to support a finding of a hostile work environment.[88] Similarly, in *Rabidue v. Osceola Refining Co.*, a workplace where pictures of nude and scantily clad women abounded (including one, which hung on a wall for eight years, of a woman with a golf ball on her breasts and a man with his golf club standing over her and yelling "Fore!"), and where a coworker, never disciplined despite repeated complaints, routinely referred to women as "whores," "cunts," "pussies," and "tits," was judged by a lower court not to be a sufficiently hostile environment to constitute sexual harassment.[89] Notice, by contrast, that the Senate Arms Services Committee, in its recent hearings, regarded an environment in which known homosexuals are simply doing their duty in the military to be too hostile an environment in which to ask male heterosexuals to serve.

Yet why should we accept the Supreme Court's characterization of sexual harassment, especially given its unwelcomeness and pervasiveness requirements?[90] As the Supreme Court interprets sexual harassment, a person's behavior must be unwelcome in a fairly strong sense before it constitutes sexual harassment. But why should a woman have to prove that the offer "If you don't sleep with me, you will be fired" is unwelcome before it constitutes sexual harassment?[91] Isn't such an offer objectively unwelcome? Isn't it just the kind of offer that those in positions of power should not be making to their subordinates – an offer that purports to make their continuing employment conditional upon providing sexual favors? Surely, unless we are dealing with some form of legalized prostitution, and maybe not even then, such offers are objectively unwelcome.[92] Given, then, that such offers are objectively unwelcome, why is there any need to show that they are also subjectively unwelcome before regarding them as violations of Title VII of the Civil Rights Act? The requirement of subjective unwelcomeness is simply a gratuitous obstacle that makes the plaintiff's case far more difficult to prove than it should be.[93]

In addition, if the plaintiff is fired after refusing such an offer, the Supreme Court requires her to prove that the firing occurred because the offer was refused, which is very difficult to do unless one is a perfect employee. Wouldn't it be fairer to require the employer to prove that the plaintiff would have been fired even if she had said "yes" to the offer?[94] Of course, employers could avoid this burden of proof simply by not making any such offers in the first place.[95] But when they do make objectively unwelcome offers, why shouldn't the burden of proof be on them to show that any subsequent firing was clearly unrelated to the plaintiff's refusal of the offer? Fairness is particularly relevant in this context because we are committed to equal opportunity in the workplace, which requires employing women and men on equal terms. Accordingly, we must guard against imposing special burdens on women in the workplace, when there are no comparable burdens imposed on men. Feminist justice, with its ideal of a gender-free or androgynous society, will be satisfied with nothing less.[96]

The demand for equal opportunity in the workplace also appears to conflict with the Supreme Court's pervasiveness requirement for establishing a hostile environment. Citing a lower court, the Supreme Court contends that, to be actionable, sexual harassment "must be sufficiently severe or pervasive 'to alter the conditions of the [victim's] employment and create an abusive working environment.'"[97] But as this standard has been interpreted by lower courts, the pervasiveness of certain forms of harassment in the workplace has become grounds for tolerating them. In *Rabidue*, the majority argued

> [I]t cannot seriously be disputed that in some work environments, humor and language are rough hewn and vulgar. Sexual jokes, sexual conversations and girlie magazines abound. Title VII was not meant to or can change this. Title VII is the federal court mainstay in the struggle for equal employment opportunity for the female workers of America. But it is quite different to claim that Title VII was designed to bring about a magical transformation in the social mores of American workers.[98]

The Supreme Court itself seems to sound a similar theme by emphasizing the application of Title VII to only extreme cases of sexual harassment as found in *Vinson*.

However, as the EEOC interprets Title VII, the law has a broader scope. It affords employees the right to work in an environment free from discriminatory intimidation, ridicule, and insult. According to the EEOC, sexual harassment violates Title VII where conduct creates an intimidating, hostile, or offensive environment or where it unreasonably interferes with work performance.[99]

But how are we to determine what unreasonably interferes with work performance? In *Rabidue*, the majority looked to prevailing standards in the workplace to determine what was reasonable or unreasonable. Yet Justice Keith, in dissent, questioned this endorsement of the status quo, arguing that, just as a Jewish employee can rightfully demand a change in her working environment if her employer maintains an anti-Semitic work force and tolerates a workplace in which "kike" jokes, displays of Nazi literature, and anti-Jewish conversation "may abound," surely women can rightfully demand a change in the sexist practices that prevail in their working environments.[100] In *Henson v. Dundee*, the majority also drew an analogy between sexual harassment and racial harassment:

> Sexual harassment which creates a hostile or offensive environment for members of one sex is every bit the arbitrary barrier to sexual equality at the workplace that racial harassment is to racial equality. Surely, a requirement that a man or woman run a gauntlet of sexual abuse in return for the privilege of being allowed to work and make a living can be as demeaning and disconcerting as the harshest of racial epithets.[101]

And this passage is also quoted approvingly by the Supreme Court in *Vinson*.

Moved by such arguments, the majority in *Ellison v. Brady* proposed that, rather than looking to prevailing standards to determine what is reasonable, we should look to the standard of a reasonable victim or, given that most victims of sexual harassment are women, the standard of a reasonable woman.[102] They contend that this standard may be different from the standard of a "reasonable man." For example, what male superiors may think is "harmless social interaction" may be experienced by female subordinates as offensive and threatening.[103]

Nevertheless, if we are concerned to establish the equal opportunity in the workplace that feminist justice with its ideal of a gender-free or androgynous society demands, there should be no question about what standard of reasonableness to use here. It is not that of a reasonable woman, nor that of a reasonable man for that matter, but the standard of what is reasonable for everyone to accept. For equal opportunity is a moral requirement, and moral requirements are those which are reasonable for everyone to accept. This assumes that apparent conflicts over what is reasonable to accept – for example, conflicts between the standard of a reasonable woman and that of a reasonable man – are conflicts that can and should be resolved by showing that one of these perspectives is more reasonable than the other, or that some still other perspective is even more reasonable. However, at least in the context of sexual harassment, this standard of what is reasonable for everyone to accept will accord closely with the standard of a reasonable woman, given that once women's perspectives are adequately taken into account, the contrasting perspective of a reasonable man will be seen as not so reasonable after all.

In its decision in *Harris v. Forklift Systems Inc.* (1993), the Supreme Court took an important step toward a more reasonable stance on sexual harassment. In this case, Teresa Harris worked as a rental manager at Forklift Systems. Charles Hardy, Forklift's president, said to Harris on several occasions, in the presence of other employees,

"You're a woman, what do you know?" and "We need a man as the rental manager." Again in front of others, he suggested that the two of them "go to the Holiday Inn to negotiate [Harris's] raise." Hardy occasionally asked Harris and other female employees to get coins from his front pants pockets. On other occasions, he threw objects on the ground in front of Harris and other women and asked them to pick the objects up. He made sexual innuendoes about Harris's and other women's clothing. On one occasion, while Harris was arranging a deal with one of Forklift's customers, Hardy asked her, in front of other employees, "What did you do, promise some [sex] Saturday night?" Soon after, Harris quit her job at Forklift.

In this case, the Supreme Court struck down the district court's requirement that in order for sexual harassment to be established Harris needed to show that Hardy's conduct had "seriously affected her psychological well-being." This was an important decision, but obviously it does not go far enough in specifying a reasonable standard for sexual harassment.

It is also important to recognize here that achieving equal opportunity in the workplace as required by the ideal of a gender-free or androgynous society will conflict, to some degree, with freedom of speech. Consider the recent case of *Robinson v. Jacksonville Shipyards*, in which a United States District Court upheld claims of sexual harassment on hostile work environment grounds and issued extensive remedial orders.[104] Plaintiff Lois Robinson was one of a very small number of female skilled craftworkers employed at the Shipyards – one of six out of 832 craftworkers. Her allegations of sexual harassment centered around "the presence in the workplace of pictures of women in various stages of undress and in sexually suggestive or submissive poses, as well as remarks by male employees and supervisors which demean women." Although there was some evidence of several incidents in which the sexually suggestive pictures and comments were directed explicitly at Robinson, most were not.

In analyzing this case, Nadine Strossen, past president of the ACLU, argues that even sexually offensive speech should be protected unless it is explicitly directed at a particular individual or group of individuals.[105] Accordingly, Strossen endorses the ACLU's amicus brief in the *Robinson v. Jacksonville Shipyards* case, which considered the court's ban on the public display of sexually suggestive material without regard to whether the expressive activity was explicitly directed toward any employee as too broad. However, in light of the fact that Jacksonville Shipyards had itself banned all public displays of expressive activity except sexual materials, the amicus brief went on to favor the imposition of a workplace rule that would right the balance and permit the posting of other materials as well – materials critical of such sexual expression, as well as other political and religious or social messages that are currently banned. Such a rule would implement a "more speech" approach in an effort to counter offensive speech.

But would such a rule work? Would it succeed in protecting the basic interests of women, especially their right to equal opportunity in the workplace? It is not clear that it would be effective in male-dominated workplaces like Jacksonville Shipyards, where women are a tiny minority of the work force, and so are likely to have their voices drowned out in the free market of expression that this rule would permit.

Nor does Strossen's distinction between offensive speech explicitly directed at a particular person or group and offensive speech that is not so directed seem all that useful, given that most sexual harassment is directed at women, not because they are Jane Doe or Lois Robinson, but because they are women. So why should we distinguish between sexual harassment that is explicitly directed at a particular woman because she is a woman, and sexual harassment that is only directed at a particular woman because it is explicitly directed at all women? Of course, sexually harassing speech can be more or less offensive, and maybe its offensiveness does correlate, to some degree, with the manner in which that harassment is directed at women. Nevertheless, what is crucial here is that the offensiveness of sexually harassing speech becomes unacceptable from the standpoint of feminist justice when it undermines the equal opportunity of women in the workplace – that is, when it imposes special burdens on women in the workplace where there are no comparable burdens on men. It is at this point that feminist justice demands that we impose whatever limitations on sexually harassing speech are needed to secure equal opportunity in the workplace.

I have argued in this chapter that the achievement of feminist justice requires a number of important changes in our society. It requires changes in traditional family structures so that children, irrespective of their sex, will have the same type of upbringing and mothers and fathers have the same opportunities for education and employment. It requires changes in the distribution of economic power in our society through programs of affirmative action and equal pay for comparable work that remove the structural violence against women. It requires the changes that are necessary to put an end to overt violence against women in the form of rape, battery, and sexual abuse. Last, it requires changes to implement new programs against sexual harassment in the workplace in order to achieve the equal opportunity that feminist justice promises to everyone. All of these changes, and more, are required by feminist justice's ideal of a gender-free or androgynous society.

Obviously, these requirements impose obligations on us individually and collectively, to do what can be reasonably expected of us to change societal institutions in order to achieve these various goals of feminist justice. In general, these requirements also impose an obligation on women to use what opportunities are available to them to develop themselves and further the cause of feminist justice, as well as an obligation on men to renounce unfair opportunities that would enable them to advance themselves at the expense of women. Yet, important as it is to bring about all of these changes required by a feminist ideal of a gender-free or androgynous society, I will argue in the next chapter that this ideal of feminist justice should not be pursued alone.

Chapter 5

From Feminism to Multiculturalism

Despite its obvious importance, it would be a mistake to pursue feminist justice alone, given that it is both theoretically and practically connected to other forms of justice. Moreover, a peacemaking way of doing philosophy demands that we work out just such connections in order to build as broad a political consensus as possible. Accordingly, in this chapter, I will be focusing on both the theoretical and the practical connections of feminist justice to three other forms of justice: racial justice, homosexual justice, and multicultural justice.

I. THE THEORETICAL CONNECTION

While feminist justice seeks to remedy the injustice of sexism, racial justice seeks to remedy the injustice of racism, homosexual justice seeks to remedy the injustice of heterosexism, and multicultural justice seeks to remedy the injustice of Eurocentrism. As it turns out, each of these injustices is supported by similar theoretical arguments. The more blatant argument begins by noting certain differences among either individuals, groups, or cultures. It then claims that these differences are grounds for regarding some individuals, groups, or cultures as superior to other individuals, groups, or cultures. This superiority is then claimed to legitimate the domination of some individuals, groups, and cultures by other individuals, groups, and cultures.[1] In each case, the theoretical argument moves from a claim of difference to a claim of superiority and then to a claim of domination. In the case of sexism, the biological differences between men and women, or other differences claimed to be linked to these biological differences, are said to be grounds for regarding men as superior to women; this superiority is then claimed to legitimate the domination of women by men. In the case of racism, specifically the principal form of racism in the United States,[2] the biological differences between whites and blacks, or other differences

101

claimed to be linked to these biological differences, are said to be grounds for regarding whites as superior to blacks; this superiority is then claimed to legitimate the domination of blacks by whites. In the case of heterosexism, the biological or acquired differences between heterosexuals and homosexuals are said to be grounds for regarding heterosexuals as superior to homosexuals; this superiority is then claimed to legitimate the domination of homosexuals by heterosexuals. In the case of Eurocentricism, the cultural differences between Western culture and non-Western cultures are said to be grounds for regarding Western culture as superior to non-Western cultures; this superiority is then claimed to legitimate the domination of non-Western cultures by Western culture. In response, feminist justice, racial justice, homosexual justice, and multicultural justice claim that none of these forms of domination can be justified.

Sometimes, however, the theoretical argument for sexism, racism, heterosexism, or Eurocentricism takes a less blatant form. This argument begins by renouncing forms of domination adopted in the past as unjustified. Simply to deny people equal opportunity on the basis of their sex, race, sexual orientation, or culture is claimed to be wrong by this version of the argument.[3] But the argument further claims that people now, for the most part, are no longer being denied equal opportunity on the basis of sex, race, sexual orientation, or culture. Accordingly, it is claimed that the ways in which men are still favored over women, whites over blacks, heterosexuals over homosexuals, or Western culture over non-Western cultures must either be grounded in a legitimate superiority of one over the other or be a residue of past injustices that cannot be removed without doing additional injustice. Of course, those who employ this form of argument do not usually think of themselves as supporting sexism, racism, heterosexism, or Eurocentricism, but, as I shall show, they are nonetheless.

There is no denying that, under current societal structures, men are still favored over women, whites over blacks, heterosexuals over homosexuals, and Western culture over non-Western cultures. As we have seen, in the case of women in the United States, 20 percent are raped at some time during their lives; between one-quarter and one-third of women are battered in their homes by husbands and lovers; 50 percent of women in the workplace say they have been sexually harassed; and 38 percent of little girls are sexually molested inside or outside the family.[4] Women employed full-time still earn only seventy-two cents for every dollar men earn.[5] In the world at large, women are responsible for 66 percent of all work done (paid and unpaid), yet they receive only 10 percent of the salaries. Men own 99 percent of all the property in the world, and women only 1 percent.[6] All of these statistics show that men are clearly favored over women.

In the case of blacks in the United States, almost half of all black children live in poverty. Black unemployment is twice that of white. The infant mortality rate in many black communities is twice that of whites. Blacks are twice as likely as whites to be robbed, seven times more likely to be murdered or to die of tuberculosis. A male living in New York's Harlem is less likely to reach age sixty-five than a resident of Bangladesh. Blacks comprise 50 percent of maids and garbage collectors but only 4 percent of managers and 3 percent of physicians and lawyers.[7] While one study of the nation's ten largest cities showed that blacks and whites rarely interact outside the workplace, another revealed that about 86 percent of available jobs do not appear in classified advertisements and that 80 percent of executives find their jobs through networking, thus showing the importance for employment of contacts outside the workplace.[8] According to another study, black children adopted by white middle-class families score significantly better on the Wechsler Intelligence Scale than black children adopted by black middle-class families, and the scoring difference is of the magnitude typically found between the average scores of black and white children.[9] Thus, there is plenty of evidence that, at least in the United States, whites are significantly favored over blacks.

In the case of homosexuals in the United States, annual studies by the National Gay and Lesbian Task Force have consistently found that over 90 percent of homosexuals have been victims of violence or harassment in some form because of their sexual orientation.[10] According to another study, 33 percent of all respondents were chased or followed; 23 percent had had objects thrown at them; 17 percent were punched, hit, kicked, or beaten; another 17 percent reported vandalism or arson against their property; 11 percent were spit at; and 8 percent were assaulted with a weapon – all just for being perceived to be gay or lesbian.[11] In 1985, the U.S. Supreme Court let stand a lower-court ruling that allows Ohio to fire homosexual teachers on the basis of their sexual orientation alone.[12] Currently, federal civil rights law bars private-sector discrimination in housing, employment, and public accommodations on the basis of race, national origin, ethnicity, gender, religion, age, or disability, but not on the basis of sexual orientation.[13] In 1986, the U.S. Supreme Court, in *Bowers v. Hardwick*, ruled that the constitutional right to privacy, which extends to possessing and reading obscene material in the privacy of one's home, does not extend to homosexual acts performed in the privacy of one's home.[14] Relatedly, in custody cases, judges are quick to remove children from openly lesbian mothers, claiming that, as admitted felons for violating state laws against homosexual acts, the mothers are obviously unfit.[15] Clearly, there is no doubt that heterosexuals are favored over homosexuals in U.S. society.

In the case of non-Western cultures, virtually the entire U.S. educational system is directed at assimilating its citizens into the dominant Western culture. Very little is being done to educate citizens about non-Western cultures. For example, according to John Searle, no advocate of multiculturalism himself, the only radical change in Stanford University's much discussed revision of its Western civilization course was the introduction of an *optional* eighth-track version of the course.[16] In this eighth-track version, the required elements of the European canon remain, but they are read along with works of Spanish-American, American-Indian and African-American authors. However, even these minimal changes were roundly attacked. For example, then Secretary of Education William Bennett paid a visit to Stanford to criticize the changes.[17] George Will, in his national column, wrote that courses at Stanford should "affirm this fact: America is predominantly a product of the Western tradition and is predominantly good because that tradition is good."[18] William Buckley declared that "from Homer to the nineteenth century no great book has emerged from any non-European source."[19] In agreement with Buckley, Saul Bellows remarked, "When the Zulus have a Tolstoy, we will read him."[20] Such opposition to opening up the educational canon to non-Western sources is particularly striking when one recognizes that over 50 percent of the undergraduate students at Stanford, as well as at Berkeley and UCLA, are nonwhite, as are over 30 percent of all U.S. undergraduate students.[21] Reflecting on this data, there is no doubt that the dominant Western culture is favored over non-Western cultures in U.S. educational institutions across the country.

II. RACISM AND SEXISM

Of course, whether the more blatant or less blatant argument for sexism, racism, heterosexism, or Eurocentricism is employed depends on how plausible it is to claim that people now are no longer denied equal opportunity by one or another of these forms of domination. Clearly, only with respect to men and women or blacks and whites does the claim seem even remotely plausible. So, as would be expected, it is only in these two contexts that the less blatant argument tends to be used, maintaining as it does that the ways in which men are still favored over women, and whites over blacks, must either be grounded in a legitimate superiority of one over the other or be a residue of past injustices that cannot be removed without doing additional injustice. Still, it is difficult to defend even this argument, because data like that noted above makes it difficult to maintain that equal opportunity currently exists, either between men and women or between whites and blacks. As a consequence, those who employ this form of the argument usually try to show that most of the inequality that does exist is a residue of past injustices that cannot be removed without doing additional injustice. Specifically, they attack both affirmative action and comparable worth as attempts to correct for past injustices that produce new injustices.

Affirmative Action

Affirmative action with respect to women and minorities is a policy of preferring qualified women and minority candidates who have been disadvantaged by past injustices over equally or more qualified white male candidates who have not been similarly disadvantaged. In fact, it is generally the case that the white male candidates who are passed over by a policy of affirmative action have themselves benefited from past injustices suffered by women and minority candidates (e.g., unequal educational opportunities). To be justified, however, such a policy of affirmative action must favor only candidates whose qualifications are such that, when their selection or appointment is combined with a suitably designed educational enhancement program, they will normally turn out, within a reasonably short time, to be as qualified as, or even more qualified than, their peers.[22] Such candidates have the potential to be as qualified as, or more qualified than, their peers, but that potential has not yet been actualized because of past injustices. Affirmative action, with its suitably designed educational enhancement program, purports to actualize just that potential. In this way, persons who receive affirmative action are like runners in a race who, for a time, are forced to compete at a disadvantage with the other runners, say, by having weights tied to their legs, but later are allowed to compete against those other runners by first having the weights removed and then receiving some special assistance for an appropriate period of time so that the results of the race will turn out to be fair. Affirmative action, therefore, is a policy that is directed at only those women and minority candidates who are highly qualified yet, because of past discrimination and prejudice, are less qualified than they would otherwise be; it seeks to provide such candidates with a benefit that will nullify the effects of past injustices by enabling them to become as qualified as or more qualified than their peers.

Now affirmative action is said to lead to injustice for the following reasons:

1) It is not required to compensate for unjust institutions of the distant past.
2) It harms those who receive it.

3) It is directed at the wrong people.
4) It is not directed at all of those who deserve it.
5) It is unfair to the white males whom it discriminates against.

In support of the first objection, Christopher Morris argues that affirmative action is not required by the existence of unjust institutions in the distant past such as American slavery because compensation for past injustices is owed only to individuals who would have been better off except for those past injustices.[23] With respect to individual African Americans living today, however, it is not true that they would have been better off if there had been no American slavery, because, given the contingencies of procreation, African Americans who are living today would not even have been born if their ancestors had not been forcibly uprooted from Africa, enslaved, and brought to this country. Of course, in the absence of American slavery and the racism it engendered, some Africans would surely have emigrated to this country, but they would have done so more like other immigrants, and their contemporary descendants would be different individuals from present-day African Americans who trace their history through the practice of American slavery.

I think the best response to this objection is not to deny that most African Americans today are the product of American slavery and would not have existed without it, but only to point out that the injustices for which present-day African Americans deserve compensation are actually of more recent vintage.[24] For example, they are the injustices of poor housing, unequal education, job discrimination, inadequate health and welfare programs, and an unfair criminal justice system, all of which African Americans today would certainly be better off without. Of course, these current injustices do have their origins in the injustices of the past, particularly the institutions of American slavery and the Jim Crow law which succeeded it, but the grounds that present-day African Americans can claim for compensation are not the injustices of the distant past, but rather the ongoing injustices that currently make them worse off as individuals – injustices that other contemporary Americans are responsible for and could do something about, in part by endorsing affirmative action programs.

In support of the second objection, Charles Murray claims that affirmative action harms those who receive it by placing women and minorities into positions for which they are not qualified.[25] Murray cites examples, from his personal experience and the personal experiences of others, of women and minorities that were harmed in this way. In one example, a black woman is hired for a position for which she lacks the qualifications and, as a result, her responsibilities are reduced, making her job a dead-end position. Yet, according to our earlier account, when affirmative action has such an effect, it is not justified. To be justified, affirmative action must be directed at candidates whose qualifications are such that when their selection or appointment is combined with a suitably designed educational enhancement program, they will normally turn out, within a reasonably short time, to be as qualified as, or even more qualified than, their peers. So if affirmative action is properly applied and carried out, it will not harm those who receive it.[26]

In support of the third objection, James Fishkin claims that affirmative action benefits the most qualified, who are actually the least deserving because they are the least discriminated against.[27] Yet the most qualified who benefit from affirmative action may not have been subjected to less discrimination; they may simply have resisted discrimination more vigorously. And even supposing that the most qualified were subject to less discrimination in the past, why wouldn't affirmative action be the appropriate response to the degree of discrimination to which they were subjected? If we assume that affirmative action is provided only to those candidates whose qualifications are such that when their selection or appointment is actually combined with a suitably designed educational enhancement program, they will normally turn out, within a reasonably short time, to be as qualified as or even more qualified than their peers, then affirmative action does seem to be appropriately directed at the most qualified candidates among those who have suffered from past discrimination. More severe forms of discrimination, whose effects upon a person's qualifications and potential are even more detrimental, would require correctives other than affirmative action, such as remedial education and job-training programs.

In support of the fourth objection that affirmative action is not directed at all of those who deserve it, Carl Cohen claims, "Compensatory affirmative action, if undertaken at all, must be undertaken for every person who qualifies on some reasonably objective standard, a standard free of racial (or sexual) orientation."[28] Robert Simon agrees, maintaining that there are candidates besides women and minorities who have suffered from discrimination and prejudice, or simply from being economically disadvantaged.[29] Cohen mentions Appalachian whites and impoverished Finns from upper Michigan as additional candidates for affirmative action.[30] Why should affirmative action not be directed at these people as well as at women and minorities?

Why not indeed! Surely if other individuals have suffered comparable hardships from discrimination and prejudice, or from simply being economically disadvantaged, some remedy would be appropriate. So Cohen's and Simon's objection is not an objection to affirmative action per se, but rather an objection to affirmative action as a narrowly conceived rather than a broadly conceived program. So, in fact, Cohen's and Simon's analyses point to the need for a more broadly conceived affirmative action program.

It should be noted, however, that if affirmative action is to be extended in this way to remedy other injustices in society, it must become a larger program. The few positions that have been targeted for affirmative action candidates have been created with the idea of simply remedying injustices suffered by women and minorities. If we now wish to remedy other comparable injustices in society as well, we will need to create many more positions to deal with the increased scope of affirmative action. Properly understood, Cohen's and Simon's analyses point to the need for just such an expansion.

Nevertheless, there might be good moral grounds for using the law to correct for sexual and racial discrimination but not for discrimination against Appalachian whites and impoverished Finns from upper Michigan, given that sexual and racial discrimination are two of the deepest and most pervasive forms of discrimination in our society. The law, it may be argued, should not be thought to be the instrument for correcting every injustice, but only for the gravest and most pervasive injustices.

In support of the fifth objection, Barry Gross claims that affirmative action is unfair to white males because it deprives them of equal opportunity by selecting or appointing women or minority candidates over more qualified white male candidates. To help fix ideas, consider the following two programs. Program A first hires women and minority candidates who are qualified over equally or more qualified white male candidates and then puts them through a six-month training program, after which it lets go any trainees who are not as qualified as, or more qualified than, anyone else in the hiring pool. Program B first admits certain highly qualified women and minority candidates into a six-month training program for which white male candidates are not eligible, and then hires just those women and minority candidates who, after completing the program, are equally qualified as, or more qualified than, anyone else in the hiring pool. I take it that Gross would object to Program A because it involves hiring women and minority candidates who are less qualified, but he need not object to program B, because he need not object to every attempt to compensate women and minorities for past discrimination but only to programs (like Program A) that he believes to be unfair because they involve hiring woman and minority candidates who are less qualified over more qualified white male candidates.

In response, Bernard Boxill denies that affirmative action is unfair to white males who are passed over for affirmative action candidates. After all, although these white males may not actually have discriminated against women and minorities themselves, Boxill argues that they have benefited from the discrimination of others, for example, through unequal educational opportunities. Hence, women and minorities do deserve compensation for this unjust discrimination, and, moreover, affirmative action seems to be an appropriate form of compensation. It also is difficult to understand how the opponent of affirmative action could object to attempts to remedy past discrimination like Program A while accepting attempts like Program B, given that they are so similar.

Of course, there are white males holding desirable positions in society who have benefited more from past discrimination than have the white males who would lose out to women or minority affirmative action candidates. So, ideally, an affirmative action program should be demanding sacrifices from these well-positioned white males as well. This could be done by requiring them to retire early, or by reducing their workweek in order to avoid having to lay off affirmative action hires, or by allowing affirmative action considerations to take precedence over seniority rules when actual layoffs become necessary.[31] Maybe we could target, among others, white male college professors who have taught for more than twenty years. Yet while it would be morally preferable to place the burdens of affirmative action on those who have benefited most from past discrimination, when the political power to do so is lacking it would still be morally permissible to place the burden primarily on white males who are competing for jobs and positions with affirmative action candidates, given that they still have benefited from past discrimination, although not as much as others.[32]

Comparable Worth

While affirmative action is a policy of preferring qualified women and minority candidates who have been disadvantaged by past injustices, comparable worth is the policy of correcting for existing wage discrimination by providing equal pay for comparable work. Its implementation would require significant changes in existing income distributions. In the United States, only a few jobs are substantially integrated by sex. Of the 503 occupations listed in the U.S. census, only 87 are integrated by sex – that is, are 30 to 50 percent female.[33] In addition, men in male-dominated occupations are usually paid more than women in female-dominated occupations. According to one study, men employed as stockroom attendants made much more than women employed as dental hygienists. In another study, women employed as school librarians were paid less than men employed as groundskeepers. Although in each of these cases the women earned at least 20 percent less than the men, the women's jobs when evaluated in terms of skill, responsibility, effort, and working conditions were given equal or higher scores than the men's jobs with which they were compared. Nor are these isolated examples. In fact, it would be difficult to come up with a single example of a male job paying less than a comparable female job.[34] There is also evidence that racial as well as sex discrimination exists with respect to comparable jobs. In San Francisco, for example, job evaluations revealed that janitors, mostly minority males, received 97 evaluation points and $18,000 in pay, while truck drivers, mostly white males, had 98 evaluation points but $27,000 in pay.[35] Consequently, paying women and minorities the same as white men earn in comparable jobs would involve a significant shift of income from men to women and from whites to blacks and other racial minorities.

Now comparable worth is objected to on grounds of justice for the following reasons:

1) It undermines the free market.
2) It eliminates nondiscriminatory wage gaps.
3) It purports to compare jobs that cannot be compared.

In support of the first objection, Clifford Hackett argues that comparable worth would destroy the link between work and marketplace evaluation.[36] In the private sector, Hackett claims that this link is vital to keeping a company competitive. In government, he claims that paying employees without regard to their cost in the local job market destroys confidence in the government's ability to match the efficiency of business. Moreover, it could be argued that a free market itself eliminates discrimination, because if some employers, for example, discriminate against women, any other employer can save money by hiring women in men's jobs for less than they currently pay men in such jobs. Presumably, some profit-maximizing employers will do this, and when enough of them do it, the discrimination against women will cease. This tendency of a free market to undermine discrimination is minimized, however, by the fact that many companies have internal labor markets that keep those outside the company from effectively competing for the higher-paying jobs within the company. For such companies, the only impact a free market has is on entry-level positions. Thus, even if a free market were to function optimally with respect to these entry-level positions, it would take a very long time for the market to eliminate discrimination in employment all the way up the employment ladder.[37] In addition, as Elaine Sorensen points out, it took new laws and court rulings to eliminate some of the most blatant discriminatory practices that prevailed in the U.S. labor market in the past.[38] So here, too, with regard to equal pay for comparable work, we will need to constrain the free market in order to produce that result within a reasonable length of time.

With respect to the second objection to comparable worth, Solomon Polachek argues that much of the wage gap between women and men is due to nondiscriminatory factors for which no corrective is needed.[39] Some of the gap, it is claimed, is attributable to women's roles as wives and mothers, which affect their pay by reducing their years of employment experience.[40] As evidence of this, it is pointed out that the gap between never-married men and never-married women is considerably smaller than the overall wage gap between women and men.[41] Advocates of comparable worth, however, argue that studies show that less than half of the wage gap between women and men can be accounted for by nondiscriminatory factors such as years of employment and willingness to choose a lower-paying job if it provides more flexible working hours.[42] In addition, the smaller wage gap between never-married women and never-married men can be accounted for by the higher level of human capital in terms of education and job experience of never-married women compared to never-married men.[43] So this still leaves a significant wage gap between women and men that can only be accounted for by discrimination.

In support of the third objection, Ellen Paul argues that job evaluations are inherently subjective, like comparing apples and oranges.[44] In response, it should be pointed out that companies already do compare people working at different jobs. In fact, two-thirds of American workers have their salaries set by job evaluations.[45] Hence, all that comparable worth requires is that the same job evaluation procedures currently used by management be used for a different purpose, that is, to compare the work done by women and men in different jobs.

Moreover, comparable worth is a policy that has been put into practice. Twenty states have enacted comparable worth policies, and twenty-two other states and Washington, D.C., have conducted or are conducting studies to determine if their wage-setting systems require comparable worth adjustments.[46] The state of Minnesota has gone the farthest in this regard by passing legislation that requires all local jurisdiction to undertake comparable worth policies. The state has 855 cities, 435 school districts, and 87 counties, all of which have undertaken some form of comparable worth policy.[47] Other countries have made even greater strides through comparable worth programs. For example, in Australia women now earn more than eighty cents for every dollar men earn, and in Sweden women now earn more than ninety cents for every dollar men earn.[48]

Conceivably, people who raise these flimsy objections to affirmative action or comparable worth, all the while remaining culpably ignorant of the gross inequalities in opportunities that favor whites over blacks[49] or men over women, do not think of themselves as racists or sexists, but I think that the unreasonableness of the stances they take convicts them of racism or sexism nonetheless. This is because one can be a racist and a sexist not only by unjustifiably intending harm to blacks and women but also by unjustifiably denying them important benefits they should have, like affirmative action and comparable worth. Likewise, people who ignore the even grosser inequalities presently favoring heterosexuals over homosexuals, or Western culture over non-Western cultures, and who maintain that any attempt to correct for past injustices in these areas only ends up doing additional injustice, convict themselves of either heterosexism or Eurocentrism respectively.

III. HETEROSEXISM

Typically, however, neither heterosexists nor Eurocentrists argue in this roundabout way for their view. Instead, they endorse the more blatant argument for heterosexism or Eurocentrism and maintain that there are certain differences between heterosexuals and homosexuals or between Western culture and non-Western cultures that ground the superiority of the former over the latter. This superiority is then further claimed to legitimate the domination of homosexuals by heterosexuals, or non-Western cultures by Western culture.

With regard to homosexuals, prohibitions against homosexuality have ancient roots, but the enforcement of such prohibitions has almost always been haphazard at best. This is because when one is dealing with acts between consenting adults, it can be difficult to find a complainant. Even so, twenty-four states still have statutes on the books prohibiting homosexual acts. Penalties range from one month's imprisonment and a fifty-dollar fine to life imprisonment.[50]

Moreover, what these statutes prohibit is sodomy, which involves more than just homosexual acts. For example, the Georgia statute whose constitutionality was upheld by the U.S. Supreme Court in *Bowers v. Hardwick* holds that "a person commits the offense of sodomy when he performs or submits to any sexual act involving the sex organs of one person and the mouth or anus of another."[51] The reason why sodomy is defined so broadly here is that the main complaint against homosexual acts – that they are unnatural – also applies to a range of other acts. More specifically, it applies to oral and anal intercourse between heterosexuals, masturbation, and bestiality, as well as homosexual acts.

Now it is important to understand what is considered to be "unnatural" about all these acts.[52] One sense of "natural" refers to what is found in nature as contrasted with what is artificial or the product

112

of human artifice. In this sense, homosexuality would seem to be natural, since it is found in virtually every human society. But even if homosexuality is understood to be a product of a certain type of upbringing or socialization, and hence artificial, that would hardly seem to be grounds for condemning it, as a great deal of human behavior has a similar origin.

Another sense of "natural" refers to what is common or statistically normal as contrasted with what is uncommon or statistically abnormal. In this sense, homosexuality would not be natural because most people are not homosexuals, despite the fact that according to one study about half of all American males have engaged in homosexual acts at some time in their lives.[53] But being unnatural in this sense could not be grounds for condemning homosexuality, for many traits we value in people, for example, being a genius, are also statistically abnormal and hence unnatural in this sense.

Still another sense of "natural" refers to a thing's proper function, and it is this sense of "natural" that is frequently used to condemn homosexuality. For if we maintain that the proper function of human sexual organs is simply procreation, then any use of those organs for a purpose other than procreation would be unnatural. Hence, homosexuality, contraception, masturbation, and bestiality would all be unnatural in this sense. But clearly the proper function of human sexual organs is not limited to procreation; these organs are also used to express love and to provide pleasure to oneself and others. Given that our sexual organs can be properly used for these other purposes, we would need an argument that every use of these organs must serve their procreative function in order to be able to condemn homosexuality. But no nontheologically based argument has succeeded in establishing this conclusion.[54] Moreover, once we grant, for example, that contraception and masturbation are morally permissible, there seem to be no grounds left, based on the proper functioning of our sexual organs, for denying that homosexual acts are morally permissible as well.

Now it might be objected here that what is wrong with acts of contraception, masturbation, and homosexuality is that they all violate the principle that one should never (intentionally) do evil that good may come of it, where it is claimed that the evil involved in these acts is that of interfering with or frustrating the human procreative process. But if interfering with or frustrating the human procreative process is always evil, whom does it harm? Surely if evil is done, someone is harmed, and if no one is harmed then the actions in question cannot be evil. But is there always someone who is harmed by acts of contraception, masturbation, and homosexuality? Clearly, under certain circumstances, there might be people who are harmed by a refusal to procreate, for example, in a community suffering from underpopulation.[55] But those who engage in acts of contraception, masturbation, and homosexuality need not refuse to procreate – even gays and lesbians can choose to be parents – and so these acts need not be harmful even under these fairly unusual circumstances. Moreover, even if heterosexists were able to establish that people are sometimes harmed by homosexual acts, that would not be enough. What they need to establish is that people are always, or at least generally, harmed by homosexual acts, and this heterosexists clearly have not done.[56]

Yet heterosexists still maintain that the "unnaturalness" of homosexuality supports the superiority of heterosexuality, and that this superiority legitimates the domination of homosexuals by heterosexuals. But the homosexuality that heterosexists oppose as unnatural is either completely biologically determined, or completely the product of socialization and choice, or partly biologically determined and partly the product of socialization and choice. Now, on the one hand, if homosexuality is completely biologically determined, then any attempt to suppress it will be unjustified because it will be ineffectual, unless, that is, we plan to change human biology. On the other hand, if homosexuality is completely the product of socialization and choice, then, in the absence of evidence showing that an (unpersecuted) homosexual lifestyle would lead to unhappiness or lack of human fulfillment for homosexuals, and in the absence of evidence showing that failure to suppress homosexuals would have unacceptable consequences for the rest of society, any attempt to suppress homosexuality will be unjustified. Similarly, if homosexuality is partly biologically determined and partly the product of socialization and choice, then any attempt to suppress the biologically determined part of homosexuality will be unjustified because it will be ineffectual, and, in the absence of evidence showing that an (unpersecuted) homosexual lifestyle would lead to unhappiness or lack of human fulfillment for homosexuals, and in the absence of evidence showing that failure to suppress homosexuals would have unacceptable consequences for the rest of society, any attempt to suppress that part of homosexuality which is a product of socialization and choice will be unjustified. Thus, the suppression of homosexuality is only justified if it can be shown that an (unpersecuted) homosexual lifestyle would lead to unhappiness or lack of human fulfillment for homosexuals or that failure to suppress homosexuals would have unacceptable consequences for the rest of society.

Unfortunately, most attempts to assess the happiness or unhappiness of homosexual lives totally ignore the effects of societal persecution. Yet even when such effects are ignored, studies have shown homosexuals to be no more psychologically and emotionally disturbed than the population as a whole.[57] According to one study, male homosexuals were even more masculine than the average male soldier.[58] So, on the basis of present evidence, there is no reason to think that unpersecuted homosexuals would be less happy or fulfilled than random members of the population as a whole. One might even wonder how much higher homosexuals might score on such evaluations if they were not the objects of societal persecution. As for evidence showing that failure to suppress homosexuals would have unacceptable consequences for the rest of society, what would such evidence look like? Would it indicate that there would be a sizable increase in the numbers of homosexuals? Such an increase, of course, could only occur if homosexuality is in whole or in part the product of socialization and choice. But suppose homosexuality were in whole or in part the product of socialization and choice, and that without persecution there would be a sizable increase in homosexuality, would this lead to unacceptable consequences for society as a whole? How could it, if homosexuals are just as psychologically adjusted as heterosexuals? There is also evidence that the suppression of at least male homosexuality is linked to a need to bolster "machismo" male roles and the sexual exploitation of women.[59] Specifically, gay men are targeted because they have broken ranks with male heterosexuality by, among other things, allowing themselves to be penetrated and treated as sexual objects.[60] What this suggests is that ceasing to suppress homosexuality might also have beneficial effects on women in their relationships with men.

In *Bowers v. Hardwick* (1986), the issue before the Supreme Court was whether the Georgia sodomy statute violates the Federal Constitution. Justice White, delivering the opinion of the Court, argued that the statute does not violate the Federal Constitution because the Constitution does not confer a fundamental right on homosexuals to engage in sodomy. While in previous cases the Federal Constitution was interpreted to confer a right to decide whether or not to beget or bear a child and a right not to be convicted for possessing and reading obscene material in the privacy of one's home, White argued that the Federal Constitution cannot analogously be interpreted to confer a fundamental right on homosexuals to engage in sodomy. Justice Burger concurred, stressing the ancient roots of sodomy statutes. In reaching its decision, the majority of the Court also drew an insupportable distinction between heterosexual sodomy and homosexual sodomy, permitting the one while proscribing the other.

In dissent, Justice Blackmun, joined by Justices Brennan and Marshall, argued that notwithstanding the ancient roots of prohibitions against homosexuality, a right to be let alone, which was the underpinning of previous court decisions, justifies in this case a right to engage in sodomy, at least in the privacy of one's home. In this case, the majority of the Court reached their conclusion by interpreting previous decisions in an excessively literal manner, in much the same way that the majority of the Court ruled in *Olmstead v. United States* (1928) that warrantless wiretapping did not violate the Fourth Amendment prohibition against search and seizure because the framers of the amendment were not explicitly prohibiting this particular method of obtaining incriminating evidence. But just as the Supreme Court later repudiated its decision in *Olmstead v. United States,* the Court may be moving toward something comparable in its recent decision on *Romer v. Evans* (1996).[61]

In *Romer v. Evans,* the issue before the Supreme Court was whether an amendment to the constitution of Colorado precluding any governmental action designed to protect the status of persons based on their "homosexual, lesbian or bisexual orientation, conduct, practices or relationship" violates the Equal Protection Clause of the Fourteenth Amendment. Justice Kennedy, writing for the majority, held that it did, because the amendment imposes a broad disability on homosexuals that is not rationally related to any legitimate government interest. Thus, the Court rejected Colorado's contention that its amendment was doing nothing more than denying special rights to homosexuals. Instead, the Court held that Colorado was imposing a special legal burden on homosexuals by denying them a protection that other people simply take for granted in a free society. Accordingly, it is difficult not to see this decision as in some sense a repudiation of *Bowers v. Hardwick.* As Justice Scalia noted in his dissent, how could it be constitutionally permissible for other states to make homosexual conduct criminal but not constitutionally permissible for Colorado to enact this amendment? Yet it may be that what the majority of the Court were objecting to in *Romer v. Evans* was the imposition of a legal disability on the basis of a person's *status* as a homosexual rather than on the basis of his or her conduct, as in *Bowers v. Hardwick.*[62] But even if this is the case, and *Romer v. Evans* cannot be viewed as a straightforward repudiation of *Bowers v. Hardwick,* this decision still is an important victory for the cause of homosexual justice.

IV. EUROCENTRISM AND MULTICULTURALISM

Unfortunately, the same blatant form of argument is used on behalf of Eurocentrism, which maintains that there are certain differences between Western culture and non-Western cultures that establish the superiority of the former over the latter and that this superiority then legitimates the domination of non-Western cultures by Western culture. Now, in this book, I have argued that rationality understood as non-question-beggingness requires us to endorse morality over both egoism and pure altruism (Chapter 2). I have also argued that even the minimal morality of the libertarian ideal of liberty requires us to endorse a right to welfare and a right to equal opportunity, and that these two rights both lead to something like the equality that socialists endorse (Chapter 3) and to the androgyny that many feminists defend (Chapter 4). But if these arguments are to be morally defensible, they must be able to survive in a comparative evaluation with other moral and political ideals, including non-Western ones. What are the chances of these rights actually surviving such a comparative evaluation?

At the moment, the chances seem to be quite good, because any defensible moral and political ideal, whether Western or non-Western, would seemingly have to endorse the rational requirement of non-question-beggingness that supports a moral point of view. Similarly, the "Ought" Implies "Can" Principle and its contrapositive, the Conflict Resolution Principle, would seem to be basic to a moral point of view, and in virtue of upholding these principles, any defensible moral and political ideal would also have to endorse a right to welfare and a right to equal opportunity, since the "Ought" Implies "Can" Principle and its contrapositive, the Conflict Resolution Principle secure these rights even within the minimal morality of a libertarian political ideal.[63] Nor is it easy to see how any defensible moral and political ideal could go beyond the requirements of these two rights. Given that these two rights lead both to something like the equality that socialists endorse (see Chapter 3) and to the androgyny that many feminists defend (see Chapter 4), it is difficult to see how a defensible moral and political ideal could be still more demanding.

American Indian Culture

Nevertheless, it may be that Western moral and political ideals are not demanding enough because they have not adequately faced the question of who is to count in ways that at least some non-Western moral and political ideals have done. For example, many, if not all, American Indian tribes regard animals, plants, and assorted other natural things as persons in their own right with whom it is possible to enter into complex social intercourse requiring mutual respect.[64] The type of respect required is illustrated by the following account of how a Sioux elder advised his son to hunt the four-legged animals of the forest.

> (S)hoot your four-legged brother in the hind area, slowing it down but not killing it. Then, take the four-legged's head in your hands, and look into his eyes. The eyes are where all the suffering is. Look into your

brother's eyes and feel his pain. Then, take your knife and cut the four-legged under his chin, here, on his neck, so that he dies quickly. And as you do, ask your brother, the four-legged, for forgiveness for what you do. Offer also a prayer of thanks to your four-legged kin for offering his body to you just now, when you need food to eat and clothing to wear. And promise the four-legged that you will put yourself back into the earth when you die, to become the nourishment of the earth, and for the sister flowers, and for the brother deer. It is appropriate that you should offer this blessing for the four-legged and, in due time, reciprocate in turn with your body in this way, as the four-legged gives life to you for your survival.[65]

Wooden Leg, a Cheyenne, provides a similar account.

The old Indian teaching was that it is wrong to tear loose from its place on the earth anything that may be growing there. It may be cut off, but it should not be uprooted. The trees and the grass have spirits. Whenever one of such growths may be destroyed by some good Indian, his act is done in sadness and with a prayer for forgiveness because of necessities. . . . [66]

Moreover, this respect for nonhuman nature shared by American Indians is based on a perceived identity with other living things. According to Luther Standing Bear, a Sioux chief,

We are the soil and the soil is us. We loved the birds and beasts that grew with us on this soil. They drank the same water as we did and breathed the same air. We are all one in nature. Believing so, there was in our hearts a great peace and a welling kindness for all living growing things.[67]

Arguably, it is this respect for nonhuman nature that has enabled American Indians to live in their natural environment with greater harmony than we in Western culture are presently doing.

Is there, then, something that we in Western culture can learn from American Indian culture? At the very least, an appreciation for American Indian culture should lead us to consider whether we have legitimate grounds for failing to constrain our own interests for the sake of nonhuman nature. In Western culture, people tend to think of themselves as radically separate from and superior to nonhuman nature, so as to allow for domination over it. To justify this perspective, people in Western culture often appeal to the creation story in Genesis. In the Priestly version of this story, God tells humans to "Be fruitful and multiply, and fill the earth and subdue it. Have dominion over the fish of the sea, the birds of the air, cattle, and all the animals that crawl on the earth" (Genesis 1:28). One interpretation of this directive is that humans are required or permitted to dominate nonhuman nature, that is, to use animals and plants for whatever purposes we happen to have, giving no independent weight at all to the interests of animals and plants. They are simply means to our ends.[68] Another interpretation, however, understands dominion, not as domination, but as a caring stewardship toward nonhuman nature, which imposes limits on the ways that we can use animals and plants in pursuit of our own purposes, thereby making it possible for other living things to flourish.[69]

Obviously, this second interpretation accords better with the perspective found in American Indian culture. However, it is the first interpretation that is most widely accepted throughout Western culture. Given these conflicting interpretations of the Genesis story, it is clear that an appeal to the Bible is not going to be decisive in determining how anyone should treat nonhuman nature. Accordingly, we need to determine whether reason alone can provide any compelling grounds for thinking that we are superior to nonhuman nature in ways that would justify our domination of it. In the next chapter, I take up this question and argue that there are no grounds for thinking that we are superior to nonhuman nature in ways that would justify our domination of it. If this argument is correct, then those of us within Western culture can learn an important lesson from American Indian culture. It is that the intrinsic value of nonhuman species places an significant constraint on how we pursue our own interests. As we shall see, this will require that we reinterpret our basic rights to welfare and equal opportunity so as to rule out the domination of nonhuman nature.

Multiculturalism and Applying Basic Rights

Yet even where the rights to welfare and equal opportunity do not need to be reinterpreted in light of non-Western ideals, knowledge of non-Western cultures is still required for the application of these rights. In particular, the application of these rights to distant peoples requires knowledge of the cultures in which distant peoples live in order to determine what is necessary for a basic-needs minimum and for equal opportunity. Unfortunately, many First World aid programs have been designed without careful consideration of the local cultures, with disastrous results. Probably the best well-known example of the failure to take into account the knowledge available in local cultures is the so-called Green Revolution.[70]

The Green Revolution was initially carried out in northwest Mexico and in the Punjab region of India. It was publicized as a political and technological achievement unprecedented in human history. It was proclaimed as a strategy for peace through the creation of abundance.

In 1970, Norman Borlaug received the Nobel Peace Prize because of his role in the Green Revolution.

The essential ingredient in the Green Revolution was the development of high-yielding seeds. These seeds, initially wheat and later rice, produced their high yield only in conjunction with the intensive application of chemical fertilizers. Native wheat seeds, when subjected to intensive applications of chemical fertilizers, would respond by producing a larger plant but not more grain; Borlaug's miracle seeds produced a dwarf plant with a higher grain yield. But these miracle seeds not only required the intensive use of chemical fertilizers, they also required more water than indigenous seeds. Unfortunately, when Borlaug's miracle seeds were being advocated for use in Mexico and India, their liabilities compared with the advantages of local alternatives were not well considered.

In 1905, Sir Albert Howard was dispatched to India by the British government to investigate methods of improving Indian agriculture. He found that their crops were free from pests, and that insecticides and fungicides had no place in their system of agriculture. He wrote: "I could not do better than watch the operations of these peasants, and acquire their traditional knowledge as rapidly as possible. For the time being, therefore, I regarded them as my professor of agriculture."[71] Earlier, in 1889, Dr. John Augustus Voeleker, in his report to the Royal Agricultural Society of England, stated:

> I may be bold to say that it is a much easier task to propose improvements in English agriculture than to make really valuable suggestions for that of India. To take the ordinary acts of husbandry, no where would one find better instances of keeping land scrupulously clean from weeds, of ingenuity in device of water raising appliances, of knowledge of soils and their capacities as well as of the exact time to sow and to reap as one would in Indian agriculture....[72]

However, after World War II, agriculture in India did experience setbacks, some having to do with the decline of export markets and others stemming from partition. In the mid-1960s the World Bank and USAID offered to provide the financial resources to implement the Green Revolution technology that was being pushed by the Ford and Rockefeller foundations. In 1966, Lyndon Johnson refused to commit food aid to India beyond one month in advance until it adopted the Green Revolution as national agricultural policy. So, under pressure, India signed on.

Initially, it appeared that the miracle seeds were working, but soon problems began to emerge. First, without crop rotation, the miracle seeds attracted pests and diseases and, hence, required the widespread use of pesticides and fungicides. Second, in three to five years, the miracle seeds became so pest-and disease-prone that new seeds had to be developed. Third, chemical fertilizers, unlike farmland manure, did not replace all the nutrients that crops were removing from the soil, so in time the soil lost its fertility and yields began to decline. Fourth, the increased water requirements of the miracle seeds led to waterlogging and salinization of the land as well as conflicts over water rights. Fifth, the new technology was not sustainable, dependent as it was on the availability of chemical fertilizers, new strains of seeds, pesticides, and fungicides.

Were there better alternatives? Surely there were, and they could have been found by working with the knowledge available in the local cultures. Before the Green Revolution, there had been important research programs in both Mexico and India on a wide variety of seeds traditionally cultivated by peasants. These programs were consciously undermined by the advocates of the Green Revolution. In India, the Cuttack Institute was working on ways to increase yields of rice based on indigenous knowledge and genetic resources. Nevertheless, for political reasons, the Indian minister of agriculture demanded that the Cuttack Institute turn over its rice-germ plasm to an institute set up by the Ford and Rockefeller foundations. When the director resisted, he was removed. Another Indian rice institute operating on a small budget had collected over twenty thousand indigenous varieties of rice and was working on a high-yield strategy based on tribal knowledge. It was closed down due to pressure from the World Bank because it had reservations about sending its rice-germ plasm to the institute set up by the Ford and Rockefeller foundations.

Thus, the failure of the Green Revolution could have been prevented by taking into account the knowledge already available in local cultures. Lack of respect for these local cultures lay at the heart of the failure of the Green Revolution as a foreign aid program. Clearly, then, the application of rights to welfare and equal opportunity must proceed with adequate knowledge of the cultures in which people live in order to determine what is necessary to secure these rights.

Multiculturalism and the Educational Canon

Much of the recent discussion of multiculturalism has focused on its application to educational institutions. In this context, it has been argued that multicultural justice requires increased enrollment of minority students, increased hiring of minority faculty, and substantial changes in the canon of what should be taught. Here I want to focus on the third implication of multicultural justice: the need for substantial changes in the canon of what should be taught – particularly as this relates to moral and political philosophy. The central questions that must be addressed here are: What should be included in the common curriculum? How much of the classics of Western culture should be left undisturbed in the common curriculum? How much from non-Western cultures should be added to the common curriculum?

Obviously, the answers that you give to these questions depend on how valuable you consider Western culture to be. If Western culture is the source of your oppression, you will probably not think that you have a lot to learn from it. But what if Western culture is in some respects the source of your oppression and in other respects also a means to your liberation? If that is the case, you will probably not want to discard Western culture entirely; you will want to salvage those parts of Western culture that can serve as a means to your liberation. In the area of moral and political philosophy, this means that even the oppressed will have good reason to retain those works of Western culture that support the rights to welfare and to equal opportunity, given that recognition of these rights worldwide and into the future would virtually put an end to their oppression.[73]

Suppose, then, that those works of Western culture which support the rights to welfare and equal opportunity are retained in the common curriculum. Will there be room left in the educational canon for any other works in moral and political philosophy? Could it be that even a selection of the greatest works of Western moral and political philosophy will just about take up the entire curriculum? Surely, this could not happen, because if the basic rights that are derived from Western moral and political philosophy are to be defensible, they must be able to survive a comparative evaluation with other moral and political ideals, including non-Western ones. So there is no escaping an adequate representation of non-Western moral and political philosophy in the common curriculum.

What, then, would a common curriculum that appropriately combines Western and non-Western works in moral and political philosophy look like? My anthology, *Social and Political Philosophy: Classical Western Texts in Feminist and Multicultural Perspectives,* is actually an attempt to answer this question.[74] In this text, a survey of some of the greatest works of Western moral and political philosophy is combined with some of the greatest related works of non-Western moral and political philosophy. Some of these non-Western works were chosen because they parallel the views defended in the Western works (for example, Confucius's work parallels that of Plato or Aristotle). But other non-Western works were chosen because they challenge the views defended in the Western works (for example, American Indian works provide an interesting challenge to the Western social contract tradition of Hobbes, Locke, and Rousseau). Obviously, these challenges to Western moral and political philosophy can lead to reinterpretations of the Western works – for example, along the lines suggested by our brief examination of American Indian culture in this chapter. In any case, what is clear is that the defensibility of Western moral and political philosophy depends on the results of just such a comparative evaluation.

V. THE PRACTICAL CONNECTION

I have argued for a theoretical connection between feminist justice, racial justice, homosexual justice, and multicultural justice. To achieve each of these forms of justice, we need to expose either a blatant argument that moves from a claim of difference to a claim of superiority and then to a claim of domination, or a less blatant argument that renounces past domination as unjustified but goes on to claim that people are no longer denied equal opportunity on the basis of sex, race, sexual orientation, or culture, so that whatever inequalities do remain must either be grounded in a legitimate superiority or constitute a residue of past injustices that cannot be removed without doing additional injustice. In view of this theoretical connection between feminist justice, racial justice, homosexual justice, and multicultural justice, the practical connection between these forms of justice is quite straightforward: It is that these forms of justice should be pursued together, as much as possible, because, given the theoretical connection between these forms of justice, failure to pursue them together will be looked upon with suspicion and distrust by anyone whose cause is excluded. In fact, this has already happened. Failure to pursue racial justice along with feminist justice has left some black feminists, like Audre Lorde and bell hooks, wondering about the commitments of at least some advocates of feminist justice; and failure to pursue homosexual justice and multicultural justice along with feminist justice has left some lesbian feminists and non-Western feminists, like Maria Lugones and Gloria Anzaldua, wondering about the commitments of at least some heterosexual and Western feminists.[75] Suspicion and distrust can be aroused in the opposite direction as well. Advocates of racial, homosexual, or multicultural justice may not express a commitment to feminist justice, thereby arousing doubts among feminists about the commitments of these advocates. There is another reason for recognizing a practical connection between these forms of justice: the fact that 50 percent of those who need racial or multicultural justice, and probably 50 percent of those who need homosexual justice, need feminist justice as well.

Of course, it can be difficult to pursue all these forms of justice together. To build a political movement strong enough to effect the necessary changes, it may be necessary to focus attention on the pursuit of just one of these forms of justice. Yet even when this is necessary, it is possible to recognize the need for the other forms of justice while still focusing primarily on only one form of justice. For example, advocates of feminist justice can recognize the need to achieve racial, homosexual, and multicultural justice as well as feminist justice. Similarly, advocates of racial, homosexual, and multicultural justice can also recognize the need to achieve feminist justice. Thus, being as inclusive as possible can serve to bring together as many people as possible in support of one's cause, and also to signal to supporters and nonsupporters alike the uncompromising justice of that cause. Surely, given the theoretical and practical connections between these forms of justice, a peacemaking way of doing philosophy concerned to fashion a conception of justice for here and now can be satisfied with nothing less.

Chapter 6

From Anthropocentrism to Nonanthropocentrism

A central debate, if not the most central debate, in contemporary environmental ethics is between those who defend an anthropocentric ethics and those who defend a nonanthropocentric ethics. This debate pits deep ecologists like George Sessions against reform or shallow ecologists like John Passmore.[1] It divides biocentric egalitarians like Paul Taylor from social ecologists like Murray Bookchin.[2] In this chapter I propose to go some way toward resolving this debate in accord with a peacemaking model of doing philosophy by showing that, when the most morally defensible versions of each of these perspectives are laid out, they do not lead to different practical requirements. In this way I hope to show how it is possible for defenders of anthropocentric and nonanthropocentric environmental ethics, despite their theoretical disagreement concerning whether humans are superior to members of other species, to agree on a common set of principles for achieving environmental justice.[3] I also propose to show how this approach to environmental justice can be extended to deal with environmental racism.

I. NONANTHROPOCENTRISM

Consider first the nonanthropocentric perspective. In support of this perspective, it can be argued that we have no non-question-begging grounds for regarding the members of any living species as superior to the members of any other. It allows that the members of species differ in a myriad of ways, but argues that these differences do not provide grounds for thinking that the members of any one species are superior to the members of any other. In particular, it denies that the differences between species provide grounds for thinking that humans are superior to the members of other species. Of course, the nonanthropocentric perspective recognizes that humans have distinctive traits which the members of other species lack, like rationality and moral agency. It just points out that the members of nonhuman species also have distinctive traits that humans lack, like the homing ability of pigeons, the speed of the cheetah, and the ruminative ability of sheep and cattle.

Nor will it do to claim that the distinctive traits that humans have are more valuable than the distinctive traits that members of other species possess, because there is no non-question-begging standpoint from which to justify that claim. From a human standpoint, rationality and moral agency are more valuable than any of the distinctive traits found in nonhuman species, since, as humans, we would not be better off if we were to trade in those traits for the distinctive traits found in nonhuman species. Yet the same holds true of nonhuman species. Generally, pigeons, cheetahs, sheep, and cattle would not be better off if they were to trade in their distinctive traits for the distinctive traits of other species.[4]

Of course, the members of some species might be better off if they could retain the distinctive traits of their species while acquiring one or another of the distinctive traits possessed by some other species. For example, we humans might be better off if we could retain our distinctive traits while acquiring the ruminative ability of sheep and cattle.[5] But many of the distinctive traits of species cannot be, even imaginatively, added to the members of other species without substantially altering the original species. For example, in order for the cheetah to acquire the distinctive traits possessed by humans, presumably it would have to be so transformed that its paws became something like hands to accommodate its humanlike mental capabilities; thereby it would lose its distinctive speed and cease to be a cheetah. So possessing distinctively human traits would not be good for the cheetah.[6] And, with the possible exception of our nearest evolutionary relatives, the same holds true for the members of other species: They would not be better off having distinctively human traits. Only in fairy tales and in the world of Disney can the members of nonhuman species enjoy a full array of distinctively human traits. So there would appear to be no non-question-begging perspective from which to judge that distinctively human traits are more valuable than the distinctive traits possessed by other species. Judged from a non-question-begging perspective, we would seemingly have to regard the members of all species as equals.

It might be useful at this point to make my argument even more explicit. Here is one way this could be done.[7]

1) We should not aggress against any living being unless there are either self-evident or non-question-begging reasons for doing so.

126

(It would be difficult to reject this principle given the various analogous principles we accept, such as the principle of formal equality: Equals should be treated equally and unequals unequally.)

2) To treat humans as superior overall to other living beings is to aggress against them by sacrificing their basic needs to meet the nonbasic needs of humans. (Definition)
3) Therefore, we should not treat humans as superior overall to other living beings unless we have either self-evident or non-question-begging reasons for doing so. (From 1 and 2)
4) We do not have either self-evident or non-question-begging reasons for treating humans as superior overall to other living beings. (That we do not have any non-question-begging reasons for treating humans as superior overall to other living beings was established by the previous argument.[8] That we do not have any self-evident reasons for doing so, I take it, is obvious.)
5) Therefore, we should not treat humans as superior overall to other living beings. (From 3 and 4)
6) Not to treat humans as superior overall to other living beings is to treat them as equal overall to other living beings.[9] (Definition)
7) Therefore, we should treat humans as equal overall to other living beings. (From 5 and 6)

Nevertheless, I want to go on to claim that regarding the members of all species as equals still allows for human preference in the same way that regarding all humans as equals still allows for self-preference.

First of all, human preference can be justified on grounds of defense. Thus, we have

A Principle of Human Defense: Actions that defend oneself and other human beings against harmful aggression are permissible even when they necessitate killing or harming animals or plants.[10]

This Principle of Human Defense allows us to defend ourselves and other human beings from harmful aggression, first, against our persons and the persons of other human beings to whom we are committed or happen to care about and, second, against our justifiably held property and the justifiably held property of other humans beings to whom we are committed or happen to care about.[11]

This principle is analogous to the principle of self-defense that applies in human ethics[12] permitting actions in defense of oneself or other human beings against harmful human aggression.[13] In the case of human aggression, however, it will sometimes be possible to effectively defend oneself and other human beings by first suffering the aggression and then securing adequate compensation later. Since in the case of nonhuman aggression, this is unlikely to obtain, more harmful preventive actions such as killing a rabid dog or swatting a mosquito will be justified. There are simply more ways to effectively stop aggressive humans than there are to stop aggressive nonhumans.

Second, human preference can also be justified on grounds of preservation. Accordingly, we have

> *A Principle of Human Preservation:* Actions that are necessary for meeting one's basic needs or the basic needs of other human beings are permissible even when they require aggressing against the basic needs of animals and plants.[14]

Now needs, in general, if not satisfied, lead to lacks or deficiencies with respect to various standards. The basic needs of humans, if not satisfied, lead to lacks or deficiencies with respect to a standard of a decent life. The basic needs of animals and plants, if not satisfied, lead to lacks or deficiencies with respect to a standard of a healthy life. The means necessary for meeting the basic needs of humans can vary widely from society to society. By contrast, the means necessary for meeting the basic needs of particular species of animals and plants are more invariant.[15] Of course, while only some needs can be clearly classified as basic, and others clearly classified as nonbasic, there still are other needs that are more or less difficult to classify. Yet the fact that not every need can be clearly classified as either basic or nonbasic, as is true of a whole range of dichotomous concepts like moral/immoral, legal/illegal, living/nonliving, human/nonhuman, should not immobilize us from acting, at least with respect to clear cases.[16]

In human ethics, there is no principle that is strictly analogous to this Principle of Human Preservation.[17] There is a principle of self-preservation in human ethics that permits actions necessary for meeting one's own basic needs or the basic needs of other people, even if this requires *failing to meet* (through an act of omission) the basic needs of still other people. For example, we can use our resources to feed ourselves and our family even if this necessitates failing to meet the basic needs of people in Third World countries. But, in general, we don't have a principle that allows us to *aggress against* (through an act of commission) the basic needs of some people in order to meet our own basic needs or the basic needs of other people to whom we are committed or happen to care about. Actually, the closest we come to permitting aggressing against the basic needs of other people in order to meet our own basic needs or the basic needs of people to whom we are committed or happen to care about is our acceptance of the outcome of life-and-death struggles in lifeboat cases, where no one has an antecedent right to the available resources. For example, if you had to fight off others in order to secure the last place in a lifeboat for yourself or for a member of your family, we might say that you justifiably aggressed against the basic needs of those whom you fought to meet your own basic needs or the basic needs of the member of your family.[18]

Nevertheless, our survival requires a principle of preservation that permits aggressing against the basic needs of at least some other living things whenever this is necessary to meet our own basic needs or the basic needs of other human beings. Here there are two possibilities. The first is a principle of preservation that allows us to aggress against the basic needs of both humans and nonhumans whenever it would serve our own basic needs or the basic needs of other human beings. The second is the principle, stated above, that allows us to aggress against the basic needs of only nonhumans whenever it would serve our own basic needs or the basic needs of other human beings. The first principle does not express any general preference for the members of the human species, and thus it permits even cannibalism, provided that it serves to meet our own basic needs or the basic needs of other human beings. In contrast, the second principle does express a degree of preference for the members of the human species in cases where their basic needs are at stake. Of course, it would be theoretically possible to interact with the members of one's own species on the basis of the first principle of preservation considered above – the one that permits even cannibalism as a means for meeting basic needs. In the case of humans, adopting such a principle would clearly reduce the degree of predation of humans on other species, and so would be of some benefit to other species. Yet implicit nonaggression pacts based on a reasonable expectation of a comparable degree of altruistic forbearance from fellow humans have been enormously beneficial and probably were necessary for the survival of the human species. So it is difficult to see how humans could be justifiably required to forgo such benefits. Moreover, to require humans to extend these benefits to the members of all species would, in effect, be to require humans to be saints, and surely morality is not in the business of requiring anyone to be a saint. Given, then, that this greater altruism cannot be morally required, the degree of preference for the members of our own species sanctioned by the above Principle of Human Preservation is justified, even if we were to adopt a nonanthropocentric perspective.[19]

Nevertheless, preference for humans can go beyond bounds, and the bounds that are compatible with a nonanthropocentric perspective are expressed by the following:

A Principle of Disproportionality: Actions that meet nonbasic or luxury needs of humans are prohibited when they aggress against the basic needs of animals and plants.

This principle is strictly analogous to the principle in human ethics mentioned previously that prohibits meeting some people's nonbasic or luxury needs by aggressing against the basic needs of other people.[20]

Without a doubt, the adoption of such a principle with respect to nonhuman nature would significantly change the way we live our lives. Such a principle is required, however, if there is to be any substance to the claim that the members of all species are equal. We can no more consistently claim that the members of all species are equal and yet aggress against the basic needs of some animals or plants whenever this serves our own nonbasic or luxury needs than we can consistently claim that all humans are equal and aggress against the basic needs of some other human beings whenever this serves our nonbasic or luxury needs.[21] Consequently, if species equality is to mean anything, it must be the case that the basic needs of the members of nonhuman species are protected against aggressive actions which only serve to meet the nonbasic needs of humans, as required by the Principle of Disproportionality.[22] So while a nonanthropocentric perspective allows for a degree of preference for the members of the human species, it also significantly limits that preference.[23]

To see why these limits on preference for the members of the human species are all that is required for recognizing the equality of species, we need to understand the equality of species by analogy with the equality of humans. We need to see that, just as we claim that humans are equal yet justifiably treat them differently, so too we can claim that all species are equal yet justifiably treat them differently. In human ethics, various interpretations are given to human equality that allow for different treatment of humans. In ethical egoism, everyone is *equally at liberty* to pursue his or her own interests, but this allows us always to prefer ourselves to others, who are understood to be like opponents in a competitive game. In libertarianism, everyone has an *equal right to liberty*, but although this imposes some limits on the pursuit of self-interest, it is said to allow us to refrain from helping others in severe need. In welfare liberalism, everyone has an *equal right to welfare and opportunity*, but this need not commit us to providing everyone with exactly the same resources. In socialism, everyone has an *equal right* to self-development, and although this may commit us to providing everyone with something like the same resources, it still sanctions some degree of self-preference. So just as there are these various ways to interpret human equality that still allow us to treat humans differently, there are various ways that we can interpret species equality that allow us to treat species differently.

Now one might interpret species equality in a very strong sense, analogous to the interpretation of equality found in socialism. But the kind of species equality that I have defended is more akin to the equality found in welfare liberalism or in libertarianism than it is to the equality found in socialism. In brief, this form of equality requires that we not aggress against the basic needs of the members of other species for the sake of the nonbasic needs of the members of our own species (the Principle of Disproportionality), but it permits us to aggress against the basic needs of the members of other species for the sake of the basic needs of the members of our own species (the Principle of Human Preservation), and it also permits us to defend the basic and even the nonbasic needs of the members of our own species against harmful aggression by members of other species (the Principle of Human Defense). In this way, I have argued that we can accept the claim of species equality while avoiding imposing an unreasonable sacrifice on oneself or the members of our own species.[24]

II. INDIVIDUALISM AND HOLISM

It might be objected here that I have not yet taken into account the conflict within a nonanthropocentric ethics between holists and individualists. According to holists, the good of a species or the good of an ecosystem or the good of the whole biotic community can trump the good of individual living things.[25] According to individualists, the good of each individual living thing must be respected.[26]

Now one might think that holists would require that we abandon my Principle of Human Preservation. Yet consider. Assuming that people's basic needs are at stake, how could it be morally objectionable for them to try to meet those needs, even if this were to harm nonhuman individuals, or species, or whole ecosystems, or even, to some degree, the whole biotic community?[27] Of course, we can *ask* people in such conflict cases not to meet their basic needs in order to prevent harm to nonhuman individuals or species, ecosystems, or the whole biotic community. But if people's basic needs are at stake, we cannot reasonably demand that they make such a sacrifice. We could demand, of course, that people do all they reasonably can to keep such conflicts from arising in the first place, for, just as in human ethics, many severe conflicts of interest can be avoided simply by doing what is morally required early on.[28] Nevertheless, when people's basic needs are at stake, the individualist perspective seems incontrovertible. We cannot reasonably require people to be saints.[29]

At the same time, when people's basic needs are not at stake, we would be justified in acting on holistic grounds to prevent serious harm to nonhuman individuals, or species, or ecosystems, or the whole biotic community. Obviously, it will be difficult to know when our interventions will have this effect, but when we can be reasonably sure that they will, such interventions (e.g., culling elk herds in wolf-free ranges or preserving the habitat of endangered species) would be morally permissible, and maybe even morally required.[30] This shows that it is possible to agree with individualists when the basic needs of human beings are at stake, and to agree with holists when they are not.

Yet this combination of individualism and holism appears to conflict with the equality of species by imposing greater sacrifices on the members of nonhuman species than it does on the members of the human species. Fortunately, appearances are deceiving here. Although the proposed resolution only justifies imposing holism when people's basic needs are not at stake, it does not justify imposing individualism at all.[31] Rather, it would simply permit individualism when people's basic needs *are* at stake. Of course, we could impose holism under all conditions. But given that this would, in effect, involve going to war against people who are simply striving to meet their own basic needs in the only way they can, as permitted by the Principle of Human Preservation, intervention is such cases would not be justified. It would involve taking away the means of survival from other people, even when these means are not required for one's own survival.[32]

Nevertheless, this combination of individualism and holism may leave animal liberationists wondering about the further implications of this resolution for the treatment of animals. Obviously, a good deal of work has already been done on this topic. Initially, philosophers thought that humanism could be extended to include animal liberation, and eventually environmental concern.[33] Then Baird Callicott argued that animal liberation and environmental concern were as opposed to each other as they were to humanism.[34] The resulting conflict Callicott called "a triangular affair." Agreeing with Callicott, Mark Sagoff contended that any attempt to link together animal liberation and environmental concern would lead to "a bad marriage and a quick divorce."[35] Yet more recently, such philosophers as Mary Ann Warren have tended to play down the opposition between animal liberation and environmental concern, and even Callicott now thinks he can bring the two back together again.[36] There are good reasons for thinking that such a reconciliation is possible.

Right off, it would be good for the environment if people generally, especially people in the First World, were to adopt a more vegetarian diet of the sort that animal liberationists are recommending. This is because a good portion of livestock production today consumes grains that could be more effectively used for direct human consumption. For example, 90 percent of the protein, 99 percent of the carbohydrate, and 100 percent of the fiber value of grain is wasted by cycling it through livestock, and currently, as we noted earlier, 30 percent of worldwide production of grain and 70 percent of U.S. production is fed to livestock.[37] So by adopting a more vegetarian diet, people generally, and especially people in the First World, could significantly reduce the amount of farmland that has to be kept in production to feed the human population. This, in turn, could have beneficial effects on the whole biotic community by eliminating the amount of soil erosion and environmental pollutants that result from raising livestock. For example, it has been estimated that 85 percent of U.S. topsoil lost from cropland, pasture, range land, and forest land is directly associated with raising livestock.[38] So, in addition to preventing animal suffering, there are these additional reasons to favor a more vegetarian diet.[39]

However, even though a more vegetarian diet seems in order, it is not clear that the interests of farm animals would be well served if all of us became complete vegetarians. Sagoff assumes that in a completely vegetarian human world people would continue to feed farm animals as before.[40] But it is not clear that we would have any obligation to do so. Moreover, in a completely vegetarian human world, unless production were increased considerably, we would probably need most of the grain we now feed livestock to meet the still unmet nutritional needs of people, particularly in Second and Third World countries. There simply would not be enough grain to go around. And then there would be the need to conserve cropland for future generations. So, in a completely vegetarian human world, it seems likely that the population of farm animals would be decimated, relegating many of the farm animals that remain to zoos. On this account, it would seem to be more in the interest of farm animals generally that they be maintained under healthy conditions, and hence not in the numbers sustainable only with factory farms, but then killed relatively painlessly and eaten, rather than that they not be maintained at all.[41] So a completely vegetarian human world would not seem to serve the interest of farm animals.[42]

Nor, it seems, would it be in the interest of wild species that no longer have their natural predators not to be hunted by humans. Of course, where possible, it maybe preferable to reintroduce natural predators. But this may not always be possible because of the proximity of farm animals and human populations, and then if action is not taken to control the populations of wild species, disaster could result for the species and their environments. For example, deer, rabbits, squirrels, quail, and ducks reproduce rapidly, and in the absence of predators can quickly exceed the carrying capacity of their environments. So it may be in the interest of certain wild species and their environments that humans intervene periodically to maintain a balance. Of course, there will be many natural environments where it is in the interest of the environment and the wild animals that inhabit it to be simply left alone. But here too animal liberation and environmental concern would not be in conflict. For these reasons, animal liberationists would have little reason to object to the proposed combination of individualism and holism within a nonanthropocentric environmental ethics.

It still might be objected that, while it is morally permissible within a nonanthropocentric environmental ethics to defend and preserve oneself and other human beings, even when this necessitates killing or harming animals or plants, it should also be morally permissible to defend and preserve nonhumans, even when this necessitates killing or harming human beings.[43] If the members of all species are equal, why shouldn't it be morally permissible to defend and preserve innocent nonhumans as well as to defend and preserve innocent humans? There are at least two reasons for rejecting this interpretation of the equality of species. First, it is not morally permissible for us to preserve *nonhumans* by killing or taking the basic resources of other humans who can reasonably expect this degree of altruistic forbearance from us.[44] Second, it is not morally permissible for us to help defend nonhumans against attempts by humans to preserve themselves because that would constitute an unreasonable imposition on humans, effectively denying them a right to self-preservation. We may, of course, provide alternative ways for humans to preserve themselves by killing or harming these nonhumans rather than killing or harming those nonhumans, but what we cannot do is deprive them of any way of effectively preserving themselves by killing or harming nonhumans unless our own self-preservation or the self-preservation of other humans is at stake. We owe humans this degree of altruistic forbearance, which we do not owe nonhumans unless we can also reasonably expect a comparable degree of altruistic forbearance from them. So, even within a nonanthropocentric environmental ethics, at least this degree of preference for humans would be morally justifiable.

III. ANTHROPOCENTRISM

Suppose, however, we were to reject the central contention of the nonanthropocentric perspective and deny that the members of all species are equal. We might claim, for example, that humans are superior because, through culture, they "realize a greater range of values" than members of nonhuman species, or we might claim that humans are superior in virtue of their "unprecedented capacity to create ethical systems that impart worth to other life-forms."[45] Or we might offer some other grounds for human superiority.[46] Suppose, then, we adopt this anthropocentric perspective. What follows?

First of all, we shall still need a principle of human defense. However, there is no need to adopt a different principle of human defense from the principle favored by a nonanthropocentric perspective. Whether we judge humans to be equal or superior to the members of other species, we shall still want a principle that allows us to defend ourselves and other human beings from harmful aggression, even when this necessitates killing or harming animals or plants.

Second, we will also need a principle of human preservation. But here too there is no need to adopt a different principle from the principle of human preservation favored by a nonanthropocentric perspective. Whether we judge humans to be equal or superior to the members of other species, we will still want a principle that permits actions that are necessary for meeting our own basic needs or the basic needs of other human beings, even when this requires aggressing against the basic needs of animals and plants.

The crucial question is whether we will need a different principle of disproportionality. If we judge humans to be superior to the members of other species, will we still have grounds for protecting the basic needs of animals and plants against aggressive action to meet the nonbasic or luxury needs of humans?

Here it is important to distinguish between two degrees of preference that we noted earlier. First, we could prefer the basic needs of animals and plants over the nonbasic or luxury needs of humans when to do otherwise would involve *aggressing against* (by an act of commission) the basic needs of animals and plants. Second, we could prefer the basic needs of animals and plants over the nonbasic or luxury needs of humans when to do otherwise would involve simply *failing to meet* (by an act of omission) the basic needs of animals and plants.

Now in human ethics, when the basic needs of some people are in conflict with the nonbasic or luxury needs of others, the distinction between failing to meet and aggressing against basic needs seems to have little moral force. In such conflict cases, both ways of not meeting basic needs are objectionable.[47] But in environmental ethics, whether we adopt an anthropocentric or a nonanthropocentric perspective, we would seem to have grounds for morally distinguishing between the two cases, favoring the basic needs of animals and plants when to do otherwise would involve *aggressing against* those needs in order to meet our own nonbasic or luxury needs, but not when it would involve simply *failing to meet* those needs in order to meet our own nonbasic or luxury needs. This degree of preference for the members of the human species would be compatible with the equality of species, because humans can reasonably expect this degree of altruistic forbearance from their fellow members but not from members of other species.

Even so, this theoretical distinction would have little practical force, since most of the ways we have of preferring our own nonbasic needs over the basic needs of animals and plants actually involve aggressing against their basic needs to meet our own nonbasic or luxury needs rather than simply failing to meet their basic needs.[48]

Yet even if most of the ways we have of preferring our own nonbasic or luxury needs do involve aggressing against the basic needs of animals and plants, wouldn't human superiority provide grounds for preferring ourselves or other human beings in these ways? Or, put another way, shouldn't human superiority have more theoretical and practical significance than I am allowing? Not, I claim, if we are looking for the most morally defensible position to take.

For consider: Given that we have shown that nonhumans have excellences of their own, the claim that humans are superior to the members of other species, if it can be justified at all, is something like the claim that a person came in first in a race where others came in second, third, fourth, and so on. It would not imply that the members of other species are without intrinsic value, because they do have excellences of their own. In fact, it would imply just the opposite – that the members of other species are also intrinsically valuable, although not as intrinsically valuable as humans, just as the claim that a person came in first in a race implies that the persons who came in second, third, fourth, and so on are also meritorious, although not as meritorious as the person who came in first.

This line of argument draws further support once we consider the fact that many animals and plants are superior to humans in one respect or another – for example, the sense of smell of the wolf, or the acuity of sight of the eagle, or the survivability of the cockroach, or the photosynthetic power of plants.[49] So any claim of human superiority must allow for the recognition of excellences in nonhuman species, even for some excellences that are superior to their corresponding human excellences. In fact, it demands that recognition.

Moreover, if the claim of human superiority is to have any moral force, it must rest on non-question-begging grounds. Accordingly, we must be able to give a non-question-begging response to the nonanthropocentric argument for the equality of species. Yet for any such argument to be successful, it would have to recognize the intrinsic value of the members of nonhuman species. Even if it could be established that human beings have greater intrinsic value, we would still have to recognize that nonhuman nature has intrinsic value as well.

So the relevant question is: How are we going to recognize the pre-sumably lesser intrinsic value of nonhuman nature?

Now if human needs, even nonbasic or luxury ones, are always preferred to even the basic needs of the members of nonhuman species, we would not be giving any recognition to the intrinsic value of nonhuman nature. But what if we allowed the nonbasic or luxury needs of humans to trump the basic needs of nonhuman nature half the time, and half the time allowed the basic needs of nonhuman nature to trump the nonbasic or luxury needs of humans? Would that be enough? Certainly, it would be a significant advance over what we are presently doing. For what we are presently doing is meeting the basic needs of nonhuman nature, at best, only when it serves our own needs or the needs of those we are committed to or happen to care about, and that does not recognize the intrinsic value of nonhuman nature at all.[50] A fifty-fifty arrangement would indeed be an advance; but it would not be enough.

The reason why it would not be enough is that the claim that humans are superior to nonhuman nature no more supports the practice of aggressing against the basic needs of nonhuman nature to satisfy our own nonbasic or luxury needs than the claim that a person came in first in a race would support the practice of aggressing against the basic needs of those who came in second, third, fourth, and so on to satisfy the nonbasic or luxury needs of the person who came in first. A higher degree of merit does not translate into a right of domination, and to claim a right to aggress against the basic needs of nonhuman nature in order to meet our own nonbasic or luxury needs is clearly to claim a right of domination.[51] All that our superiority as humans would justify is not meeting the basic needs of nonhuman nature when this conflicts with our nonbasic or luxury needs. What it does *not* justify is aggressing against the basic needs of nonhuman nature when this conflicts with our nonbasic or luxury needs.

IV. OBJECTIVE AND SUBJECTIVE VALUE THEORY

Now it might be objected that my argument so far presupposes an objective theory of value which regards things as valuable because of the qualities they actually have rather than a subjective theory of value which regards things as valuable simply because humans happen to value them. However, I contend that when both these theories are defensibly formulated, they will lead to the same practical require-ments.

Consider. Suppose we begin with a subjective theory of value that regards things as valuable simply because humans value them. Of course, some things would be valued by humans instrumentally, others intrinsically, but, according to this theory, all things would have the value they have, if they have any value at all, simply because they are valued by humans either instrumentally or intrinsically.

One problem facing such a theory is why should we think that humans alone determine the value that things have? For example, why not say that things are valuable because the members of other species value them? Why not say that grass is valuable because zebras value it, and that zebras are valuable because lions value them, and so on? Or why not say, assuming God exists, that things are valuable because God values them?

Nor would it do simply to claim that we authoritatively determine what is valuable for ourselves, that nonhuman species authoritatively determine what is valuable for themselves, and that God authoritatively determines what is valuable for the Godhead. For what others value should at least be relevant data when authoritatively determining what is valuable for ourselves.

Another problem for a subjective theory of value is that we probably would not want to say that just anything we happen to value determines what is valuable for ourselves. For surely we would want to say that at least some of the things that people value, especially people who are evil or deficient in certain ways, are not really valuable, even for them. Merely thinking that something is valuable doesn't make it so.[52]

Suppose, then, we modified this subjective theory of value to deal with these problems. Let the theory claim that what is truly valuable for people is what they would value if they had all the relevant information (including, where it is relevant, the knowledge of what others would value) and reasoned correctly.[53] Of course, there will be many occasions where we are unsure that ideal conditions have been realized – unsure, that is, that we have all the relevant information and have reasoned correctly. And even when we are sure that ideal conditions have been realized, we may not always be willing to act upon what we come to value due to weakness of will.

Nevertheless, when a subjective theory of value is formulated in this way, it will have the same practical requirements as an objective theory of value that is also defensibly formulated. For an objective theory of value holds that what is valuable is determined by the qualities things actually have. But in order for the qualities things actually have to be valuable in the sense of being capable of being valued, they must be accessible to us, at least under ideal conditions – that is, they must be the sort of qualities that we would value if we had all the relevant information and reasoned correctly.[54] But this is just what is valuable according to our modified subjective theory of value. So once a subjective theory of value and an objective theory of value are defensibly formulated in the manner I propose, they will lead us to value the same things.[55]

Now it is important to note here that with respect to some of the things we value intrinsically, such as animals and plants, our valuing them depends simply on our ability to discover the value they actually have based on their qualities, whereas for other things that we value intrinsically, such as our aesthetic experiences and the objects that provided us with those experiences, the value these things have depends significantly on the way we are constituted. So that if we were constituted differently, what we valued aesthetically would be different as well. Of course, the same holds true for some of the things that we value morally. For example, we morally value not killing human beings because of the way we are constituted. Constituted as we are, killing is usually bad for any human whom we would kill. But suppose that we were constituted differently such that killing human beings was immensely pleasurable for those humans we killed, following which they immediately sprang back to life asking us to kill them again.[56] If human beings were constituted in this way, we would no longer morally value not killing. In fact, constituted in this new way, I think we would come to morally value *killing* and the relevant rule for us might be "Kill human beings as often as you can." But while such aesthetic and moral values are clearly dependent on the way we are constituted, they still are not anthropocentric in the sense that they imply human superiority. Such values can be recognized from both an anthropocentric and a nonanthropocentric perspective.

It might be objected, however, that while the intrinsic values of an environmental ethics need not be anthropocentric in the sense that they imply human superiority, these values must be anthropocentric in the sense that humans would reasonably come to hold them. This seems correct. However, appealing to this sense of anthropocentric, Eugene Hargrove has argued that not all living things would turn out to be intrinsically valuable, as a nonanthropocentric environmental ethics maintains.[57] Hargrove cites as hypothetical examples of living things that would not turn out to be intrinsically valuable the creatures in the films *Alien* and *Aliens*. What is distinctive about the creatures in these films is that they require the deaths of many other living creatures, whomever they happen upon, to reproduce and survive as a species. Newly hatched, these creatures emerge from their eggs and immediately enter host organisms, which they keep alive and feed upon while they develop. When the creatures are fully developed, they explode out of the chests of their host organisms, killing their hosts with some fanfare. Hargrove suggests that if such creatures existed, we would not intrinsically value them because it would not be reasonable for us to do so.[58]

Following Paul Taylor, Hargrove assumes that to intrinsically value a creature is to recognize a negative duty not to destroy or harm that creature and a positive duty to protect it from being destroyed or harmed by others.[59] Since Hargrove thinks that we would be loath to recognize any such duties with respect to such alien creatures, we would not consider them to be intrinsically valuable.

Surely it seems clear that we would seek to kill such alien creatures by whatever means are available to us, but why should that preclude our recognizing them as having intrinsic value any more than our seeking to kill any person who is engaged in lethal aggression against us would preclude our recognizing that person as having intrinsic value? To recognize something as having intrinsic value does not preclude destroying it to preserve other things that also have intrinsic value, when there is good reason to do so.[60] Furthermore, recognizing a prima facie negative duty not to destroy or harm something and a prima facie positive duty to protect it from being destroyed or harmed by others is perfectly consistent with recognizing an all-things-considered duty to destroy that thing when it is engaged in lethal aggression against us. Actually, all we are doing here is simply applying our Principle of Human Defense, and, as I have argued earlier, there is no reason to think that the application of this principle would preclude our recognizing the intrinsic value of every living being.

In sum, I have argued that whether we endorse an anthropocentric or a nonanthropocentric environmental ethics, we should favor a Principle of Human Defense, a Principle of Human Preservation, and a Principle of Disproportionality, as I have interpreted them. In the past, failure to recognize the importance of a Principle of Human Defense and a Principle of Human Preservation has led philosophers to overestimate the amount of sacrifice required of humans.[61] By contrast, failure to recognize the importance of a Principle of Disproportionality has led philosophers to underestimate the amount of sacrifice required of humans.[62] I claim that, taken together, these three principles strike the right balance between concerns of human welfare and the welfare of nonhuman nature.

V. ENVIRONMENTAL RACISM

Let us now turn to the problem of environmental racism. First, some relevant facts.

1) Penalties under hazardous waste laws at sites having the greatest white population were 500 percent higher than penalties at sites with the greatest minority population, averaging $335,566 for the white areas, compared with $55,318 for minority areas.[63]

2) The disparity under toxic waste law occurs by race and not by income. The average penalty in areas with the lowest median income is only 3 percent different from the average penalty in areas with the highest median income.[64]

3) For all the federal environmental laws aimed at protecting citizens from air, water, and waste pollution, penalties in white communities were 46 percent higher than in minority communities.[65]

4) Under the giant Superfund cleanup program, abandoned hazardous waste sites in minority areas take 20 percent longer to be placed on the national priority action list than those in white areas.[66]

5) In Tacoma, Washington, where paper mills and other industrial polluters ruined the salmon streams and the way of life of a Native American tribe, the government never included the tribe in assessing the pollution's impact on residents' health.[67]

6) Three out of every five black and Hispanic Americans live in a community with uncontrolled toxic waste sites.[68]

7) The developed countries ship an estimated 20 million tons of waste to the Third World each year. In 1987, dioxin-laden industrial ash from Philadelphia was dumped in Guinea and Haiti. In 1988, 4,000 tons of PCB-contaminated chemical waste from Italy was found in Nigeria, leaking from thousands of rusting and corroding drums, poisoning both soil and groundwater. In 1991, a Swiss broker negotiated on behalf of Italian companies a twenty-year deal with one faction in Somalia to ship toxic wastes into the country. According to the contract, the shipments – each 100,000 to 150,000 tons – were to yield a profit of 8–10 million dollars per shipment, with 2–3 million dollars per shipment going to the Swiss broker.[69]

Drawing on these data, we can define environmental racism as the imposition of unfair risks to health and well-being on people of color.

Although the problem of environmental racism has been with us for some time, attention only began to focus on the problem with the protest of a hazardous waste landfill in a predominantly African-American community in 1982, the publication of a U.S. Accounting Office Report on race and hazardous wastes in 1983, and a similar report issued by the United Church of Christ in 1987. A subsequent, more extensive, report by the *National Law Journal* appeared in 1992; and in February of 1994 President Clinton issued an executive order requiring that environmental justice with respect to minority and low-income populations be addressed. Attention was also focused on the problem in 1990 by a series of letters from Louisiana's Gulf Coast Tenant Leadership Development Project and the Southwest Organizing Project in Albuquerque, which accused the so-called Group of Ten consisting of the Sierra Club, Sierra Club Legal Defense Fund, Friends of the Earth, The Wilderness Society, National Audubon Society, National Resources Defense Council, Environmental Defense Fund, National Wildlife Federation, Izaak Walton League, and National Parks and Conservation Association of racist hiring practices, ignoring serious toxic hazards faced by poor and minority communities, and failing to involve minorities in policy decisions supposedly designed to protect them. As one critic put it: "The traditional environmental movement on the one hand pretends there were no indigenous people in the North American plains and forests. On the other hand, it distances itself from the cities, denying that they are part of the environment."[70] While environmental groups denied some of these charges, some of the charges were undeniable, and, in response, the groups did pledge to make some changes, particularly in their staffing.

Yet is it clear what changes are needed to eliminate environmental racism? The letters to the Group of Ten focused on procedural changes. They recommended involving minorities in the process by which projects are selected by the environmental groups. By extension, we can imagine a procedural rule that would require the participation of minorities in the selection of all environmental policies that affect them. We could formulate the rule as follows:

> *A Principle of Procedural Justice:* Everyone, especially minorities, should participate in the selection of environmental policies that affect them.[71]

Obviously such a procedural rule would go a long way toward eliminating existing environmental racism, yet unless we can specify exactly how minority interests should be weighed against majority interests, the procedural process will be left too open-ended to ensure fairness. Of course, the specification of a voting mechanism for such deliberations (such as three-quarters, two-thirds, or simple majority) will say something about how interests are to be weighed, but it can still be indeterminate or unfair in its results unless we further specify on what basis votes should be cast. What would be a fair allocation of the environmental risks to health and well-being?

Consider Robert Bullard's suggestion that "Every individual has a right to be protected from environmental degradation."[72] This seems like a reasonable principle, but what does it require? Bullard says that it requires nondiscrimination, but how should nondiscrimination be understood here? Bullard goes on to propose two helpful concrete specifications. The first is that the burden of proof be shifted to those who would impose environmental risks upon others to prove that their activities are nondiscriminatory. The second is that it does not suffice for those who impose environmental risks to have no intention of discriminating; whatever their intentions, their actions will still be discriminatory if they impose unfair burdens on anyone. Yet when are burdens unfair here?

One way to specify a fair allocation of the burdens with respect to environmental policies is the following:

A Principle of Allocating Risks by Production: One's share of the environmental risks to health and well-being should be proportionate to the amount of pollution and contaminates one produces.

According to this principle, the more pollution and contaminates one produces, the more risks to health and well-being one should have to bear. The main difficulty with this principle is that production is often driven by consumption – what consumers want or are willing and able to buy. So, to impose risks to health and well-being primarily on producers does not attack the problem at its source, the preferences of consumers. A more appropriate principle would seem to be the following:

A Principle of Allocating Risks by Consumption: One's share of the risks to health and well-being should be in proportion to the amount of resources one consumes.

According to this principle, those who consume more should bear a greater risk. This would mean, for example, that waste disposal sites should be located, other things being equal, in or near rich white communities rather than in or near poor minority communities. Moreover, if rich white communities were required to shoulder their fair share of the risks to health and well-being, they would most likely push for less production of pollutants and contaminates overall so as to reduce the size of their own share of the risk to health and well-being. Clearly, this should have beneficial consequences for everyone.

Obviously, implementing the Principle of Allocating Risk by Consumption would require drastic changes in current environmental policies. But current environmental policies have authority over us only insofar as they accord with environmental justice. So our main goal must be to bring our current environmental policies in accord with environmental justice. What I have argued is that this requires modifying our environmental policies to accord with the Principle of Procedural Justice and the Principle of Allocating Risk by Consumption so as to avoid environmental racism and to comply with the Principle of Human Defense, the Principle of Human Preservation, and the Principle of Disproportionality so as to maintain the right balance between a concern for human welfare and the welfare of nonhuman nature.

VI. OBJECTIONS AND RESPONSES

Recently, Brian Steverson has raised a number of important objections to my defense of principles of environmental justice.[73] Against my attempt to show that a nonanthropocentric perspective requires these principles, Steverson

1) criticizes my appeal to reciprocal altruism to justify the human preference permitted by the Principle of Human Preservation;
2) claims that while it is reasonable from a nonanthropocentric perspective to select the Principle of Human Preservation, one could just as well select a Principle of Nonhuman Preservation from that perspective.

Against my attempt to show that an anthropocentric perspective requires these principles, Steverson

1) questions whether intrinsic value can come in degrees as required to support the Principle of Disproportionality from an anthropocentric perspective;
2) questions whether we are always prohibited from satisfying our nonbasic needs by aggressing against the basic needs of nonhuman nature as required by the Principle of Disproportionality, even assuming that nonhuman nature has intrinsic value.

These are very serious objections to my reconciliationist argument that go right to the heart of the matter. Let me consider each of them in turn.

With respect to my appeal to reciprocal altruism to justify preferential treatment for humans – that is, my claim that the degree of human preference sanctioned by the Principle of Human Preservation is justified by the degree of reciprocal altruism that humans can reasonably expect from others humans – Steverson contends that it would be a mistake to ground all of our moral obligations in such reciprocity.[74] Actually, I agree with Steverson here. I agree, that is, that not *all* of our moral obligations can be given a foundation in reciprocal altruism. What I have argued, however, is that only some of our obligations can be so grounded in the reciprocal altruism that we can reasonably expect of other humans, and Steverson offers no objection to this more limited appeal to reciprocal altruism.

With respect to my claim that it is reasonable to select the Principle of Human Preservation from a nonanthropocentric perspective, Steverson contends that it is equally reasonable from that perspective to select a Principle of Nonhuman Preservation, which maintains that actions that are necessary for meeting the basic needs of nonhumans are permissible even when they require aggressing against the basic needs of humans.

Here I doubt that Steverson is interpreting "permissible" in the same sense or applying the notion in the same way in both of these principles. This is because, as I interpret the Principle of Human Preservation, when it maintains that it is permissible to meet one's own basic needs or the basic needs of other humans even when this requires aggressing against the basic needs of animals and plants, this implies that other humans should not interfere with that aggression. Let us call this "strong permissibility." Now, if we similarly interpret "permissible" in the Principle of Nonhuman Preservation, it would imply that other humans should not interfere with any aggression that is directed against humans for the preservation of nonhumans, *even when that aggression happens to be directed against themselves!* Surely, this would be a very demanding requirement to impose on humans even from a nonanthropocentric perspective, and I doubt that Steverson wants to endorse it.

Alternatively, Steverson may want to interpret "permissible" in the same way in both principles, but in such a way that it imposes almost no practical requirements on anyone. According to this interpretation, let us call it "weak permissibility," its being permissible to meet one's own basic needs or the basic needs of other human beings by aggressing against the basic needs of nonhumans would be consistent with its being permissible for other humans to resist that aggression. And the same would hold true for the Principle of Nonhuman Preservation. Thus, its being permissible to meet the basic needs of nonhumans by aggressing against the basic needs of humans would be consistent with its being permissible for other humans to resist that aggression. On this interpretation of the two principles, since nothing is morally required or prohibited by them, what gets done obviously depends on the comparative power relations of the contending parties. Nevertheless, the problem with this interpretation is that it is certainly odd to think that morality imposes no prohibitions or requirements at all in an area of such severe conflicts of interest, given that it is in just such areas that we would expect morality to provide some sort of a resolution.

Another possibility is that Steverson may want to interpret "permissible" as strong permissibility in both principles, but then limit the scope of application of the Principle of Nonhuman Preservation so that it would be permissible for humans to aggress against their own basic needs, (i.e., sacrifice them) in order to meet the basic needs of nonhumans, but not permissible for humans to aggress against the basic needs of other humans for that purpose. Yet while this limitation on the scope of the Principle of Nonhuman Preservation seems defensible from a nonanthropocentric perspective, it also seems defensible from an anthropocentric perspective, which, of course, is just what Steverson wanted to deny. Thus, it would seem that the only defensible interpretations of the Principle of Human Preservation and the Principle of Nonhuman Preservation turn out to support rather than oppose my reconciliationist argument.

In objecting to my claim that intrinsic value can come in degrees, Steverson cites Tom Regan as having shown that such a claim makes a category mistake, like claiming that two persons can be half-married to each other.[75] Yet whether or not a category mistake is involved here depends on the particular notion of intrinsic value that one is using. In this context, there are at least two notions of intrinsic value that need to be distinguished. According to one notion of intrinsic value, which we can call agent-centered intrinsic value, to say that *X has intrinsic value* is to say that *X is good as an end for some agent Y*, as opposed to saying that *X has instrumental value*, which is to say that *X is good as a means for some agent Y*. Now, according to this notion, intrinsic value does not come in degrees; one can't have more or less of it.[76] But there is another notion of intrinsic value, which we can call recipient-centered intrinsic value, according to which to say that *X has intrinsic value* is to say that *the good of X ought to constrain the way that others use X in pursuing their own interests*.[77] Now it seems to me that recipient-centered intrinsic value, unlike agent-centered intrinsic value, does allow for the possibility of different degrees of intrinsic value, provided we can show that the good of some Xs should constrain others more than the good of other Xs. In fact, however, this is just what I have argued – that there *are* good reasons why the good of humans should constrain other humans more than the good of nonhumans. Specifically, they are the reasons of reciprocal altruism and reasons of permissible defense and preservation as captured by the Principle of Human Defense and the Principle of Human Preservation.[78] These reasons require a degree of preference for humans over nonhumans when the relevant needs of humans are at stake.[79] Assuming, then, that it is possible to show in this way that humans can be legitimately constrained more by the good of humans than by the good of nonhumans, it is possible to claim that humans have a greater degree of intrinsic value than nonhumans.[80]

Steverson further argues that those who accept an anthropocentric perspective would still have plausible grounds for rejecting the constraint of the Principle of Disproportionality, even assuming that nonhumans have intrinsic value, although less intrinsic value than humans. Specifically, Steverson denies that humans are always prohibited from satisfying their nonbasic needs by aggressing against the basic needs of nonhumans, despite the intrinsic value of nonhumans.

But the only reason that Steverson offers for rejecting this prohibition is that the satisfaction of *many* nonbasic needs of humans may turn out in some utilitarian calculation to outweigh the frustration of a *few* basic needs of nonhumans.[81] Yet when this sort of reasoning is applied to humans, many utilitarians have been reluctant to embrace it,[82] because it would seem to justify such practices as the sacrifice of the lives of Roman gladiators for the sake of the pleasure of the large crowds who witnessed those gladiatorial contests. Instead of defending the morality of such contests, utilitarians have been inclined to favor alternative social practices that preserve the lives of the few while still securing comparable pleasures for the many. It is also understandable why utilitarians have been reluctant to allow such trade-offs of the few for the many. The idea that a person's basic needs can be aggressed against to meet nonbasic needs of others seems opposed to the fundamental respect that we think is reasonably due to each and every person. So while utilitarians admit the theoretical possibility of such trade-offs, they tend to argue that, practically speaking, such trade-offs are unattainable, and so, even from a utilitarian perspective, the principles that we need to appeal to in order to carry on our affairs should not take such trade-offs into account.[83]

Moreover, in considering such trade-offs with respect to our human/nonhuman cases, it is difficult to see how the numbers could turn out to be the way that they must turn out in order to be justified – with the satisfaction of nonbasic needs of *many* humans weighed against aggression against the basic needs of only a *few* nonhumans. Usually the numbers seem to be the other way round, with aggression against the basic needs of many nonhumans weighed against the satisfaction of the nonbasic needs of only a few humans. Nevertheless, just as in the analogous case involving only humans, we may not be able to theoretically rule out the possibility of trade-offs involving aggression against the basic needs of a few nonhumans for the sake of the satisfaction of the nonbasic needs of many humans. Nevertheless, even from a utilitarian perspective, we can rule them out practically speaking, excluding them, as I have done, from the principles of environmental justice.[84]

In formulating these answers to Brian Steverson's objections to my reconciliationist argument, I have been led to develop my argument further than I had previously done. Specifically, I have clarified the requirements for others that follow from the actions that are permitted by the Principle of Human Defense and the Principle of Human Preservation. I have also clarified the notion of intrinsic value that I am endorsing and the grounds on which my claim of greater intrinsic value for humans rests.

Still another objection that might be raised to my reconciliationist argument is that my view is too individualistic, as evidenced by the fact that my principles of environmental justice refer to individual humans, plants, and animals but not specifically to species or ecosystems.[85] Now, I would certainly agree with Paul Taylor that all individual living beings can be benefited or harmed and have a good of their own and, hence, qualify as moral subjects.[86] But Taylor goes on to deny that species themselves are moral subjects with a good of their own, because he regards "species" as a class name, and classes, he contends, have no good of their own.[87] Yet here I would disagree with Taylor, because species are unlike abstract classes in that they evolve, split, bud off new species, become endangered, go extinct, and have interests distinct from the interests of their members.[88] For example, a particular species of deer but not individual members of that species can have an interest in being preyed upon. Hence, species can be benefited and harmed and have a good of their own, and so should qualify on Taylor's view, as well as my own, as moral subjects.[89] So, too, ecosystems can qualify as moral subjects, when they can be benefited and harmed and have a good of their own, having features and interests not shared by their components.[90] Following Lawrence Johnson, we can go on to characterize moral subjects as living systems in a persistent state of low entropy sustained by metabolic processes for accumulating energy whose organic unity and self-identity is maintained in equilibrium by homeostatic feedback processes.[91] Thus, modifying my view in order to take into account species and ecosystems requires the following changes in my first three principles of environmental justice:

A Principle of Human Defense: Actions that defend oneself and other human beings against harmful aggression are permissible even when they necessitate killing or harming individual animals or plants or even destroying whole species or ecosystems.

A Principle of Human Preservation: Actions that are necessary for meeting one's basic needs or the basic needs of other human beings are permissible even when they require aggressing against the basic needs of individual animals and plants or even of whole species or ecosystems.

A Principle of Disproportionality: Actions that meet nonbasic or luxury needs of humans are prohibited when they aggress against the basic needs of individual animals and plants, or of whole species or ecosystems.[92]

But while this modification is of theoretical interest because it allows that species and ecosystems as well as individuals count morally, it actually has little or no practical effect on the application of these principles. This is because, for the most part, the positive or negative impact the application of these principles would have on species and ecosystems is correspondingly reflected in the positive or negative impact it would have on the individual members of those species or ecosystems. As a consequence, actions that are permitted or prohibited with respect to species and ecosystems according to the modified principles are already permitted or prohibited respectively through their correspondence with actions that are permitted or prohibited according to the unmodified principles.

However, this is not always the case. In fact, considerations about what benefits nonhuman species or subspecies as opposed to individuals of those species or subspecies have already figured in my previous argument. For example, I have argued for culling elk herds in wolf-free ranges, but this is primarily for the good of herds or species of elk and certainly not for the good of the particular elk who are being culled from those herds. I also have argued that it would be for the good of farm animals generally that they be maintained under healthy conditions, and then killed relatively painlessly and eaten, rather than that they not be maintained at all. But clearly this is an argument about what would be good for existing flocks or herds, or species or subspecies of farm animals. It is not an argument about what would be good for the existing individual farm animals who would be killed relatively painlessly and eaten.[93] Nevertheless, for the most part, because of the coincidence between the welfare of species and ecosystems and the welfare of individual members of those species and ecosystems, the two formulations of the first three principles turn out be practically equivalent.[94]

Of course, the practical implications of all five of my principles for environmental justice will include: proposals for allocating wastes, particularly toxic wastes; proposals for conserving existing resources, particularly nonrenewable resources; proposals for converting to renewable resources; proposals for redistributing resources to meet the basic needs of both humans and nonhumans; and proposals for population control, many of them implemented principally by educational changes and changes in the tax and incentive structures of our society. Each of these practical proposals needs to be worked out in detail. Here I have simply sought to provide the nonanthropocentric and anthropocentric grounding for such proposals in a common set of conflict resolution principles that are required to achieve environmental justice. In this way, I hope to have shown that a peacemaking way of doing philosophy can lead to peacemaking of a different sort by motivating us to put an end to the widespread violence against nature in which we are presently engaged.

It should be pointed out that the first three of my principles for environmental justice are actually modeled after traditional principles of just war theory. Thus it is appropriate that in the next chapter I discuss just war theory itself. I go on to argue that when just war theory is given its most morally defensible interpretation, it can in fact be reconciled with the pacifism to which it is usually opposed.

Chapter 7

From Just War Theory to Pacifism

Traditionally, pacifism and just war theory have represented radically opposed responses to aggression. Pacifism has been interpreted to rule out any use of violence in response to aggression. Just war theory has been interpreted to permit a measured use of violence in response to aggression.[1] It has been thought that the two views might sometimes agree in particular cases – for example, that pacifists and just war theorists might unconditionally oppose nuclear war – but beyond that it has been generally held that the two views lead to radically opposed recommendations. In this chapter, by applying a peacemaking model of doing philosophy to the analysis of these two views, I hope to show that this is not the case. Specifically, I will argue that pacifism and just war theory, in their most morally defensible interpretations, can be substantially reconciled both in theory and in practice.

I. JUST WAR THEORY AND PACIFISM

In traditional just war theory there are two basic elements: an account of just cause and an account of just means. Just cause is usually specified as follows:

1) There must be substantial aggression.
2) Nonbelligerent correctives must be either hopeless or too costly.
3) Belligerent correctives must be neither hopeless nor too costly.

Needless to say, the notion of substantial aggression is a bit fuzzy, but it is generally understood to be the type of aggression that violates people's most fundamental rights. To suggest some specific examples of what is and is not substantial aggression, usually the taking of hostages is regarded as substantial aggression while the nationalization of particular firms owned by foreigners is not so regarded. But even when substantial aggression occurs, frequently nonbelligerent

151

correctives are neither hopeless nor too costly. And even when non-belligerent correctives are either hopeless or too costly, in order for there to be a just cause, belligerent correctives must be neither hopeless nor too costly.

Traditional just war theory assumes, however, that there are just causes and goes on to specify just means as imposing two requirements:

1) Harm to innocents should not be directly intended as an end or a means.
2) The harm resulting from the belligerent means should not be disproportionate to the particular defensive objective to be attained.

While the just means conditions apply to each defensive action, the just cause conditions must be met by the conflict as a whole.

It is important to note that these requirements of just cause and just means are not essentially about war at all. Essentially, they constitute a theory of just defense that can apply to war but can also apply to a wide range of defensive actions short of war. Of course, what needs to be determined is whether these requirements can be justified. Since just war theory is usually opposed to pacifism, to secure a non-question-begging justification for the theory and its requirements we need to proceed as much as possible from premises that are common to pacifists and just war theorists alike. The difficulty here is that there is not only one form of pacifism but many. So we need to determine which form of pacifism is most morally defensible.

Now when most people think of pacifism they tend to identify it with a theory of nonviolence. We can call this view "nonviolent pacifism." It maintains that

Any use of violence against other human beings is morally prohibited.

It has been plausibly argued, however, that this form of pacifism is incoherent. In a well-known article, Jan Narveson rejects nonviolent pacifism as incoherent because it recognizes a right to life yet rules out any use of force in defense of that right.[2] The view is incoherent, Narveson claims, because having a right entails the legitimacy of using force in defense of that right, at least on some occasions.

Given the cogency of objections of this sort, some have opted for a form of pacifism that does not rule out all violence but only lethal violence. We can call this view "nonlethal pacifism." It maintains that

Any lethal use of force against other human beings is morally prohibited.

In defense of nonlethal pacifism, Cheyney Ryan has argued that there is a substantial issue between the pacifist and the nonpacifist concerning whether we can or should create the necessary distance between ourselves and other human beings in order to make the act of killing possible.[3] To illustrate, Ryan cites George Orwell's reluctance to shoot at an enemy soldier who jumped out of a trench and ran along the top of a parapet half-dressed and holding up his trousers with both hands. Ryan contends that what kept Orwell from shooting was that he couldn't think of the soldier as a thing rather than a fellow human being.

However, it is not clear that Orwell's encounter supports nonlethal pacifism. For it may be that what kept him from shooting the enemy soldier was not his inability to think of the soldier as a thing rather than a fellow human being, but rather his inability to think of a soldier who was holding up his trousers with both hands as a threat or a combatant. Under this interpretation, Orwell's decision not to shoot would accord well with the requirements of just war theory.

Let us suppose, however, that someone is attempting to take your life. Why does that permit you, the defender of nonlethal pacifism might ask, to kill the person making the attempt? The most cogent response, it seems to me, is that killing in such a case is not evil, or at least not morally evil, because anyone who is wrongfully engaged in an attempt upon your life has already forfeited his or her right to life by engaging in such aggression.[4] So, provided that you are reasonably certain that the aggressor is wrongfully engaged in an attempt on your life, you would be morally justified in killing, assuming that it is the only way of saving your own life.

There is, however, a form of pacifism that remains untouched by the criticisms I have raised against both nonviolent pacifism and nonlethal pacifism. This form neither prohibits all violence nor even all uses of lethal force. We can call the view "antiwar pacifism," because it holds that

> Any participation in the massive use of lethal force in warfare is morally prohibited.[5]

In defense of antiwar pacifism, it is undeniable that wars have brought enormous amounts of death and destruction in their wake and that many of those who have perished in them were noncombatants or innocents. In fact, the tendency of modern wars has been to produce higher and higher proportions of noncombatant casualties, making it more and more difficult to justify participation in such wars. Furthermore, strategies for nonbelligerent conflict resolution are rarely intensively developed and explored before nations choose to go to war, making it all but impossible to justify participation in such wars.[6]

II. THE INTENTIONED/FORESEEN DISTINCTION

To determine whether the requirements of just war theory can be reconciled with those of antiwar pacifism, however, we need to consider whether we should distinguish between harm intentionally inflicted upon innocents and harm whose infliction on innocents is merely foreseen? On the one hand, we could favor a uniform restriction against the infliction of harm upon innocents that ignores the intended/foreseen distinction. On the other hand, we could favor a differential restriction that is more severe against the intentional infliction of harm upon innocents but less severe against the infliction of harm that is merely foreseen. What needs to be determined, therefore, is whether there is any rationale for favoring this differential restriction on harm over a uniform restriction. But this presupposes that we can, in practice, distinguish between what is foreseen and what is intended, and some have challenged whether this can be done. So first we need to address this challenge.

Now the practical test that is frequently appealed to in order to distinguish between foreseen and intended elements of an action is the Counterfactual Test, according to which, two questions are relevant:

1) Would you have performed the action if only the good consequences would have resulted and not the evil consequences?
2) Would you have performed the action if only the evil consequences resulted and not the good consequences?

If an agent answers yes to the first question and no to the second, some would conclude that (1) the action is an intended means to the good consequences, (2) the good consequences are an intended end, and (3) the evil consequences are merely foreseen.

But how well does this Counterfactual Test work? Douglas Lackey has argued that the test gives the wrong result in any case where the "act that produces an evil effect produces a larger good effect."[7] He cites the bombing of Hiroshima as an example. That bombing is generally thought to have had two effects: the killing of Japanese civilians and the shortening of the war. Now suppose we were to ask:

1) Would Truman have dropped the bomb if only the shortening of the war would have resulted but not the killing of Japanese civilians?
2) Would Truman have dropped the bomb if only Japanese civilians would have been killed and the war not shortened?

And suppose the answer to the first question is that Truman would have dropped the bomb if only the shortening of the war would have resulted but not the killing of Japanese civilians, and that the answer to the second question is that Truman would not have dropped the bomb if only Japanese civilians would have been killed and the war not shortened. Lackey concludes from this that the killing of civilians at Hiroshima, self-evidently a means for shortening the war, is by the Counterfactual Test classified not as a means but as a mere foreseen consequence. On these grounds, Lackey rejects the Counterfactual Test as an effective device for distinguishing between the foreseen and the intended consequences of an action.

Unfortunately, this is to reject the Counterfactual Test only because one expects too much from it. It is to expect the test to determine all of the following:

1) Whether the action is an intended means to the good consequences;
2) Whether the good consequences are an intended end of the action;
3) Whether the evil consequences are simply foreseen consequences.

In fact, this test is capable of meeting only the first two of these expectations. And the test clearly succeeds in doing this for Lackey's own example, where the test shows the bombing of Hiroshima to be an intended means to shortening the war, and shortening the war an intended consequence of the action.

To determine whether the evil consequences are simply foreseen, however, an additional test is needed, which I shall call the Nonexplanation Test. According to this test, the relevant question is:

Does the bringing about of the evil consequences help explain why the agent undertook the action as a means to the good consequences?

If the answer is no, that is, if the bringing about of the evil consequences does not help explain why the agent undertook the action as a means to the good consequences, the evil consequences are merely foreseen. But if the answer is yes, the evil consequences are an intended means to the good consequences.

Of course, there is no guaranteed procedure for arriving at an answer to the Nonexplanation Test. Nevertheless, when we are in doubt concerning whether the evil consequences of an act are simply foreseen, seeking an answer to the Nonexplanation Test will tend to be the best way of reasonably resolving that doubt. For example, applied to Lackey's example, the Nonexplanation Test comes up with a yes, since the evil consequences in this example do help explain why the bombing was undertaken to shorten the war. For, according to the usual account, Truman ordered the bombing to bring about the civilian deaths, which by their impact upon Japanese morale were expected to shorten the war. So, by the Nonexplanation Test, the civilian deaths were an intended means to the good consequences of short-ening the war.[8]

Assuming, then, that we can distinguish in practice between harm intentionally inflicted upon innocents and harm whose infliction on innocents is merely foreseen, we need to determine whether there is any rationale for favoring a differential restriction that is more severe against the intentional infliction of harm upon innocents but less se-vere against the infliction of harm that is merely foreseen, over a uni-form restriction against the infliction of harm upon innocents that ignores the intended/foreseen distinction.

Let us first examine the question from the perspective of those suf-fering the harm. Initially, it might appear to matter little whether the harm was intended or merely foreseen by those who caused it. From the perspective of those suffering harm, it might appear that what matters is simply that the overall amount of harm be restricted, irre-spective of whether it is foreseen or intended. But consider. Don't those who suffer harm have more reason to protest when the harm is done to them by agents who are directly engaged in causing harm to them than when it is done incidentally by agents whose ends and means are good? Don't we have more reason to protest when we are being used by others than when we are affected by them only inci-dentally?

Moreover, if we examine the question from the perspective of those causing the harm, additional support for this line of reasoning can be found. For it would seem that we have more reason to protest a re-striction against foreseen harm than we do to protest a comparable restriction against intended harm. This is because a restriction against foreseen harm limits our actions when our ends and means are good, whereas a restriction against intended harm only limits our actions when our ends or means are evil or harmful, and it would seem that we have stronger grounds for acting when both our ends and means are good than when they are not. Consequently, because we have more reason to protest when we are being used by others than when we are being affected by them only incidentally, and because we have more reason to act when both our ends and means are good than when they are not, we should favor the foreseen/intended distinction that is incorporated into just means.

It might be objected, however, that, at least sometimes, we could produce greater good overall by violating the foreseen/intended dis-tinction of just means and acting with the evil means of intentionally harming innocents. On this account, it might be argued that it should be permissible, at least sometimes, to intentionally harm innocents in order to achieve greater good overall.

Now it seems to me that this objection is well taken insofar as it is directed against an absolute restriction upon intentional harm to innocents. It seems clear that there are exceptions to such a restriction when intentional harm to innocents is:

1) trivial (e.g., as in the case of stepping on someone's foot to get out of a crowded subway);
2) easily reparable (e.g., as in the case of lying to a temporarily depressed friend to keep her from committing suicide); or
3) greatly outweighed by the consequences of the action, especially to innocent people (e.g., as in the case of shooting one of two hundred civilian hostages to prevent, in the only way possible, the execution of all two hundred).

Yet though we need to recognize these exceptions to an absolute restriction upon intentional harm to innocents, there is good reason not to permit simply maximizing good consequences overall, because that would place unacceptable burdens upon particular individuals. More specifically, it would be an unacceptable burden on innocents to allow them to be intentionally harmed in cases other than the exceptions we have just enumerated. And, allowing for these exceptions, we would still have reason to favor a differential restriction against harming innocents that is more severe against the intentional infliction of harm upon innocents but less severe against the infliction of harm upon innocents that is merely foreseen. Again, the main grounds for this preference is that we would have more reason to protest when we are being used by others than when we are being affected by them only incidentally, and more reason to act when both our ends and means are good than when they are not.

III. JUST CAUSE AND JUST MEANS

So far, I have argued that there are grounds for favoring a differential restriction on harm to innocents that is more severe against intended harm and less severe against foreseen harm. I have further argued that this restriction is not absolute, so that when the evil intended is trivial, easily reparable, or greatly outweighed by the consequences, intentional harm to innocents can be justified. Moreover, there is no reason to think that antiwar pacifists would reject either of these conclusions. Antiwar pacifists are opposed to any participation in the massive use of lethal force in warfare, yet this need not conflict with the commitment of just war theorists to a differential but nonabsolute restriction on harm to innocents as a requirement of just means.[9] Where just war theory goes wrong, according to antiwar pacifists, is not in its restriction on harming innocents but rather in its failure adequately to determine when belligerent correctives are too costly to constitute a just cause or are lacking in the proportionality required by just means. According to antiwar pacifists, just war theory provides insufficient restraint in both of these areas. Now, to evaluate this criticism, we need to consider a wide range of cases where killing or inflicting serious harm on others in defense of oneself or others might be thought to be justified, beginning with the easiest cases to assess from the perspectives of antiwar pacifism and the just war theory and then moving on to cases that are more difficult to assess from those perspectives.

Case (1): where only the intentioned or foreseen killing of an unjust aggressor would prevent one's own death.[10] This case clearly presents no problems. In the first place, antiwar pacifists adopted their view because they were convinced that there were instances of justified killing. And, in this case, the only person killed is an unjust aggressor. So surely antiwar pacifists would have to agree with just war theorists that one can justifiably kill an unjust aggressor if it is the only way to save one's life.

Case (2): where only the intentioned or foreseen killing of an unjust aggressor and the foreseen killing of one innocent bystander would prevent one's own death and that of five other innocent people.[11] In this case, we have the foreseen killing of an innocent person as well as the killing of the unjust aggressor, but since it is the only way to save one's own life and the lives of five other innocent people, antiwar pacifists and just war theorists alike would have reason to judge it morally permissible. In this case, the intended life-saving benefits to six innocent people is judged to outweigh the foreseen death of one innocent person and the intended or foreseen death of the unjust aggressor.

Case (3): where only the intentioned or foreseen killing of an unjust aggressor and the foreseen killing of one innocent bystander would prevent the death of five innocent people. In this case, despite the fact that we lack the justification of self-defense, saving the lives of five innocent people in the only way possible should still provide antiwar pacifists and just war theorists with sufficient grounds for granting the moral permissibility of killing an unjust aggressor, even when the killing of an innocent bystander is a foreseen consequence. In this case, the intended life-saving benefits to five innocent people would still outweigh the foreseen death of one innocent person and the intended or foreseen death of the unjust aggressor.

Case (4): where only the intentioned or foreseen killing of an unjust aggressor and the foreseen killing of five innocent people would prevent the death of two innocent people. In this case, neither antiwar pacifists nor just war theorists would find the cost and proportionality requirements of just war theory to be met. Too many innocent people would have to be killed to save too few. Here, the fact that the deaths of the innocents would be merely foreseen does not outweigh the fact that we would have to accept the deaths of five innocents and the unjust aggressor in order to be able to save two innocents.

Notice that, up to this point in interpreting these cases, we have simply been counting the number of innocent deaths involved in each case and opting for the solution that minimized the resulting loss of innocent lives. Suppose, however, that an unjust aggressor is not threatening the lives of innocents but only their welfare or property. Would the taking of the unjust aggressor's life in defense of the welfare and property of innocents be judged proportionate? Consider the following the case.

Case (5): where only the intentioned or foreseen killing of an unjust aggressor would prevent serious injury to oneself and/or five other innocent people. Since in this case the intentioned or foreseen killing of the unjust aggressor is the only way of preventing serious injury to oneself and/or five other innocent people, then, by analogy with Cases 1–3, both antiwar pacifists and just war theorists alike would have reason to affirm its moral permissibility. Of course, if there were any other way of stopping unjust aggressors in such cases short of killing them, that course of action would clearly be required. Yet, if there is no alternative, the intentioned or foreseen killing of the unjust aggressor to prevent serious injury to oneself and/or five other innocent people would be justified.

In such cases, the serious injury could be bodily injury, as when an aggressor threatens to break one's limbs, or it could be serious psychological injury, as when an aggressor threatens to inject mind-altering drugs, or it could be a serious threat to property. Of course, in most cases where serious injury is threatened, there will be ways of stopping aggressors short of killing them. Unfortunately, this is not always possible.

In still other kinds of cases, stopping an unjust aggressor would require indirectly inflicting serious harm, but not death, upon innocent bystanders. Consider the following cases.

Case (6): where only the intentioned or foreseen infliction of serious harm upon an unjust aggressor and the foreseen infliction of serious harm upon one innocent bystander would prevent serious harm to oneself and five other innocent people.

Case (7): where only the intentioned or foreseen infliction of serious harm upon an unjust aggressor and the foreseen infliction of serious harm upon one innocent bystander would prevent serious harm to five other innocent people.

In both of these cases, serious harm is indirectly inflicted upon one innocent bystander in order to prevent greater harm from being inflicted by an unjust aggressor upon other innocent people. In Case 6, we also have the justification of self-defense, which is lacking in Case 7. Nevertheless, with regard to both cases, antiwar pacifists and just war theorists should agree that preventing serious injury to five or six innocent people in the only way possible renders it morally permissible to inflict serious injury upon an unjust aggressor, even when the serious injury of one innocent person is a foreseen consequence. In these cases, by analogy with Cases 2 and 3, the foreseen serious injury of one innocent person and the intended or foreseen injury of the unjust aggressor should be judged proportionate, given the intended injury-preventing benefits to five or six other innocent people.

Up to this point there has been the basis for general agreement among antiwar pacifists and just war theorists as to how to interpret the proportionality requirement of just means, but in the following case this no longer obtains.

Case (8): where only the intentioned or foreseen killing of an unjust aggressor and the foreseen killing of one innocent bystander would prevent serious injuries to the members of a much larger group of innocent people. The interpretation of this case is crucial. Here, we are asked to sanction the loss of an innocent life in order to prevent serious injuries to the members of a much larger group of innocent people. Unfortunately, neither antiwar pacifists nor just war theorists have explicitly considered this case. Both antiwar pacifists and just war theorists agree that we can inflict serious injury upon an unjust aggressor and an innocent bystander to prevent greater injury to other innocent people, as in Cases 6 and 7, and that one can even intentionally or indirectly kill an unjust aggressor to prevent serious injury to oneself or other innocent people, as in Case 5. Yet neither antiwar pacifists nor just war theorists have explicitly addressed the question of whether we can indirectly kill an innocent bystander in order to prevent serious injuries to the members of a much larger group of innocent people. Rather, they have tended to confuse Case 8 with Case 5, where it is agreed that one can justifiably kill an unjust aggressor in order to prevent serious injury to oneself or five other innocent people. In Case 8, however, one is doing something quite different: one is killing an innocent bystander in order to prevent serious injury to oneself and a much larger group of innocent people.

Now this kind of trade-off is not accepted in standard police practice. Police officers are regularly instructed not to risk innocent lives simply to prevent serious injury to other innocents. Nor is there any reason to believe that a trade-off which is unacceptable in standard police practice would be acceptable in larger-scale conflicts. Thus, for example, even if the Baltic republics could have effectively freed themselves from the Soviet Union by infiltrating into Moscow several bands of saboteurs who had then attacked several military and government installations in

Moscow, causing an enormous loss of innocent lives, such a trade-off would not have been justified. Accordingly, it follows that if the proportionality requirement of just war theory is to be met, we must save more innocent lives than we cause to be lost, we must prevent more injuries than we inflict, and we must not kill innocents, even indirectly, simply to prevent serious injuries to ourselves and others.

Of course, sometimes our lives and well-being are threatened at the same time. Or better, if we are unwilling to sacrifice our well-being then our lives are threatened. Nevertheless, if we are justified in our use of lethal force to defend ourselves in cases where we will indirectly kill innocents, it is because our lives are also threatened, not simply our well-being. And the same holds for when we are defending others.

What this shows is that the constraints imposed by just war theory on the use of belligerent correctives are actually much more severe than antiwar pacifists have tended to recognize.[12] In determining when belligerent correctives are too costly to constitute a just cause or are lacking in the proportionality required by just means, just war theory, under its most morally defensible interpretation:

1) allows the use of belligerent means against unjust aggressors only when such means minimize the loss and injury to innocent lives overall;
2) allows the use of belligerent means against unjust aggressors to indirectly threaten innocent lives only to prevent the loss of innocent lives, not simply to prevent injury to innocents;
3) allows the use of belligerent means to directly or indirectly threaten or even take the lives of unjust aggressors when it is the only way to prevent serious injury to innocents.

It might be objected that all that I have shown through the analysis of the above eight cases is that killing in defense of oneself or others is morally permissible, not that it is morally required or morally obligatory. That is true. I have not established any obligation to respond to aggression with lethal force in these cases, but only that it is morally permissible to do so. For one thing, it is difficult to ground an obligation to use lethal force on self-defense alone, as would be required in Case 1 or in one version of Case 5. Obligations to oneself appear to have an optional quality that is absent from obligations to others. In Cases 2, 3, and 5–7, however, the use of force would prevent serious harm or death to innocents, and here I contend that it would be morally obligatory, if either the proposed use of force required only a relatively small personal sacrifice from us or if we were fairly bound by convention or by a mutual defense agreement, to come to the aid of others. In such cases, I think we can justifiably speak of a moral obligation to kill or seriously harm in defense of others.

Another aspect of Cases 1–3 and 5–7 to which someone might object is that it is the wrongful actions of others that put us into situations where I am claiming that we are morally justified in seriously harming or killing others.[13] Were it not for the actions of unjust aggressors, we would not be in situations where I am claiming that we are morally permitted or required to seriously harm or kill.

Yet doesn't something like this happen in a wide range of cases when wrongful actions are performed? Suppose I am on the way to the bank to deposit money from a fundraiser, and someone accosts me and threatens to shoot if I don't hand over the money. If I do hand over the money, I will have been forced to do something I don't want to do, something that involves a loss to myself and others. But surely it is morally permissible for me to hand over the money in this case. And it may even be morally required for me to do so if resistance would lead to the shooting of others in addition to myself. So it does seem that bad people, by altering the consequences of our actions, can alter our obligations as well. What our obligations are under nonideal conditions are different from what they would be under ideal conditions. If a group of thugs comes into a classroom where I am lecturing and make it very clear that they intend to shoot me if each of my students doesn't give them one dollar, I think, and I would hope that my students would also think, that each of them now has an obligation to give the thugs one dollar, when before they had no such obligation. Likewise, I think that the actions of unjust aggressors can put us into situations where it is morally permissible, or even morally required, for us to seriously harm or kill, when before it was not.

Now it might be contended that antiwar pacifists would concede the moral permissibility of Cases 1–3 and 5–7 but still maintain that any participation in the massive use of lethal force in warfare is morally prohibited. The scale of the conflict, antiwar pacifists might contend, makes all the difference. Of course, if this simply means that many large-scale conflicts will have effects that bear no resemblance to Cases 1–3 or 5–7, this can hardly be denied. Still, it is possible for some large-scale conflicts to bear a proportionate resemblance to the above cases. For example, it can plausibly be argued that India's military action against Pakistan in Bangladesh and the Tanzanian incursion into Uganda during the rule of Idi Amin resemble Cases 3, 5, or 7 in their effects upon innocents.[14] What this shows is that antiwar pacifists are not justified in regarding every participation in the massive use of lethal force in warfare as morally prohibited. Instead, antiwar pacifists must allow that, at least in some real-life cases, wars and other large-scale military operations both have been and will be morally permissible.

This concession from antiwar pacifists, however, needs to be matched by a comparable concession from just war theorists themselves, because too frequently they have interpreted their theory in morally indefensible ways.[15] When just war theory is given a morally defensible interpretation, I have argued that the theory favors a strong just means prohibition against intentionally harming innocents. I have also argued that the theory favors the use of belligerent means only when such means (1) minimize the loss and injury to innocent lives overall, (2) threaten innocent lives only to prevent the loss of other innocent lives, not simply to prevent injury to innocents, and (3) threaten or even take the lives of unjust aggressors when it is the only way to prevent serious injury to innocents.

Obviously, just war theory, so understood, is going to place severe restrictions on the use of belligerent means in warfare. In fact, most of the actual uses of belligerent means in warfare that have occurred turn out to be unjustified. For example, the U.S. involvement in Nicaragua, El Salvador, and Panama, the Soviet Union's involvement in Afghanistan, Israeli involvement in the West Bank and the Gaza Strip all violate the just cause and just means provisions of just war theory as I have defended them. Even the recent U.S.-led war against Iraq violated both the just cause and just means provisions of just war theory.[16] In fact, one must strain to find examples of justified applications of just war theory in recent history. Two examples I have already referred to are India's military action against Pakistan in Bangladesh and the Tanzanian incursion into Uganda during the rule of Idi Amin. But after mentioning these two examples it is difficult to go on. What this shows is that, when just war theory and antiwar pacifism are given their most morally defensible interpretations, both views can be reconciled. In this reconciliation, the few wars and large-scale conflicts that meet the stringent requirements of just war theory are the only wars and large-scale conflicts to which antiwar pacifists cannot justifiably object.[17] We can call the view that emerges from this reconciliation "just war pacifism,"[18] and it is the view which claims that, due to the stringent requirements of just war theory, only very rarely will participation in a massive use of lethal force in warfare be morally justified.[19] Assuming that objections to the view can be met, it is a view that a peacemaking model of doing philosophy, with its goal of reconciling alternative moral and political perspectives, can rest content.

IV. FURTHER OBJECTIONS

Now if my proposed reconciliation of just war theory and antiwar pacifism is to be morally acceptable, it must be possible to answer the objections that have been raised to various aspects of just war theory and its reconciliation with antiwar pacifism. Some of the most important are the following: a conventionalist objection to just means, a collectivist objection to just means, a feminist objection to just cause and just means, and a pacifist objection to the reconciliation of just war theory and antiwar pacifism. Let us consider each of these in turn.

A Conventionalist Challenge to Just Means

As one would expect, the criteria of just means have been incorporated to some degree into the military codes of different nations and adopted as international law. Yet rarely has anyone contended that the criteria of just means ought to be met simply because they have been incorporated into military codes or adopted as international law. Surprisingly, however, George Mavrodes has defended just such a conventionalist view.[20] Mavrodes arrives at this conclusion largely because he finds the standard attempts to specify the convention-independent basis for condition (2) of just means to be so totally unsuccessful. All such attempts, Mavrodes claims, are based on an identification of innocents with noncombatants. But by any plausible standard of guilt and innocence that has moral content, Mavrodes contends, noncombatants can be guilty and combatants innocent. For example, noncombatants who are doing everything in their power to support an unjust war financially would be morally guilty, and combatants who were forced into military service and intended never to fire their weapons at anyone would be morally innocent. Consequently, the guilt/innocence distinction will not support the combatant/noncombatant distinction.

Hoping to support the combatant/noncombatant distinction, Mavrodes suggests that the distinction might be grounded on a convention to observe it. This would mean that our moral obligation to abide by condition (2) of just means would be a convention-dependent obligation. Nevertheless, Mavrodes does not deny that we have some convention-independent obligations. Our obligation to refrain from wantonly murdering our neighbors is given as an example of a convention-independent obligation, as is our obligation to reduce the pain and death involved in combat. But to refrain from harming noncombatants when harming them would be the most effective way of pursuing a just cause is not included among our convention-independent obligations.

Yet Mavrodes does not claim that our obligation to refrain from harming noncombatants is *purely* convention-dependent. He allows that, in circumstances in which the convention of refraining from harming noncombatants does not exist, we might still have an obligation to unilaterally refrain from harming noncombatants, provided that our action will help give rise to a convention prohibiting such harm with its associated good consequences. According to Mavrodes, our primary obligation is to maximize good consequences, and this obligation requires that we refrain from harming noncombatants when that will help bring about a convention prohibiting such harm. By contrast, someone who held that our obligation to refrain from harming noncombatants was purely convention-dependent would never recognize an obligation to unilaterally refrain from harming noncombatants. On a purely convention-dependent account, obligations can only be derived from existing conventions; the expected consequences from establishing a particular convention could never ground a purely convention-dependent obligation. But while Mavrodes does not claim that our obligation to refrain from harming noncombatants is purely convention-dependent, he does claim that this obligation generally arises only when there exists a convention prohibiting such harm. According to Mavrodes, the reason for this is that, generally, only when there exists a convention prohibiting harm to noncombatants will our refraining from harming them, while pursuing a just cause, actually maximize good consequences.

But is there no other way to support our obligation to refrain from harming noncombatants? Mavrodes would deny that there is. Consider, however, Mavrodes's own example of the convention-independent obligation not to wantonly kill our neighbors. There are at least two ways to understand how this obligation is supported. Some would claim that we ought not to wantonly kill our neighbors because this would not maximize good consequences. This appears to be Mavrodes's view. Others would claim that we ought not to wantonly kill our neighbors, even if doing so would maximize good consequences, simply because it is not reasonable to believe that our neighbors are engaged in an attempt upon our lives. Both of these ways of understanding how the obligation is supported account for the convention-independent character of the obligation; but the second approach can also be used to show how our obligation to refrain from harming noncombatants is convention-independent. According to this approach, since it is not reasonable to believe that noncombatants are engaged in an attempt upon our lives, we have an obligation to refrain from harming them. So interpreted, our obligation to refrain from harming noncombatants is itself convention-independent, although it will certainly give rise to conventions.

Of course, some may argue that whenever it is not reasonable to believe that persons are engaged in an attempt upon our lives, an obligation to refrain from harming such persons will also be supported by the maximization of good consequences. Yet even if this were true, which seems doubtful, all it would show is that there exists a utilitarian or forward-looking justification for a convention-independent obligation to refrain from harming noncombatants; it would not show that such an obligation is a convention-dependent obligation, as Mavrodes claims.

A Collectivist Challenge to Just Means

Now according to a collectivist challenge to just means, more people should be included under the category of combatants than the standard interpretation of just means allows. Just means, as we noted earlier, imposes two requirements:

1) Harm to innocents should not be directly intended as an end or a means.
2) The harm resulting from the belligerent means should not be disproportionate to the particular defensive objective to be attained.

According to advocates of this challenge to just means, the problem is that the standard interpretation of (1) does not assume that the members of a society are collectively responsible for the actions of their leaders unless they have taken radical steps to oppose or disassociate themselves from those actions, for example, by engaging in civil disobedience or emigration. Of course, those who are unable to take such steps, particularly children, would not be responsible in any case; but, for the rest, advocates of this collectivist challenge contend that failure to take the necessary radical steps when one's leaders are acting aggressively has the consequence that one is no longer entitled to full protection as a noncombatant. Some of those who press this objection against the just means criteria of just war theory, like Gregory Kavka, contend that the members of a society can be directly threatened with nuclear attack to secure deterrence but then deny that carrying out such an attack could ever be morally justified.[21] Others, like James Child, contend that the members of a society who fail to take the necessary radical steps can be both indirectly threatened and indirectly attacked with what would otherwise be a disproportionate attack.[22]

In response to this collectivist challenge, the first thing to note is that people are more responsible for disassociating themselves from the unjust acts of their leaders than they are for opposing those same acts. For there is no general obligation to oppose all unjust acts, even all unjust acts of one's leaders. Nevertheless, there is a general obligation to disassociate oneself from unjust acts and to minimize one's contribution to them. Of course, how far one is required to disassociate oneself from the unjust acts of one's leaders depends upon how much one is contributing to those actions. If one's contribution is insignificant, as presumably a farmer's or a teacher's would be, only a minimal effort to disassociate oneself would be required, unless one's action could somehow be reasonably expected, in cooperation with the actions of others, to put a stop to the unjust actions of one's leaders. However, if one's contribution is significant, as presumably a soldier's or a munitions worker's would be, a maximal effort at disassociating oneself would be required immediately, unless by delaying one could reasonably expect to put a stop to the unjust actions of one's leaders.

In support of this collectivist challenge to just war theory, James Child offers the following example:

> A company is considering engaging in some massively immoral and illegal activity – pouring large quantities of arsenic into the public water supply as a matter of ongoing operations, let us say. A member of the board of directors of the company, when the policy is before the board, votes no but does nothing else. Later, when sued in tort (or charged in crime) with these transgressions of duty, she pleads that she voted no. What would our reaction be? The answer is obvious! We would say, you are responsible as much or nearly as much, as your fellow board members who voted yes. You should have blown the whistle, gone public or to regulatory authorities, or at the very least, resigned from the board of so despicable a company. Mere formal dissent in this case does almost nothing to relieve her liability, legal or moral.[23]

But while one might agree with Child that in this case the member of the board of directors had at least the responsibility to disassociate herself from the actions of the board by resigning, this does not show that farmers and teachers are similarly responsible for disassociating themselves from the unjust action of their leaders either by engaging in civil disobedience or by emigration. This is because neither their contributions to the unjust actions of their leaders nor the effect of their disassociation on those unjust actions would typically be significant enough to require such a response.

This is not to deny that some other response (e.g., political protest or remunerations at the end of the war) would not be morally required. However, to meet this collectivist challenge, it suffices to show that not just any contribution to the unjust actions of one's leaders renders the contributor subject to attack or threat of attack; one's contribution must be significant enough to morally justify such a response.

A Feminist Challenge to Just Cause and Just Means

As it turns out, a formidable challenge to both the just cause and just means criteria of just war theory comes from feminism. According to the feminist challenge to just war theory, sexism and militarism are inextricably linked in society. They are linked, according to Betty Reardon, because sexism is essentially a prejudice against all manifestations of the feminine, and militarism is a policy of excessive military preparedness and eagerness to go to war that is rooted in a view of human nature as limited to masculine characteristics.[24] Seen from a militarist perspective, other nations are competitive, aggressive, and averse to cooperation, the same traits that tend to be fostered primarily in men in a sexist society. By contrast, the traits of openness, cooperativeness, and nurturance that promote peaceful solutions to conflicts tend to be fostered primarily in women, who are then effectively excluded from positions of power and decision making in a sexist society. Consequently, if we are to rid society of militarism, Reardon argues, we need to rid society of sexism as well.

But even granting that sexism and militarism are inextricably linked in society in just the way Reardon maintains, how does this effect the validity of just war theory? As just war theory expresses the values of proportionality and respect for the rights of innocents, how can it be linked to militarism and sexism? The answer is that the linkage is practical rather than theoretical. It is precisely because the leaders in militarist/sexist society have been socialized to be competitive, aggressive, and averse to cooperation that they will tend to misapply just war theory when making military decisions. This represents an important practical challenge to just war theory. And the only way of meeting this challenge, as far as I can tell, is to rid society of its sexist and militarist attitudes and practices so as to increase the chances that just war theory will be correctly applied in the future.

A Pacifist Challenge to the Reconciliation of Just War Theory and Antiwar Pacifism

In "The Irreconciliability of Pacifism and Just War Theory," Eric Reitan raises a pacifist challenge to my reconciliation thesis, claiming that the most morally defensible interpretation of antiwar pacifism cannot be reconciled with just war theory.[25] According to Reitan, this is because there is an interpretation of the restriction on harm to innocents, which he calls nonaggressor immunity, that separates the antiwar pacifists from just war theorists. According to this interpretation, aggressors are defined as persons who are engaged in, or are preparing to engage in, unjust aggression against others. Nonaggressors are defined as persons who are not aggressors, and it is nonaggressors so understood whom Reitan thinks should be immune from harm.

Reitan distinguishes his preferred interpretation of nonaggressor immunity from three other interpretations that he rejects. First, there is an interpretation which defines aggressors, more narrowly, as persons who are engaged in unjust aggression against others. Second, there is an interpretation which defines aggressors, more broadly, as persons who are engaged in or preparing to engage in some act that would contribute toward unjust aggression against others. Third, there is an interpretation which defines aggressors, even more broadly, as persons who are associated in a supportive role with a group organized for the purpose of performing acts of aggression against others.

Reitan rejects the first of these alternative interpretations as too narrow, the third as too broad, and the second as not restrictive enough to preclude the fighting of just wars. Reitan contends that when antiwar pacifism is understood in accord with his preferred interpretation of nonaggressor immunity, it cannot be reconciled with just war theory. This is because, given this restrictive interpretation of nonaggressor immunity, antiwar pacifism will never sanction any large-scale military engagement whatsoever. Unfortunately, taking antiwar pacifism to accord with Reitan's preferred interpretation of nonaggressor immunity is both too weak and too strong to be morally acceptable.

It is too weak because nonaggressor immunity, as Reitan interprets it, together with a requirement that there must be a reasonable chance of success, are the *only* moral constraint on defense against unjust aggression. So as long as one's defensive actions are directed against someone who is engaged in or is preparing to engage in unjust aggression and there is a reasonable chance of success, it does not matter how many innocent bystanders one unintentionally kills or harms as a result. Aiming at an appropriately defined aggressor and the requirement that there must be a reasonable chance of success are the only constraints that Reitan imposes on antiwar pacifism. More specifically, Reitan fails to incorporate any proportionality restriction into his account of antiwar pacifism. So interpreted, antiwar pacifism would allow the indirect killing of thousands of innocents in defense of just one life against a bona fide aggressor. Obviously, such a specification of antiwar pacifism is too weak to be a morally defensible. It permits actions that no morally defensible account would permit.

Reitan's specification of antiwar pacifism is also too strong. It is too strong because he defines aggressors *metaphysically* as persons who are engaged in or are preparing to engage in unjust aggression, rather than *epistemologically* as persons of whom it is reasonable for defenders to believe they are engaged in or are preparing to engage in unjust aggression.[26] Because Reitan takes a metaphysical view of aggressors, he thinks that frontline soldiers who intend only to fire their weapons over the heads of their enemies should be immune from harm even when they appear to be engaged in an unjust aggression. But this is clearly to impose too strong a requirement on morally justified defensive action. In order for defensible action to be morally justified, it is not necessary that one's defense be directed only at persons who are *actually* engaged in or are *actually* preparing to engage in unjust aggression; rather it suffices if one's defense is directed at persons whom one reasonably believes are engaged in or are preparing to engage in unjust aggression. Accordingly, frontline soldiers who *appear* to be attacking, despite the fact that they only intend to fire their weapons over the heads of their enemies, would not be immune from harm.

It is also inappropriate for Reitan to rule out defensive actions against military patrols simply on the grounds that failure to do so would lead antiwar pacifists to justify participation in at least some just wars.[27] There has to be an independent moral reason for declaring such actions to be beyond the bounds of a morally justified defense. It is also difficult to see what this reason could be, given that military patrols have always been an inextricable part of aggressive military actions.

Accordingly, once we recognize that aggressors should be defined *epistemologically* as persons of whom it is reasonable for defenders to believe that they are engaged in or are preparing to engage in unjust aggression, rather than *metaphysically* as persons who are actually engaged in or are actually preparing to engage in unjust aggression, we can see why it is reasonable to deny nonaggressor immunity, not only to soldiers generally, but also to those who work in munitions factories or who are in other ways inextricably tied to aggressive military actions. Given this availability of legitimate targets, it becomes possible for there to be large-scale military engagements or wars to which neither antiwar pacifists nor just war theorists could reasonably object.

Of course, both antiwar pacifists and just war theorists agree that before any belligerent means can be employed, all nonbelligerent correctives must be either hopeless or too costly.[28] And both antiwar pacifists and just war theorists also agree that in most cases nonbelligerent correctives will be neither hopeless nor too costly. In fact, as I have argued, once antiwar pacifism and just war theory are given their most morally defensible interpretations, there is little reason to think that antiwar pacifists and just war theorists would have anything to disagree about at all. In any case, Reitan's morally objectionable interpretation of antiwar pacifism does not give us any reason to doubt that such a practical reconciliation obtains.[29]

Obviously, the defense of any view is never final, especially if one is committed to a peacemaking model of doing philosophy. So it is always possible to raise further objections to what I have argued. But I think enough has been said to make a convincing case for the reconciliation of just war theory and pacifism. Nevertheless, one might wonder why, if such a convincing case can be made for the reconciliation of just war theory and pacifism, have there not been more reconciliationists? The answer, I believe, is fairly obvious. It is that, until recently, neither just war theory nor pacifism has been presented in sufficient detail so as to be able to determine how such a practical reconciliation would, in fact, be possible. For example, until the recent work of Duane Cady and Robert Holmes, the relevant forms of pacifism had not been clearly distinguished and assessed in terms of moral defensibility, nor until recently had the proportionality requirements of just war theory been sufficiently teased out through an analysis of particular cases.[30] However, once antiwar pacifism emerges as the most morally defensible form of pacifism, and once the requirements of just war theory are worked out in enough detail, then the case for a practical reconciliation of just war theory and pacifism can be seen to be truly compelling – possibly for the first time. In this way, we can appreciate how a peacemaking model for doing philosophy leads to peacemaking of a different sort, by restricting the occasions on which wars can be legitimately fought.

Chapter 8

Conclusion: Justice for Here and Now

So what are the implications of the preceding chapters for a conception of justice for here and now? In Chapter 1, I defended peacemaking as a way of doing philosophy. With respect to moral and political philosophy, peacemaking requires that we seek the broadest justification possible for our philosophical perspectives and their practical requirements. Specifically, it requires that we (1) examine the possibility of grounding morality on the widely shared norms of rationality, (2) explore the possibility of achieving a practical reconciliation of alternative moral and political perspectives, and (3) be willing to modify or abandon our favored social and political perspective, either in whole or in part, should the weight of evidence require it. The rest of the book is an attempt to implement this peacemaking model of doing philosophy.

In Chapter 2, implementing the first requirement of a peacemaking model of doing philosophy, I took up the question of whether the norms of rationality require morality. I considered contemporary attempts by Kurt Baier and Alan Gewirth to show that rationality does require morality and discussed why they are unsuccessful. Building on the work of Baier and Gewirth, I then offered my own justification of morality and responded to both Hobbesian and Aristotelian objections that could be raised against it and to three contemporary objections that have been raised against it.

In Chapter 3, implementing the second requirement of a peacemaking model of doing philosophy, I examined the minimal morality of the libertarian's ideal of liberty and argued that, despite what libertarians claim, their ideal can be seen to support rights to welfare and equal opportunity through an application of the "Ought" Implies "Can" Principle and the Conflict Resolution Principle to conflicts between the rich and the poor. I further argued that these two rights that usually are associated with a welfare liberal ideal lead to something like the equality that socialists endorse, once distant peoples and future generations are taken into account.

In Chapter 4, further implementing the second requirement of a peacemaking model of doing philosophy, I argued that these same rights to welfare and equal opportunity also lead to the ideal of a gender-free or androgynous society that many feminists defend. This ideal requires that truly desirable traits in society be equally available to both women and men or, in the case of virtues, be equally expected of both women and men. I argued that this ideal requires changes in traditional family structures so that children, irrespective of their sex, will have the same type of upbringing and mothers and fathers the same opportunities for education and employment; changes in the distribution of economic power in our society through programs of affirmative action and comparable work that remove the structural violence against women; changes that are necessary to put an end to the overt violence against women that takes the form of rape, battery, and sexual abuse; and changes that implement new programs against sexual harassment in the workplace.

In Chapter 5, implementing still further the second requirement of a peacemaking model of doing philosophy, I explored the theoretical and practical connections between feminist justice with its ideal of a gender-free or androgynous society and three other forms of justice: racial justice, which seeks to remedy the injustice of racism; homosexual justice, which seeks to remedy the injustice of heterosexism, and multicultural justice, which seeks to remedy the injustice of Eurocentrism. I argued that similar theoretical arguments are used in favor of each of these forms of injustice and that there are practical advantages to opposing all these forms of injustice together.

In Chapter 6, I pursued peacemaking of a different sort, arguing that when the most morally defensible versions of an anthropocentric environmental ethics and a nonanthropocentric environmental ethics are laid out, despite their theoretical disagreement concerning whether or not humans are superior to members of other species, both support a Principle of Human Defense, a Principle of Human Preservation, a Principle of Disproportionality, a Principle of Procedural Justice, and a Principle of Allocating Risks by Consumption, as I have interpreted them. I claimed that, taken together, these five principles strike the right balance between concerns of human welfare and the welfare of nonhuman nature that is required to achieve environmental justice. In this context, a peacemaking model of doing philosophy leads to peacemaking of a different sort by significantly restricting the violence that humans can legitimately do to nature.

In Chapter 7, pursuing a peacemaking model of doing philosophy in the one area of social and political philosophy where peace is usually discussed, I explored the opposition between pacifism and just war theory and argued that, once antiwar pacifism is recognized as the most morally defensible form of pacifism, and the stringent requirements of just war theory are clearly specified, it becomes possible to see how the two views can be reconciled in practice. I argued that, in this reconciliation, the few wars and large-scale conflicts that meet the requirements of just war theory are the only wars and large-scale conflicts to which antiwar pacifists cannot justifiably object. I called the view that emerges from this reconciliation "just war pacifism." It is the view which claims that, due to the stringent requirements of just war theory, only very rarely will participation in a massive use of lethal force in warfare be morally justified. Here, a peacemaking model of doing philosophy leads to peacemaking of a different sort by restricting the occasions on which wars can be legitimately fought.

In sum, pursuing peacemaking as a model for doing philosophy, I have argued that, not only does rationality require morality, but even a minimal morality like libertarianism requires rights to welfare and equal opportunity that lead to socialist equality and feminist androgyny. In this way, I have brought together the moral ideals of libertarianism, welfare liberalism, socialism, and feminism into what could be called a reconciliationist conception of justice. In addition, I have argued that the pursuit of this reconciliationist conception of justice, especially in its feminist dimensions, is theoretically and practically connected to the pursuit of racial justice, homosexual justice, and multicultural justice and is further constrained by specific principles of environmental justice and just war pacifism.

It is also important to see that this reconciliationist conception of justice is only intended to be a conception of justice *for here and now*.[1] At other times and in other places, particularly in non-Western societies, the requirements of justice may be different. Given that the justification for any conception of justice always depends on the intellectual resources that are available at a particular time and place, a certain relativism in requirements of justice is to be expected. In this respect, however, moral theory is no different from scientific theory; both must always be open to revision as new information and understandings become available. Obviously, this openness to revision accords with the third requirement of a peacemaking model of doing moral and political philosophy, which requires a willingness to abandon one's favored conception of justice, either in whole or in part, should the evidence require it. Nevertheless, once one considers that the reconciliationist conception of justice defended in this book is grounded in the norms of rationality, and that its very demanding requirements of a right to welfare and a right to equal opportunity follow from even a minimal morality like libertarianism, it is difficult to see how the most morally defensible requirements of justice for other times and places could significantly differ from the basic rights required by this reconciliationist conception of justice.[2]

In light of the support, then, that can be provided for this conception of justice for here and now, when the laws of our society accord with this conception we definitely should obey them. But what should we do if the laws of our society do not accord with this conception of justice? What if the laws of our society do not guarantee all its citizens a right to welfare and a right to equal opportunity, nor make a reasonable effort to extend these rights to distant peoples and future generations in accord with the specified principles of environmental justice and just war pacifism? What if our society offers men better opportunities than women, and what if our society is not respectful of differences in race, sexual orientation, or culture? At present, all of these injustices can be found in many countries, but let us focus on their presence in the United States. As we noted earlier, 32 million Americans live below the official poverty index, and one-fifth of American children are growing up in poverty.[3] In the United States, 10 percent of families own 57 percent of the total net wealth and 86 percent of total financial assets, and 0.5 percent owns 19 percent of the total net worth and 34 percent of total financial assets.[4] From 1979 to 1993 in the United States, the average pre-tax income of families in the top 1 percent increased by 78 percent, while during roughly the same period income of the bottom 20 percent fell by 9 percent.[5] We also noted that 1.2 billion people are currently living in conditions of absolute poverty, which Robert McNamara has described as "a condition of life so characterized by malnutrition, illiteracy, disease, squalid surroundings, high infant mortality and low life expectancy as to be beneath any reasonable definition of human decency."[6] In 1991, the richest 20 percent of the world's people received 85 percent of global income and the poorest 20 percent only 1.4 percent.[7] Currently, the United States contributes only 0.22 percent of its GNP to relieve absolute poverty in the world. By any estimate, that is not enough (the Netherlands and Norway each contributes 0.7 percent), and the problem has only grown worse over the last ten years.[8] A study of a coalition of eight hundred voluntary organizations in the United States shows that charitable giving by U.S. households declined by 24 percent between 1989 and 1993.[9] So, in the United States, we have not yet secured a right to welfare for all our citizens, nor have we made a reasonable effort to extend this right to distant peoples, let alone to future generations. We have also noted the significant injustices suffered by women, blacks, homosexuals, and members of non-Western cultures in the United States.

What, then, should be done? Should we simply try to change the laws through normal politics? Should we try to change the laws through legal protest? Should we engage in civil disobedience? Should we revolt and overthrow the government?

It should be clear that we are not dealing with minor injustices here. Millions of people in the United States are being deprived of an adequate welfare and the basic opportunities to develop their abilities, and many of them are children. And the figures worldwide for those living in conditions of absolute poverty are staggering. The figures indicating the lack of equal opportunity currently experienced by women, blacks, and homosexuals are staggering as well. Surely, normal politics and legal protest should be used to secure these basic rights as far as that is possible, but since these means have already been extensively tried and major injustices persist, is there any reason to limit ourselves to these means alone? Why not, then, engage in civil disobedience or revolutionary action to secure these basic human rights? Is there any reason to think that civil disobedience or revolutionary action would not be morally justified?

It might be argued that, given that the U.S. Constitution itself fails to guarantee its citizens a right to equal opportunity and a right to welfare, we in the United States would not be justified in using civil disobedience or revolutionary action to try to secure these rights. That the Constitution fails to guarantee rights to equal opportunity and welfare seems clear enough. If we focus, by way of example, on educational opportunity, a majority of the Supreme Court determined, in *San Antonio School District v. Rodriguez* (1973), that there was no constitutional right to education. Likewise, in *Wyman v. James* (1971), the Supreme Court's decision presupposed that there was no constitutional right to welfare. The only right to welfare recognized by the Court was one that was conditional upon the state or federal government's interest in providing that welfare.

But surely, if rights to welfare and equal opportunity are fundamental requirements of the conception of justice for here and now that I have defended in this book, then, other things being equal, they must be guaranteed by any constitution that claims to be morally defensible. Since the U.S. Constitution does not guarantee these rights, it would seem to be a fundamentally flawed document.

It might be objected that this criticism of the U.S. Constitution is inappropriate because it attempts to evaluate the document, which for the most part was written two hundred years ago, by appealing to contemporary ideals. But this is to miss the point of the criticism, which is not so much directed at the Constitution as originally written as it is at the Constitution as presently amended and interpreted. For whenever a society's constitution can be seen to be morally defective in light of its acknowledged ideals, then it is incumbent upon the

members of that society to amend, or at least to reinterpret, their constitution to remedy those deficiencies. If the main argument of this
book is right – that a conception of justice for here and now supports
a right to welfare and a right to equal opportunity, constrained so as
to accord with specific principles of environmental justice and just war
pacifism – then, it would appear that the U.S. Constitution will remain
a fundamentally flawed document until it too requires these rights.[10]

Yet, clearly, few people today endorse civil disobedience and revolutionary action as a means of securing a right to welfare and a right
to equal opportunity. Why is that? To answer this question, it is useful
to consider what distinguishes existing injustices from those which
were challenged during the anti–Vietnam War movement and the civil
rights movement in the United States.

The anti–Vietnam War movement challenged the legality and morality of U.S. involvement in the war in Southeast Asia. While the most
severe harmful effects of this war were suffered by the people of
North and South Vietnam, some of its harmful effects were also
widely felt by young men of draft age and their families and friends
in the United States. The U.S. draft system required a large number
of young men, virtually all those who could not get a deferment or
an exemption, to become part of the war effort, and, for many, this
meant risking their lives in Southeast Asia. According to Kim Willenson, "Clearly the draft, with its assertion of a government right to
demand the sacrifice of young lives in a cause that it could not explain,
was the yeast that made [the anti–Vietnam War] movement rise."[11]
As a consequence, not just poor peasants in North and South Vietnam,
but also a large number of politically powerful people in the United
States had something to lose from the continuation of the war in
Southeast Asia. So, in the case of the Vietnam War, self-interest and
morality blended to create a relatively effective opposition to the war
that included acts of civil disobedience and some near revolutionary
actions.[12]

In contrast, failure to secure the basic human rights of welfare and
equal opportunity has had much less impact on those who have political power in the United States today. The conflict here is basically
between the haves and the have-nots, and in such situations it is not
surprising that the have-nots have not been very politically effective
at pressing their case. What the have-nots need in order to be more
effective are powerful allies within the current (unjust) power struc-
ture, and this is just what they do not have. So although the justice
of their cause is no less cogent than the justice of the cause of the anti–
Vietnam War movement, the have-nots of today lack the political
power to effectively press their case for basic human rights. It is this
lack of effective political power that appears to explain people's failure

to challenge presently existing injustices with civil disobedience or near revolutionary actions.

When we look to the U.S. civil rights movement, especially from 1955 to the passing of the Voting Rights Act in 1965, a similar contrast emerges. Unlike the have-nots in the United States and the world at large today, blacks at that time were united in solidarity.[13] It was this solidarity, for example, that made the Montgomery bus boycott nearly 100 percent effective, even though it lasted more than a year.[14] Clearly, no comparable solidarity exists today among the have-nots in the United States or in the world at large. The have-nots in the United States are too divided by racial, ethnic, religious, and cultural prejudices to present a united challenge to the common injustices they suffer. So, again, it is not the justice of the cause, but the comparative lack of effective political power that distinguishes the current denial of basic human rights from that denial of basic human rights which was challenged in the United States by the civil rights movement from 1955 to 1965.

Without some source of political power upon which to build, people tend not to be motivated to take the personal risk involved in civil disobedience or revolutionary action. So what explains this lack of civil disobedience and revolutionary action with respect to the current injustices is not the seriousness of the injustices themselves, because they are in every way as serious as the injustices protested by the anti–Vietnam War movement and the civil rights movement. Rather, it is the lack of sufficient political power to generate some hope of success and to motivate the personal risk required for civil disobedience and revolutionary action. Thus, while people may have a moral right to engage in civil disobedience or revolutionary action, under certain conditions, because of the risks involved, it may be reasonable for them to do so only when there is enough political power to give some hope of success.

There is, however, at least one bright spot with respect to the possibility of correcting existing injustices. It is the potential that currently exists for ridding society of the injustices against women. Because women are found in all economic levels of society, the feminist movement may more easily be able to generate the kind of political power necessary to rid society of the lack of equal opportunity for women. It may also happen that, in the process of securing justice for women, other forms of justice will be secured as well.

Of course, for the most part, the feminist movement has not been characterized by civil disobedience or revolutionary action – unless we count lesbian separatism as a form of revolutionary action, but that may simply have been a tactical error. For example, the Equal Rights Amendment for women might have been ratified in 1982 if feminists had gone further in challenging existing injustices. Some well-chosen civilly disobedient or revolutionary acts might have been just what was needed to turn the tide.[15] This might also be true today with respect to the variety of reforms that are needed to secure equal opportunity for women.[16]

Obviously, the degree to which the feminist movement or any other movement will be able to correct existing injustices remains uncertain. At the moment, however, what is clear is that many have-nots in the United States and the world at large are being denied their basic rights. Under such circumstances, it remains to be determined what it is that is permissible for the have-nots to do.

By now it goes without saying that have-nots in the United States, as elsewhere, should consider trying to change or eliminate existing injustices, first by normal politics, then by legal protest, then by civil disobedience, and only then by revolutionary action. But what if all of these means have been tried and are reasonably judged to be ineffective; or, alternatively, what if these means are reasonably judged too costly for those whom they are intended to benefit? If either of these conditions obtains, what is permissible for the have-nots to do? Is it permissible for them to engage in private illegal acts to secure those goods and resources to which they are morally entitled? Would such criminally disobedient acts be morally permissible if either of these conditions obtained? Assuming that normal politics, legal protest, civil disobedience, and revolutionary action have all been tried and reasonably judged to be ineffective, or that such means are reasonably judged too costly for those whom they are intended to benefit, then it would seem that criminally disobedient acts would be morally permissible, provided that they are directed at appropriating surplus goods from people who have more than their fair share of opportunities to lead a good life, and at appropriating such goods with a minimum of physical force. Of course, even when criminally disobedient acts are morally permissible, they will normally be engaged in only when they are likely to be successful in securing at least some of those goods and resources to which people are morally entitled.

Thus, suppose, for example, that Gretchen, who is morally entitled to a $8,000 income, receives only a $5,000 income through legal channels. Suppose further that every means of correcting this injustice, save criminal disobedience, has been tried so as to be reasonably judged to be ineffective, or that using such means is reasonably judged too personally costly for Gretchen. If this is the case, it would be morally permissible for her to be criminally disobedient, provided that her criminal activity is directed at appropriating surplus goods from people who have more than a fair share of opportunities to lead a good life, and at appropriating such goods with a minimum of physical force. Of course, Gretchen will normally engage in such criminal acts only if there is some likelihood that she will be successful at appropriating the $3,000 income to which she has a basic right.

Suppose, however, that Gretchen is caught by the legal authorities. Should they punish her? In a basically just society, the grounds for punishing a person is the judgment that the criminal, unlike the victim of crime, could have been reasonably (i.e., morally) expected to act otherwise.[17] But while this comparative opportunity judgment generally holds in a basically just society, it does not hold in the unjust society in which Gretchen lives. She could not be reasonably expected to act differently. In the society in which Gretchen lives (which appears to be strikingly similar to our own), there would be no grounds for punishing Gretchen's criminal activity.

It is important to be very clear about what characterizes cases in which punishing criminal activity would not be morally justified. First, in these cases, other options (e.g., normal politics, legal protest, civil disobedience, and revolutionary action) would have to be either ineffective for achieving reasonable progress toward a just society or reasonably judged too costly for those persons they are intended to benefit. Second, in these cases, there would be only minimal violations of the moral rights of others. This means that in these cases the criminal activity would be directed at appropriating surplus goods from people who have more than a fair share of opportunities to lead a good life, and at appropriating such goods with a minimum of physical force. Hence, criminal activity that harmed the less advantaged in society would not be morally justified. Nor would it be morally justified to kill or seriously injure the more advantaged, except in self-defense, when attempting to dispossess them of their unjust holdings. But given that all these requirements have been met, it would not only be morally permissible for persons like Gretchen to engage in criminally disobedient actions, it would also be morally required for the legal authorities to withhold punishment in such cases. What this means is that for societies, like the United States, which are making little if any progress toward correcting basic injustices, although punishment will still be morally justified with regard to most crimes against persons, it will only be morally justified for *some* crimes against property. Happily, for those who dislike this limited moral justification for punishment in societies like the United States, there is an appropriate remedy: Guarantee the basic human rights required by the reconciliationist conception of justice defended in this book and more punishment for crimes will then be morally justified.

It is interesting to note how the practical conclusions arrived at in this chapter relate to our earlier discussion of the libertarian ideal of liberty in Chapter 3. There it was argued that when we apply the

180

"Ought" Implies "Can" Principle and the Conflict Resolution Principle to the conflict of liberties that exists between the rich and the poor, the liberty of the poor not to be interfered with when taking from the surplus possessions of the rich what one requires to satisfy one's basic needs has moral priority over the liberty of the rich not to be interfered with when using their surplus possessions for luxury purposes. It was further argued that to legitimately prevent the poor from choosing when and how to exercise their "negative" liberty, the rich could institute an adequate "positive" liberty, or "positive" welfare rights, that would take moral precedence over the exercise of a "negative" liberty, or "negative" welfare right. Of course, the underlying assumption of this whole discussion is that the rich and the poor would do what is reasonably determined to be morally right within a libertarian framework.

But what if the rich refuse to do what is reasonably determined to be morally right? Specifically, what if the rich refuse to recognize the welfare rights of the poor or recognize only inadequate welfare rights, as in the United States today? Then what can the poor legitimately do? It is here that this chapter's discussion of the moral appropriateness of normal politics, legal protest, civil disobedience, revolutionary action, and criminal disobedience becomes relevant in deciding what we should be doing in the unjust world in which we live.

We have noted that many people live in societies where the basic human rights required by the reconciliationist conception of justice defended in this book are not guaranteed, yet where very little civil disobedience or revolutionary action takes place. In this chapter, I have tried to explain this absence of civil disobedience and revolutionary action in a way that provides no justification at all for the practices of these unjust societies. The absence of civil disobedience and revolutionary action is simply due to the lack of sufficient political power to inspire some hope of success. In these circumstances, civil disobedience and revolutionary action are still morally permissible, but they are unlikely to take place because there is little chance that they will be successful. I have also argued that in such societies where basic human rights have been denied, certain criminally disobedient acts thereby become morally permissible, and existing legal authorities have no right to punish them. Rather than punishment, the appropriate corrective in such cases is to make the changes required to guarantee just those basic human rights which have been denied. Only then will we secure a peace that is joined with justice for here and now.

Notes

CHAPTER 1. A PEACEMAKING WAY OF DOING PHILOSOPHY

1 It is also important to distinguish doing philosophy in the sense of establishing philosophical conclusions before one's philosophical peers from doing philosophy in the sense of teaching or explaining philosophy to students and nonphilosophers. Here I am primarily concerned with doing philosophy in the first sense.

2 For a discussion of the similarities between argument and war, see George Lakoff and Mark Johnson, *Metaphors We Live By* (Chicago: University of Chicago Press, 1980), pp. 4–6, 77–86, and Edwin Burtt, "Philosophers as Warriors," in *The Critique of War*, ed. Robert Ginsberg (Chicago: Henry Regnery Co., 1969), pp. 30–42. Lakoff and Johnson argue that these similarities between argument and war are constitutive features of the nature of argument.

3 Although names are omitted, the events described in this chapter actually did occur.

4 The question may also have been intended to express distrust of libertarian philosophers in general, but, if so, I see no grounds for it. Libertarian philosophers as a group seem no more or less trustworthy than any comparably chosen group of philosophers.

5 Janice Moulton, "A Paradigm of Philosophy: The Adversary Method," in *Discovering Reality*, ed. Sandra Harding and Merrill B. Hintikka (Dordrecht: Reidel Publishing Co., 1983), pp. 149–64. It should be noted that Moulton is also concerned to criticize this adversary model, but not for the reason I give later.

6 Ibid., p. 153.

7 See William James, *The Moral Equivalent of War* (Association for International Conciliation, 1910), and John Stuart Mill, *On Liberty* (New York: Bobbs-Merrill Co., 1956). The phrase "marketplace of ideas" is associated with the work of John Stuart Mill, but surprisingly the phrase never appears in Mill's writings and in fact is somewhat at odds with the views he actually endorsed. See Jill Gordon, "John Stuart Mill and the 'Marketplace of Ideas,'" *Social Theory and Practice*, vol. 23 (1997), pp. 235–49.

8   It might be objected that philosophers can only identify who their strong-
    est opponents are by interpreting their opponents honestly and with sym-
    pathetic understanding. But even assuming that this is the case, once
    philosophers have so identified their opponents, they may still resort to
    dishonesty and unsympathetic interpretations to achieve their ultimate
    goal of publicly defeating them.

9   This does not just happen in philosophy. In a recent feature article in the
    New York Times, Lester Thurow and Paul Krugman, both at MIT and
    known for their opposing economic views, were said to "go at it, *never
    face to face,* always in writing and public speaking, sometimes from the
    well of the same MIT lecture amphitheater, although on separate days"
    (emphasis added). *New York Times,* February 16, 1997.

10 See, for example, W. D. Hudson, ed., *The Is/Ought Question* (London: Mac-
    millan, 1969).

11 See Kurt Baier, *The Moral Point of View* (Ithaca, NY: Cornell University
    Press, 1958); Alan Gewirth, *Reason and Morality* (Chicago: University of
    Chicago Press, 1978), and Stephen Darwall, *Impartial Reason* (Ithaca, NY:
    Cornell University Press, 1983).

12 Feminists (see, e.g., the articles in the *APA Newsletter on Feminism and
    Philosophy,* vol. 88 [March 1989], and Phyllis Rooney, "Recent Work on
    Feminist Discussion of Reason," *American Philosophical Quarterly,* vol. 31
    (1994), pp. 1–21) have, of course, attacked norms of rationality in philos-
    ophy as a masculine ideal linked to competitiveness and aggression, but
    that is not how norms are to be understood here, as I am using norms
    of rationality simply to imply a commitment to consistency and non-
    question-beggingness.

13 John Rawls is typical here. See his *A Theory of Justice* (Cambridge, MA:
    Harvard University Press, 1971), p. 136.

14 For example, Alasdair MacIntyre, *After Virtue* (Notre Dame, IN: Univer-
    sity of Notre Dame Press, 1981).

15 For example, John Rawls, *Political Liberalism* (New York: Columbia Uni-
    versity Press, 1993). For Rawls, justified agreement on practical require-
    ments necessitates an overlapping consensus on political values, but
    unfortunately Rawls never establishes that there is any such overlapping
    consensus on political values. My approach in this book is different. I
    argue that there are grounds for justified agreement on practical requi-
    rements even in the absence of a consensus on political values.

16 Good examples of philosophers who have taken this approach are Will
    Kymlicka, *Contemporary Political Philosophy* (New York: Oxford University
    Press, 1990), and Seyla Benhabib, *Situating the Self* (New York: Routledge,
    1992).

17 Needless to say, the moral and political perspectives that we manage to
    consider will depend both on our starting points and on the perspectives
    that are accessible to us from those starting points. But achieving a truly
    justified perspective is always context-dependent in just this way.

18 Of course, no set of rules could fully capture a philosophical method, and
    even the above rules require sympathetic interpretation if they are to be
    applicable. It is also interesting to note how this model for doing phi-

losophy contrasts with the standard of discourse ethics proposed by Jurgen Habermas. See Jurgen Habermas, *Moral Consciousness and Communicative Action* (Cambridge, MA: MIT Press, 1984), pp. 69–73, 83–91.

According to Habermas, the central principle of the discourse ethics that he defends is the following: "Only those norms can claim to be valid that meet (or could meet) with the approval of all affected in their capacity as participants in a practical discourse." Habermas claims that this central principle of his discourse ethics is derived from a principle of universalization, which in turn is implied by the presuppositions of ordinary argumentation. One formulation of these presuppositions of argumentation, which he endorses, is as follows:

1) Every subject with the competence to speak and act is allowed to take part in the discourse.
2) Everyone is allowed to question any assertion whatsoever.
   a) Everyone is allowed to introduce any assertion whatsoever into the discourse.
   b) Everyone is allowed to express his or her attitudes, desires and needs.
3) No speaker may be prevented, by internal or external coercion, from exercising his or her rights as laid down in (1) and (2).

Habermas thinks that these presuppositions, along with the claim that one should not prejudge any issue, entail a principle of universalization from which the principle of discourse ethics in turn follows. But unless we build a lot into what it is to prejudge an issue, the presuppositions of argumentation on which Habermas grounds his account seem consistent with a slightly modified, but still objectionable, warmaking model of argumentation; they do not require a peacemaking model of argumentation as I have characterized it. This is because, according these presuppositions, although one has to give others time to present their views, one doesn't have to be fair-minded, for example, by putting the best construction on other people's views. Nor does one necessarily have to modify or abandon one's views should the weight of available evidence require it.

This raises a problem not only for the adequacy of Habermas's presuppositions of argumentation but for the central principle of his discourse ethics as well. For the norms that meet (or could meet) with the approval of all affected in their capacity as participants in a modified warmaking model of discourse may not be the norms that people in fact should abide by, or would in fact abide by if they were participants in a peacemaking model of discourse as I have characterized it. So while Habermas's account has the advantage of grounding norms in a discourse in which all parties are represented and have a chance to speak, he does not sufficiently constrain that discourse so that its results would be adequately justified.

At one point, however, Habermas does say that if the participants in discourse ethics "genuinely want to convince one another," they must make their "responses to be influenced solely by the force of the better argument" (see Jurgen Habermas, *Justification and Application*, trans. Ciaron Cronin [Cambridge, MA: MIT Press, 1993], p. 31). But the argument that best serves to convince others may not be the most defensible view. Accordingly, if the participants in Habermas's discourse ethics are primarily concerned with convincing others, that is, with winning a philosophical victory by whatever means available, they may well favor an objectionable warmaking model of doing philosophy over the peacemaking model that I have developed in this chapter, which aims at achieving the most defensible views, even if those views happen not to be endorsed by large numbers of people.

19 What this also shows is that a peacemaking model of doing philosophy is only defensible when it too is strongly committed to the values of fair-mindedness, openness, and self-criticalness in the pursuit of the most justified philosophical views.

20 Others should feel free, however, to call a model of doing philosophy that is committed to fair-mindedness, openness, and self-criticalness whatever they want.

CHAPTER 2. FROM RATIONALITY TO MORALITY

1 While egoism is an ethical perspective because it provides norms about how one should behave, it is not a moral perspective because it never requires a person to sacrifice her overall interests for the sake of others.

2 Again John Rawls is typical here. See his *A Theory of Justice* (Cambridge, MA: Harvard University Press, 1971), p. 136.

3 Ibid.

4 See Richard B. Brandt, *Ethical Theory* (Englewood Cliffs, NJ: Prentice-Hall, 1959), chap. 1.

5 See Knud Rasmussen, *The People of the Polar North* (London: Kegan Paul, Trench, Trubner and Co., 1908), pp. 106ff.; and Peter Freuchen, *Book of the Eskimos* (New York: World Publishing Co., 1961), pp. 193–206. And cf. Hans Reusch, *Top of the World* (New York: Pocket Books, 1951), pp. 123–26.

6 See Mary Douglas, *Purity and Danger* (London: Praeger, 1966), p. 39.

7 It may be possible, however, to show that even those who deny that the fetus is a person should still oppose abortion in a wide range of cases. See my "Abortion and the Rights of Distant Peoples and Future Generations," *Journal of Philosophy*, vol. 77 (1980), pp. 424–40; *How to Make People Just* (Totowa, NJ: Rowman and Littlefield, 1988), and "Response to Nine Commentators," *Journal of Social Philosophy*, vol. 22 (1991), pp. 100–18.

8 This is not to deny that it would have been a good thing to avoid carcinogens in the Middle Ages, it is just that without the concept of a carcinogen, there couldn't have been any moral requirement to do so.

9 For more on this requirement, see my *Contemporary Social and Political Philosophy* (Belmont, CA: Wadsworth Publishing Co., 1995), pp. 2–5. It should also be pointed out that this requirement necessitates interpreting the Kantian notion of acts that accord with duty in particular circum-

stances as acts that certain moral agents, but not necessarily all moral agents, would have a duty to do in those circumstances.

10 See W. T. Stace, *The Concept of Morals* (New York: Macmillan, 1937), chaps. 1 and 2.

11 Kurt Baier: *The Moral Point of View* (Ithaca, NY: Cornell University Press, 1958); "The Social Source of Reason," *Proceedings and Addresses of the American Philosophical Association*, vol. 51 (1978), pp. 707–33; "Moral Reasons and Reasons to Be Moral," in *Values and Morals*, ed. A. I. Goldman and J. Kim (Dordrecht: Reidel Publishing Co., 1978), pp. 231–56; "Moral Reason 2," in *Midwest Studies in Philosophy*, ed. Peter French et al., vol. 3 (1982), pp. 62–74; "The Conceptual Link between Morality and Rationality," *Nous*, vol. 16 (1983), pp. 78–88; "Justification in Ethics," *Nomos*, ed. J. R. Pennock and J. W. Chapman (New York: New York University Press, 1986), vol. 28, pp. 3–27 and *The Rational and the Moral Order* (La Salle, IL: Open Court, 1995).

12 Baier, "Moral Reasons," pp. 62–74, and "Moral Reasons and Reasons to Be Moral," pp. 231–256.

13 For this interpretation, see Baier, "Moral Reasons and Reasons to Be Moral, p. 240.

14 It is sometimes argued that egoism is an inconsistent view and that it is not possible for everyone to follow its dictates. I argue against this view in my *The Demands of Justice* (Notre Dame, IN: University of Notre Dame Press, 1980), chap. 1.

15 Baier, "Moral Reasons," p. 69.

16 This assumes, of course, that egoists have not internalized the moral norms they seek to internalize in others, and so are not overcome with guilt when they violate those norms for reasons of self-interest. But it certainly seems possible for some egoists to be like this.

17 I am assuming that to act contrary to reason is one way of failing to do what is rationally required, but it need not imply that one has acted irrationally. Acting irrationally is a more egregious failure to do what is rationally required.

18 When players fail to execute their best moves it may simply be due to their lack of skill or ability, *or* they may have been tricked into not executing their best moves.

19 See Baier, "Justification in Ethics," pp. 14ff.

20 Although the egoist rejects a fairness requirement here, she would initially be inclined to accept the fair-mindedness requirement of the peace-making way of doing philosophy set out in Chapter 1 as well as the other requirements of that way of doing philosophy, provided that she need not publicly attest to the results of doing philosophy that way. This is because the egoist thinks that what would emerge from this way of doing philosophy is that egoism is the most rationally defensible view, but while the egoist surely thinks that that is the case, she also has good egoistic reasons for not wanting to say so publicly – hence the reason for the proviso that the egoist would want to impose on accepting a peace-making way of doing philosophy.

21 Baier, *The Rational and the Moral Order*. Baier's most recent defense of

morality is quite similar to David Gauthier's in his *Moral by Agreement* (Cambridge: Cambridge University Press, 1986). I discuss Gauthier's view later in this chapter.

22 Baier, *The Rational and the Moral Order*, p. 188.

23 Kurt Baier was my teacher in graduate school and my dissertation director, and so he as exerted a long-standing influence on my work, for which I have always been grateful.

24 Alan Gewirth: *Reason and Morality* (Chicago: University of Chicago Press, 1978), chaps. 1 and 2; "The Rationality of Reasonableness," *Synthese*, vol. 57 (1983), pp. 225–47; "From the Prudential to the Moral," *Ethics*, vol. 95 (1985), pp. 302–4; "Why There Are Human Rights," *Social Theory and Practice*, vol. 11 (1985), pp. 235–48; "Ethics and the Pain of Contradiction," *Philosophical Forum*, vol. 23 (1992) pp. 259–77.

25 For Gewirth's claim that the right in premise (3) is prudential, see "Replies to My Critics," in *Gewirth's Ethical Rationalism*, ed. Edward Regis (Chicago: University of Chicago Press, 1984), pp. 205–12.

26 No doubt some will find Gewirth's notion of a "prudential right" to be something of an oxymoron, but in his account the notion is clearly defined to be the equivalent of a prudential as opposed to a moral ought. So if it would help, barring a little awkwardness, it is possible to restate Gewirth's argument, as well as my response, by simply replacing every occurrence of "right" with one of "ought."

27 "Ought" presupposes "can" here. So unless people have the capacity to entertain and follow both self-interested and moral reasons for acting, it does not make any sense to ask whether they ought or ought not to do so. Moreover, moral reasons here are understood necessarily to include (some) altruistic reasons but not necessarily to exclude (all) self-interested reasons. So the question of whether it would be rational for us to follow self-interested reasons rather than moral reasons should be understood as the question of whether it would be rational for us to follow self-interested reasons exclusively rather than some appropriate set of self-interested reasons and altruistic reasons that constitutes the class of moral reasons.

28 Of course, we don't need to seek to construct a good argument in support of all of our views, but our view about whether morality or egoism has priority is an important enough question to call for the support of a good argument. I owe this point to Bernard Gert.

29 I understand the pure altruist to be the mirror image of the pure egoist. Whereas the pure egoist thinks that the interests of others count for them but not for herself except instrumentally, the pure altruist thinks that her own interests count for others but not for herself except instrumentally.

30 Self-interested reasons favor both relational and nonrelational goods for the self, while altruistic reasons favor both relational and nonrelational goods for others.

31 Nell Nodding, *Caring: A Feminine Approach to Ethics and Moral Education* (Berkeley: University of California Press, 1984); Joyce Trebilcot, ed., *Mothering* (Totowa, NJ: Rowman and Littlefield, 1983); Susan Brownmiller, *Femininity* (New York: Ballantine Books, 1984).

32 James Doyle, *The Male Experience* (Dubuque, IA: W. C. Brown & Co., 1983); Marie Richmond-Abbot, ed., *Masculine and Feminine*, 2d ed. (New York: Random House, 1991).

33 Victor Seidler, *Rediscovering Masculinity* (New York: Routledge, 1989); Larry May and Robert Strikwerda, *Rethinking Masculinity* (Lanham, MD: Rowman and Littlefield, 1992).

34 This is not to deny that we usually have greater knowledge and certainty about what is in our own self-interest than about what is in the interest of others, and that this difference in our knowledge and certainty can have a practical effect on what good we should do in particular contexts. It is just that the debate between egoism and morality gets started at the theoretical level where no assumption is made about this difference in our knowledge and certainty, since we can, and frequently do, have adequate knowledge and certainty about both what is in our own self-interest and what is in the interest of others.

35 Not all the reasons that people are or were able to acquire are *relevant* to an assessment of the reasonableness of their conduct. First, reasons that are evokable only from some logically possible set of opportunities are simply not relevant; the reasons must be evokable from the opportunities people actually possessed. Second, reasons that radically different people could have acquired are also not relevant. Instead, relevant reasons are those which people could have acquired without radical changes in their developing identities. Third, some reasons are not important enough to be relevant to a reasonable assessment of conduct. For example, a reason that I am able to acquire which would lead me to promote my own interests or that of a friend just slightly more than I am presently doing is hardly relevant to an assessment of the reasonableness of my conduct. Surely, I could not be judged as unreasonable for failing to acquire such a reason. Rather, relevant reasons are those which would lead one to avoid a *significant harm* to oneself (or others) or to secure a *significant benefit* to oneself (or others) at an acceptable cost to oneself (or others).

It is also worth noting that a given individual may not actually reflect on all the reasons that are relevant to deciding what she should do. In fact, one could do so only if one had already acquired all the relevant reasons. Nevertheless, reasonable conduct is ideally determined by a rational weighing of all the reasons that are relevant to deciding what one should do, so that failing to accord with a rational weighing of all such reasons is to act contrary to reason.

36 For a discussion of the causal links involved here, see *Marketing and Promotion of Infant Formula in Developing Countries*, Hearing before the Subcommittee of International Economic Policy and Trade of the Committee on Foreign Affairs, U.S. House of Representatives, 1980. See also Maggie McComas et al., *The Dilemma of Third World Nutrition* (1983).

37 Assume that both jobs have the same beneficial effects on the interests of others.

38 I am assuming that acting contrary to reason is a significant failing with respect to the requirements of reason, and that there are many ways of

not acting in (perfect) accord with reason that do not constitute acting contrary to reason.

39 To deal with pure sadists (if any exist) for whom malevolent reasons or the reasons on which such reasons are grounded would not have been outweighted by other self-interested reasons, we might introduce an additional argument to show that pure sadists should team up with pure masochists (if any exist)!

40 Of course, such reasons will have to be taken into account at some point in a conception of justice for here and now, but the method of integrating such reasons will simply parallel the method already used for integrating self-interested and altruistic reasons. In Chapter 6, I will consider how such reasons to promote nonhuman welfare should be integrated into a conception of justice for here and now. It is not clear how there could be any other kind of reasons that would be relevant to rational choice, but if there were such, they would have to relate to some other kind of good that we could plausibly be maintained to pursue.

41 In G. E. Moore's thought experiment of whether a beautiful world should be preferred to an ugly world if no one were to have experience of either, Moore's preference for the beautiful world was based on the assumption that humans would not be affected one way or the other by the choice. See G. E. Moore, *Principia Ethica* (Cambridge: Cambridge University Press, 1966), pp. 83–85. Moreover, although there are many aesthetic objects that we restrict our experience of in order to better preserve them, even in such cases it still seems that the value of such objects correlates with the value of the aesthetic experiences that such objects have produced in the past or could produce in the future for beings like ourselves.

42 This is because, as I shall argue, morality itself already represents a compromise between egoism and altruism. So to ask that moral reasons be weighed against self-interested reasons is, in effect, to count self-interested reasons twice – once in the compromise between egoism and altruism and then again when moral reasons are weighed against self-interested reasons. But to count self-interested reasons twice is clearly objectionable.

43 Assume that all these methods of waste disposal have roughly the same amount of beneficial effects on the interests of others.

44 It is important to point out here that this defense of morality presupposes that we can establish a conception of the good, at least to the degree that we can determine high- and low-ranking self-interested and altruistic reasons for each agent.

45 It is worth pointing out here an important difference between these self-interested and altruistic reasons that constitute moral reasons. It is that the self-interested reasons render the pursuit of self-interest permissible, whereas the altruistic reasons require the pursuit of altruism. This is because it is always possible to sacrifice oneself more than morality demands and thus act supererogatorily. Yet even here there are limits and one can sacrifice oneself too much, as presumably the pure altruist does, and consequently be morally blameworthy for doing so.

46 Actually, all of what altruism assumes is:

1) All high-ranking altruistic reasons have priority over conflicting lower-ranking self-interested reasons.
2) All low-ranking altruistic reasons have priority over conflicting higher-ranking self-interested reasons.
3) All high-ranking altruistic reasons have priority over conflicting high-ranking self-interested reasons.
4) All low-ranking altruistic reasons have priority over conflicting low-ranking self-interested reasons.

By contrast, all of what egoism assumes is:

1') All high-ranking self-interested reasons have priority over conflicting lower-ranking altruistic reasons.
2') All low-ranking self-interested reasons have priority over conflicting higher-ranking altruistic reasons.
3') All high-ranking self-interested reasons have priority over conflicting high-ranking altruistic reasons.
4') All low-ranking self-interested reasons have priority over conflicting high-ranking altruistic reasons.

And what the compromise view assumes is (1) and (1'), and it favors neither altruism nor egoism with respect to (3) and (4), (3') and (4').

47 Kai Nielson, "Why Should I Be Moral? Revisited," *American Philosophical Quarterly*, vol. 21 (1984), p. 90.

48 Since (pure) altruism requires the infliction of basic harm on oneself for the sake of nonbasic benefit to others, it also has an analogous burden of proof, although it may not be as weighty a burden given that the harm would be self-imposed, and so frequently, but not always, permissible. See note 45 above.

49 Kurt Baier, *The Moral Point of View*, abridged ed. (New York: Random House, 1965), p. 150.

50 Thomas Nagel, *Equality and Partiality* (Oxford: Oxford University Press, 1991).

51 Notice that the impersonal standpoint will coincide with the compromise view only if the impersonal standpoint is interpreted as allowing each individual to opt for a certain degree of self-preference.

52 A compromise between the personal and the impersonal would be judged too much from the personal standpoint if more consideration of others was required than the personal perspective regarded as justified. A compromise between the personal and the impersonal would be judged as too little from the impersonal standpoint if less consideration of others was required than the impersonal perspective regarded as justified.

53 The justification for blaming and censuring such persons is not based on any possibility for reforming them because we were assuming that they were incapable of reform. Rather, the justification is based on what the persons in question deserve because of their past behavior and on whatever usefulness blaming and censuring them would have in deterring others.

54　What it is rational for those who lack even the minimal capacity for altruism to do is a question that I will not take up here.

55　More precisely, to say that I am morally responsible for my lack of moral reasons in this regard is to say that (*a*) I have or had the opportunity and capacity to acquire those reasons, and (*b*) I also have, had, or could have had overwhelming good reasons of the relevant sort to utilize my capacity and opportunity to acquire those reasons.

56　For an account of what counts as relevant self-interested or moral reasons, see note 35 above.

57　Gauthier, *Moral by Agreement*. See also idem., "Morality, Rational Choice, and Semantic Representation: A Reply to My Critics," *Social Philosophy and Policy*, vol. 5 (1988), pp. 173–221; *Rationality, Justice and the Social Contract: Themes from Morals by Agreement*, ed. David Gauthier and Robert Sugden (Ann Arbor: University of Michigan Press, 1993); Peter Vallentyne, *Contractarianism and Rational Choice: Essays on David Gauthier's Moral by Agreement* (Cambridge: Cambridge University Press, 1991).

58　Gauthier, *Moral by Agreement*, chaps. 5–7.

59　Ibid., p. 169.

60　Ibid., p. 174.

61　Ibid., p. 200.

62　Ibid., p. 204. Gauthier never considers the problem of whether the injustices of slaveholders, for example, may have resulted in particular slaves being born who would not have been born otherwise. This is relevant, because if the lives of these slaves are still worth living, they would not have been made worse off than if the slaveholders had never existed, because then they would have never existed either.

63　Ibid., p. 232.

64　Ibid., pp. 227–32. Writing in 1988 in response to critics, Gauthier still maintained the same view. Referring to the situation in South Africa at the time, he wrote: "But of course, in such circumstances, although it may be rational for some persons to dispose themselves to acquiesce in the existing principles, it would be a misrepresentation to identity their disposition with one of unforced compliance. And the existing principles could not plausibly be identified with morality" (Gauthier, "Morality, Rational Choice, and Semantic Representation," p. 182). On Gauthier's view, morality does not appear to make any recommendations for such situations.

65　Stephen Darwall, *Impartial Reason* (Ithaca, NY: Cornell University Press, 1983), pp. 196–98.

66　Ibid., pp. 200–201, 208.

67　Sarah Broadie, *Ethics with Aristotle* (New York: Oxford University Press, 1991); Richard Kraut, *Aristotle on the Human Good* (Princeton, NJ: Princeton University Press, 1989); John Cooper, *Reason and Human Good in Aristotle* (Cambridge, MA: Harvard University Press, 1975); Thomas Nagel, "Aristotle on Eudaimonia," in *Essays on Aristotle's Ethics*, ed. Amelie Rorty (Berkeley: University of California Press, 1980), pp. 7–14; J. L Ackrill, "Aristotle on Eudaimonia," in *Essays on Aristotle's Ethics*, pp. 15–34;

W. F. B. Hardie, "The Final Good in Aristotle's Ethics," in *Aristotle,* ed. J. M. E. Moravcsik (New York: Anchor Books, 1967), pp. 297–322; Kathleen Wilkes, "The Good Man and the Good for Man," in *Essays on Aristotle's Ethics,* pp. 341–58; Amelie Rorty, "The Place of Contemplation in Aristotle's Nicomachean Ethics," in *Essays on Aristotle's Ethics,* pp. 377–94.

68 By a "viable Aristotelian account," I mean an account that could be plausibly considered morally defensible in Aristotle's day, or a refurbished account that could be plausibly considered morally defensible today.

69 Kraut, *Aristotle on the Human Good,* especially chap. 2.

70 It is possible that some viable Aristotelian accounts of personal flourishing will involve both kinds of compromise: a compromise within the account of personal flourishing itself between conflicting interests of the self or between conflicting selves, or something similar, and a compromise between personal flourishing and the good of others. This will occur when the compromise within the account of human flourishing itself does not fully resolve the conflict between self and others. One might think of Nagel's attempt to reconcile the personal and impersonal standpoints as a needed "second compromise," except for the fact that if the second compromise is to be done correctly in Nagel's account, it will have to undo at least some of the compromises achieved within the personal standpoint, and maybe even within the impersonal standpoint as well. With respect to the Aristotelian views requiring two compromises that I am considering here, I am assuming that there is no similar need to undo the first compromise.

71 Jeffrey Reiman, "What Ought " 'Ought' Implies 'Can' " Imply? Comments on James Sterba's *How to Make People Just," Journal of Social Philosophy,* special issue, vol. 22 (1991), pp. 73–80; Eric Mack, "Libertarianism Untamed," *Journal of Social Philosophy,* special issue, vol. 22 (1991), pp. 64–72. See also Jeffrey Reiman, *Justice and Modern Moral Philosophy* (New Haven, CT: Yale University Press, 1990), pp. 97–112.

72 There is also the additional reason, discussed earlier, that egoism fails to meet its burden of proof.

73 Mack, "Libertarianism Untamed."

74 Reiman, "What Ought " 'Ought' Implies 'Can' " Imply? Comments on James Sterba's *How to Make People Just,"* pp. 73–80. This objection was actually directed against Alan Gewirth's defense of morality, but in private correspondence Reiman has directed it against my own view as well.

75 Ibid., pp. 112–29.

76 In private correspondence, Reiman claims that, as he understands the denial of the reality of other people, it does not require solipsism but only the failure to "recognize the first-person reality of other people" (August 2, 1995). But even given this interpretation it still seems that Reiman is making too strong a claim about the egoist. For example, the egoist does not have to deny that other human beings are in pain, as would seemingly be the case if she failed to "recognize the first-person reality of other people."

77 The logical mistake of begging the question entails, in this context, preferring low-ranking self-interested reasons over high-ranking altruistic reasons or low-ranking altruistic reasons over high-ranking self-interested reasons, which, in turn, entails the material mistake of inflicting basic harm for the sake of nonbasic benefit. Likewise, the material mistake of inflicting basic harm for the sake of nonbasic benefit entails preferring low-ranking self-interested reasons over high-ranking altruistic reasons, which, in turn, entails the logical mistake of begging the question.

CHAPTER 3. FROM LIBERTY TO EQUALITY

1 F. A. Hayek, *The Constitution of Liberty* (Chicago: University of Chicago Press, 1960), p. 11.

2 John Hospers, *Libertarianism* (Los Angeles: Nash Publishing, 1971), p. 5.

3 See John Hospers, "The Libertarian Manifesto," in *Morality in Practice,* ed. James P. Sterba, 5th ed. (Belmont, CA: Wadsworth Publishing Co., 1997) p. 21.

4 See Milton Friedman, *Capitalism and Freedom* (Chicago: University of Chicago Press, 1962), pp. 161–72; Robert Nozick, *Anarchy, State, and Utopia* (New York: Basic Books, 1974), 160–64.

5 Basic needs, if not satisfied, lead to significant lacks or deficiencies with respect to a standard of mental and physical well-being, Thus, a person's needs for food, shelter, medical care, protection, companionship, and self-development are, at least in part, needs of this sort. For a discussion of basic needs, see my *How to Make People Just* (Totowa, NJ: Rowman and Littlefield, 1988), pp. 45–48.

6 It is not being assumed here that the surplus possessions of the rich are either justifiably or unjustifiably possessed by the rich. Moreover, according to Spencerian libertarians, it is an assessment of the liberties involved that determines whether the possession is justifiable.

7 See Hospers, *Libertarianism*, chap. 7, and Tibor Machan, *Human Rights and Human Liberties* (Chicago: Nelson-Hall, 1975), pp. 231ff.

8 I first appealed to this interpretation of the "Ought" Implies "Can" Principle to bring libertarians around to the practical requirements of welfare liberalism in an expanded version of an article entitled "Neo-Libertarianism," which appeared in the fall of 1979 in my edited volume, *Justice: Alternative Political Perspectives*, 1st ed. (Belmont, CA: Wadsworth Publishing Co., 1980), pp. 172–86. In 1982, T. M. Scanlon, in "Contractualism and Utilitarianism," *Utilitarianism and Beyond*, ed. Amartya Sen and Bernard Williams (Cambridge: Cambridge University Press, 1982), pp. 103–28, appealed to much the same standard to arbitrate the debate between contractarians and utilitarians. In my judgment, however, this standard embedded in the "Ought" Implies "Can" Principle can be more effectively used in the debate with libertarians than in the debate with utilitarians, because the sacrifices that libertarians standardly seek to impose on the less advantaged are more outrageous and, hence, more easily shown to be contrary to reason.

9 This linkage between morality and reason is expressed in the belief that

(true) morality and (right) reason cannot conflict. Some supporters of this linkage have developed separate theories of rationality and reasonableness, contending, for example, that, while egoists are rational, those who are committed to morality are both rational and reasonable. On this interpretation, morality is rationally permissible but not rationally required, since egoism is also rationally permissible. Other supporters of the linkage between reason and morality reject the idea of separate theories of rationality and reasonableness, contending that morality is not just rationally permissible but also rationally required, and that egoism is rationally impermissible. But despite their disagreement over whether there is a separate theory of rationality distinct from a theory of reasonableness, both groups link morality with a notion of reasonableness that incorporates a certain degree of altruism. For further discussion of these issues, see Chapter 2.

10 I am indebted to Alasdair MacIntyre for helping me make this point clearer.

11 See James P. Sterba, "Is There a Rationale for Punishment?" *American Journal of Jurisprudence*, vol. 29 (1984), pp. 29–43.

12 By the liberty of the rich to meet their luxury needs, I continue to mean the liberty of the rich not to be interfered with when using their surplus possessions for luxury purposes. Similarly, by the liberty of the poor to meet their basic needs, I continue to mean the liberty of the poor not to be interfered with when taking what they require to meet their basic needs from the surplus possessions of the rich.

13 My thanks to Tara Smith for helping me to clarify the argument in this paragraph.

14 See, for example, Eric Mack, "Individualism, Rights and the Open Society," in *The Libertarian Alternative*, ed. Tibor Machan (Chicago: Nelson-Hall, 1974), pp. 21–37.

15 Since the Conflict Resolution Principle is the contrapositive of the "Ought" Implies "Can" Principle, whatever logically follows from the one principle logically follows from the other. Nevertheless, by first appealing to the one principle and then the other, as I have here, I maintain that the conclusions I derive can be seen to follow more clearly.

16 For an analogous resolution, consider the following report of a former slave, "[I]t is all right for us poor colored people to appropriate whatever of the white folks' blessings the Lord put in our way." Julius Lester, *To Be a Slave* (New York: Dial Books, 1968), p. 102

17 As further evidence, notice that those libertarians who justify a minimal state do so on the grounds that such a state would arise from reasonable disagreements concerning the application of libertarian rights. They do not justify the minimal state on the grounds that it would be needed to keep in submission large numbers of people who could not come to see the reasonableness of those rights.

18 Under such circumstances, however, it would not be unreasonable to *ask* but not require the rich to further constrain their liberty for the sake of the poor.

19 The employment opportunities offered to the poor must be honorable

and supportive of self-respect. To do otherwise would be to offer the poor the opportunity to meet some of their basic needs at the cost of denying some of their other basic needs.

20 The poor cannot, however, give up the liberty to which their children are entitled.

21 See John Hospers, "The Libertarian Manifesto."

22 Sometimes advocates of libertarianism inconsistently contend that the duty to help others is supererogatory but that a majority of a society could justifiably enforce such a duty on everyone. See Theodore Benditt, "The Demands of Justice," in *Economic Justice*, ed. Diana Meyers and Kenneth Kipnis (Totowa, NJ: Rowman and Allanheld, 1985), pp. 108–20.

23 Sometimes advocates of libertarianism focus on the coordination problems that arise in welfare and socialist states concerning the provision of welfare and ignore the far more serious coordination problems that would arise in a night-watchperson state. See Burton Leiser, "Vagrancy, Loitering and Economic Justice," in Meyers and Kipnis, *Economic Justice*, pp. 149–60.

24 It is true, of course, that if the rich could retain the resources that are used in a welfare state for meeting the basic needs of the poor, they might have the option of using those resources to increase employment opportunities beyond what exists in any given welfare state, but this particular way of increasing employment opportunities does not seem to be the most effective way of meeting the basic needs of the poor, and it would not at all serve to meet the basic needs of those who cannot work.

25 See Sterba, "Moral Approaches to Nuclear Strategy: A Critical Evaluation," *Canadian Journal of Philosophy special issue*, vol. 12 (1986), pp. 75–109.

26 Although in this case the rich would be blameworthy for bringing about the death of (i.e., killing) the poor, it is not clear to me that they can properly be called "killers."

27 When the poor are acting collectively in conjunction with their agents and allies to exercise their negative welfare rights, they will want, in turn, to institute adequate positive welfare rights to secure a proper distribution of the goods and resources they are acquiring.

28 It is important to see how moral and pragmatic considerations are combined in this argument from negative welfare rights to positive welfare rights, as this will become particularly relevant when we turn to a consideration of distant peoples and future generations. What needs to be seen is that the moral consideration is primary and the pragmatic consideration secondary. The moral consideration is that, until positive welfare rights for the poor are guaranteed, any use by the rich of their surplus possessions to meet their nonbasic needs is likely to violate the negative welfare rights of the poor by preventing them from appropriating (some part of) the surplus goods and resources of the rich. The pragmatic consideration is that, in the absence of positive welfare rights, the rich would have to put up with the discretion of the poor, either acting by themselves or through their allies or agents, in choosing when and how to exercise their negative welfare rights.

Now obviously peoples who are separated from the rich by significant distances will be able to exercise their negative welfare rights only either by negotiating the distances involved or by having allies or agents in the right place, willing to act on their behalf. And with respect to future generations, their rights can be exercised only if they too have allies and agents in the right place and time, willing to act on their behalf. So unless distant peoples are good at negotiating distances or unless distant peoples and future generations have ample allies and agents in the right place and time, the pragmatic consideration leading the rich to endorse positive welfare rights will diminish in importance in their regard. Fortunately, the moral consideration alone is sufficient to carry the argument here and elsewhere: Libertarians should endorse positive welfare rights because it is the only way they can be assured of not violating the negative welfare right of the poor by preventing the poor from appropriating (some part of) the surplus goods and resources of the rich.

29 Richard DeGeorge, "Do We Owe the Future Anything?" in *Law and the Ecological Challenge*, vol. 2 (1978), pp. 180–90.

30 Rex Martin, *Rawls and Rights* (Lawrence: University of Kansas, 1984), chap. 2.

31 Anita Gordon and David Suzuki, *It's a Matter of Survival* (Cambridge, MA: Harvard University Press, 1990). See also Donella H. Meadows, Dennis L. Meadows, Jorgen Randers, and William W. Behrens III, *The Limits to Growth*, 2d ed. (New York: New American Library, 1974), chaps. 3 and 4.

32 For a somewhat opposing view, see M. P. Golding, "Obligations to Future Generations," *The Monist*, vol. 56 (1972), pp. 85–99.

33 Derek Parfit, "On Doing the Best for Our Children," in *Ethics and Population*, ed. Michael Baylis (Cambridge, MA: Schenkman Press, 1976). See also Derek Parfit, *Persons and Reasons* (Oxford: Clarendon Press, 1984), chap. 16.

34 Parfit qualifies his claim that the woman has not harmed the child by a further condition – namely, provided that the child's life is worth living.

35 Elsewhere I have discussed the morality of procreation and Parfit's work in this regard. See my *How to Make People Just*, chap. 8 and also note 47 below.

36 Moreover, libertarians have not restricted the class of morally legitimate claimants in this fashion. After all, the fundamental rights recognized by libertarians are universal rights, that is, rights possessed by all people, not just those who live in certain places or at certain times. Of course, to claim that these rights are universal does not mean that they are universally recognized; obviously the fundamental rights that flow from the libertarian ideal have not been universally recognized. Rather, to claim that they are universal rights, despite their spotty recognition, implies only that they ought to be recognized at all times and places by people who have or could have had good reasons to recognize these rights, whether or not they actually did or do so. Nor need these universal rights be unconditional. This is particularly true in the case of the right to welfare, which, I have argued, is conditional on people doing all that they legitimately can to provide for themselves. In addition, this right is

conditional on there being sufficient goods and resources available so that everyone's welfare needs can be met. So, where people do not do all that they can to provide for themselves or where there are not sufficient goods and resources available, people simply do not have a right to welfare.

Yet even though libertarians have claimed that the rights they defend are universal rights in the manner I have just explained, it may be that they are simply mistaken in this regard. Even when universal rights are stripped of any claim to being universally recognized or unconditional, still it might be argued that there are no such rights, that is, that there are no rights that all people ought to recognize. But how would one argue for such a view? One couldn't argue from the failure of people to recognize such rights, because we have already said that such recognition is not necessary. Nor could one argue that not everyone ought to recognize such rights because some lack the capacity to do so. This is because "ought" does imply "can" here, so that the obligation to recognize certain rights only applies to those who actually have or at some point have had the capacity to do so. Thus, the existence of universal rights is not ruled out by the existence of individuals who have never had the capacity to recognize such rights. It would be ruled out only by the existence of individuals who could recognize these rights but for whom it would be correct to say that they ought, all things considered, not to do so. But we have just seen that even a minimal libertarian moral ideal supports a universal right to welfare. And as I have argued in Chapter 2 that when "ought" is understood prudentially rather than morally, a non-question-begging conception to rationality favors morality over prudence (see Chap. 2). So for those capable of recognizing universal rights, it simply is not possible to argue that they, all things considered, ought not to do so.

37 Bob Bergland, "Attacking the Problem of World Hunger," *The National Forum*, vol. 69 (1979), p. 4.

38 *Hunger 1995: Fifth Annual Report on the State of World Hunger* (Silver Springs, MD: Bread for the World Institute, 1994), p. 10; Ruth Sivard, *World Military and Social Expenditures* (Washington, DC: World Priorities, 1993), p. 28; Frances Moore Lappe, *World Hunger* (New York: Grove Press, 1986), p. 9.

39 Lester Brown, Christopher Flavin, and Hal Kane, *Vital Signs 1996* (New York: Norton, 1996), pp. 34–35; Jeremy Rifkin, *Beyond Beef* (New York: Penguin, 1992), p. 1.

40 Lester Brown, *State of the World 1996* (New York: Norton, 1996), p. 10; Lester Brown, *State of the World 1992* (New York: Norton, 1992), p. 79.

41 Lester Brown, *Who Will Feed China?* (New York: Norton, 1995). For reasons for thinking that the additional capacity for grain production worldwide is quite limited, see pp. 104ff.

42 Henry Shue, *Basic Rights* (Princeton, NJ: Princeton University Press, 1980), chap. 7.

43 For a discussion of these causal connections, see Cheryl Silver, *One Earth, One Future* (Washington, DC: National Academy Press, 1990); Bill Mc-

Kibben, *The End of Nature* (New York: Anchor Books, 1989); Jeremy Leggett, ed., *Global Warming* (New York: Oxford University Press, 1990); and Lester Brown, ed., *The World Watch Reader* (New York: Nelson, 1991).

44 Charles Park, Jr., ed., *Earth Resources* (Washington, DC: Voice of America, 1980), chap. 13; Lester Brown, *State of the World 1995* (New York: Norton, 1992), chap. 7; Lester Brown, ed., *The World Watch Reader*, p. 268. China currently uses more coal than the U.S.A. See Lester Brown, *State of the World* (New York, 1997), p. 9.

45 G. Tyler Miller, Jr., *Living with the Environment* (Belmont, CA: Wadsworth Publishing Co., 1990), p. 20. See also Janet Besecker and Phil Elder, "Lifeboat Ethics: A Reply to Hardin," in *Readings in Ecology, Energy and Human Society*, ed. William Burch (New York: Harper and Row, 1977), p. 229. For higher and lower estimates of the impact of North Americans, see Holmes Rolston III, "Feeding People versus Saving Nature?" in *World Hunger and Morality*, 2d ed. (Englewood Cliffs, NJ: Prentice-Hall, 1996), pp. 259–60; Paul Ehrlich, Anne Ehrlich, and Gretchen Daily, *The Stork and the Plow* (New York: Grosset/Putnam, 1995), p. 26.

46 Successes in meeting the most basic needs of the poor in particular regions of developing countries (e.g., the Indian state of Kerala) should not blind us to the growing numbers of people living in conditions of absolute poverty (1.2 billion by a recent estimate) and how difficult it will be to meet the basic needs of all these people in a sustainable way that will allow future generations to have their basic needs met as well, especially when we reflect on the fact that the way we in the developed world are living is not sustainable at all!

47 In *How to Make People Just*, pp. 109–10, I argued similarly that "[f]or all practical purposes the argument from the welfare rights of distant peoples and future generations is sufficient to show that . . . there will be very few resources left over for the satisfaction of nonbasic needs." I then went on to advance a rather complicated argument that depended on a claim of symmetry between a right not to be born and a right to be born (but not on the claim that the fetus is a person) to arrive at the conclusion that, in some throughly just and hence nonsexist world that was also underpopulated (obviously not the real world we live in), abortion and even contraception might be morally impermissible in certain circumstances. Derek Parfit and others have challenged this argument in print ("A Reply to Sterba," *Philosophy and Public Affairs*, vol. 16 [1987], pp. 193–94), but Parfit later conceded in correspondence that he now thinks the argument works. After searching in vain for a mistake in it, I also think the argument works. But I also see more clearly now that the argument does little to support my case for equality, since under present conditions it justifies both abortion and contraception. So I have not used it here. My initial argument, buttressed by the new considerations that I have brought to bear, is more than sufficient to establish the conclusion I want.

48 John Rawls, *A Theory of Justice* (Cambridge, MA: Harvard University Press, 1971), chap. 2.

49 James P. Sterba, "The U.S. Constitution: A Fundamentally Flawed Document" and "A Response to Three Critics," in *Philosophical Reflections on*

the United States Constitution, ed. Christopher Gray (Lewiston, NY: Edwin Meller Press, 1989), pp. 134–61, 196–200.

50 For further discussion of a basic-needs minimum, see my *How to Make People Just*, pp. 45–48.

51 Tibor Machan, *Individuals and Their Rights* (La Salle, IL: Open Court, 1989), pp. 100–11.

52 Ibid., p. 107.

53 Alan Durning, "Life on the Brink," *World Watch*, vol. 3 (1990), p. 24.

54 Ibid., p. 29.

55 Machan also sketches another line of argument, which unfortunately proceeds from premises that contradict his line of argument that I have discussed here. The line of argument I have discussed here turns on Machan's claim that "normally, persons do not lack the opportunities and resources to satisfy their basic needs." Machan's second line of argument, by contrast, concedes that many of the poor lack the opportunities and resources to satisfy their basic needs, but then contends that this lack is the result of political oppression in the absence of libertarian institutions (see Machan, *Individuals and Their Rights*, p. 109). See also Machan's contribution to James P. Sterba, Tibor Machan et al., *Morality and Social Justice: Point and Counterpoint* (Lanham, MD: Rowman and Littlefield, 1994), pp. 59–106, where Machan develops this second line of argument in more detail. For my response to this line of argument, see "Comments by James P. Sterba," in *Morality and Social Justice: Point and Counterpoint*, pp. 110–13.

56 Tibor Machan, "The Nonexistence of Welfare Rights" (new expanded version) in *Liberty for the 21st Century*, ed. Tibor Machan and Douglas Rasmussen for the Social, Political, and Legal Philosophy Series, ed. James P. Sterba (Lanham, MD: Rowman and Littlefield, 1995), pp. 218–20.

57 Ibid.

58 Ibid.

59 Richard Rose and Rei Shiratori, eds., *The Welfare State East and West* (Oxford: Oxford University Press, 1986). In fact, the living standards of poor children in Switzerland, Sweden, Finland, Denmark, Belgium, Norway, Luxembourg, Germany, the Netherlands, Austria, Canada, France, Italy, United Kingdom, and Australia are all better than they are in the United States. See James Carville, *We're Right They're Wrong* (New York: Random House, 1996), pp. 31–32.

60 Michael Wolff, *Where We Stand* (New York: Bantam Books, 1992), pp. 23, 115; George Kurian, *The New Book of Work Rankings*, 3d ed. (New York: Facts on File, 1990), p. 73; *New York Times*, April 17, 1995.

61 Douglas Rasmussen, "Individual Rights and Human Flourishing," *Public Affairs Quarterly*, vol. 3 (1989), pp. 89–103. See also Douglas Rasmussen and Douglas Den Uyl, *Liberty and Nature* (La Salle, IL: Open Court, 1991), chaps. 2–4.

62 Rasmussen, "Individual Rights and Human Flourishing," p. 98.

63 Ibid., p. 99.

64 Ibid., p. 100.

65 Ibid., p. 101.

66 John Hospers, "Some Unquestioned Assumptions," *Journal of Social Philosophy*, vol. 22 (1991), pp. 42–51.

67 Although, given what I have said about the welfare rights of distant peoples and future generations, it would seem that (*b*) and (*c*) are unlikely to obtain.

68 Actually, the possessions in question are not truly nonsurplus, as those who have them could relatively easily produce a surplus.

69 Eric Mack, "Libertarianism Untamed," *Journal of Social Philosophy*, vol. 22 (1991), pp. 64–72.

70 Jan Narveson, *The Libertarian Idea* (Philadelphia: Temple University Press, 1988), pp. 20–21, and "Liberty, Equality and Distributive Justice," in *The Liberty–Equality Debate*, ed. Larry May (Lawrence: University of Kansas, forthcoming).

71 Jan Narveson, "Revisiting the Excursion from Liberty to Equality with Jim Sterba," unpublished circulated paper (1994), p. 2

72 Narveson, *The Libertarian Idea*, chap. 14.

73 Ibid., pp. 61, 266–67, and in "Liberty, Equality and Distributive Justice."

74 Narveson, *The Libertarian Idea*, pp. 20–21, and in his "Liberty, Equality and Distributive Justice."

75 Narveson, "Revisiting the Excursion from Liberty to Equality with Jim Sterba," p. 2.

76 Jan Narveson, "Comments on Sterba's *Ethics* Article," unpublished circulated paper (1994), p. 7. See also *The Libertarian Idea*, p. 35

77 Jan Narveson, "Sterba on Reconciling Conceptions of Justice," unpublished circulated paper (April 24, 1992). These were Narveson's comments on my symposium paper presented at the Central Division American Philosophical Association Meeting at Louisville, KY, in 1992.

78 I was so struck by the resemblance that in some of my recent work I claimed that Narveson was actually endorsing these two principles in the way I interpret them, for example, in my 1992 APA symposium paper, "Reconciling Conceptions of Justice," published in James P. Sterba et al., *Morality and Social Justice* (Lanham, MD: Rowman and Littlefield, 1994), pp. 1–38.

79 Jan Narveson, "Property Rights: Original Acquisition and Lockean Provisos," unpublished circulated paper (1991), p. 11.

80 Ibid., p. 15.

81 Ibid., p. 7.

82 I made this abundantly clear in my response to Narveson at the Central Division APA Meeting in 1992. Unfortunately, he still persists in this same misinterpretation. For example, see his "Liberty, Equality and Distributive Justice."

83 Narveson criticizes political moralities for not satisfying the interests of rational egoists. I criticize rational egoism for not meeting its own rationality requirements. For my argument see Chapter 2.

84 See, for example, John Rawls simply dismissing Hobbesian egoism out of hand in *A Theory of Justice*, pp. 124, 130–36; and many philosophers have followed his lead, despite its arbitrariness. Among libertarians, I think the work of Tibor Machan is typical here. He distinguishes between

an Aristotelian grounding for libertarian rights, which he accepts, and a Hobbesian grounding for these rights, which he rejects. See his *Individuals and Their Rights,* p. 35.

85 Narveson, "Sterba on Reconciling Conceptions of Justice," p. 10.

86 Jan Narveson, "Comments on 'From Rationality to Morality,'" unpublished circulated paper (December 23, 1993). This response has also been reiterated in subsequent conversations.

87 Narveson, *The Libertarian Idea,* pp. 61, 266–67, and in idem, "Liberty, Equality and Distributive Justice."

88 As I noted before, liberty can be characterized as a positive ideal. Likewise, equality can be characterized as a negative ideal, as in interpretations of equal opportunity where the ideal is that certain unfair constraints not be imposed on candidates for various positions.

89 But what, you might ask, is my response to the defenses of libertarianism provided by the examples from Friedman and Nozick? My response to Friedman's defense should be obvious. When basic needs are at stake, the poor can have a claim against the rich, and poor Robinson Crusoes can have a claim against rich Robinson Crusoes. My response to Nozick's defense of libertarianism is that it seems to apply only to political ideals that require an absolute equality of income. Since a welfare liberal conception of justice is not committed to an absolute equality of income, the inequalities of income generated in Nozick's example would be objectionable only if they deprived people of something to which they had a right, such as welfare or equal opportunity. And whether people are so deprived depends on to what uses the Wilt Chamberlains or Michael Jordans of the world put their greater income. Thus, it is perfectly conceivable that those who have legitimately acquired greater income may use it in ways that do not violate the rights of others.

CHAPTER 4. FROM EQUALITY TO FEMINISM

1 See, for example, Ann Ferguson, "Androgyny as an Ideal for Human Development," in *Feminism and Philosophy,* ed. Mary Vetterling-Braggin et al. (Totowa, NJ: Rowman and Littlefield, 1977), pp. 45–69; Mary Ann Warren, "Is Androgyny the Answer to Sexual Stereotyping?" in *"Femininity," "Masculinity," and "Androgyny,"* ed. by Mary Vetterling-Braggin (Totowa, NJ: Rowman and Littlefield, 1982), pp. 170–86; A. G. Kaplan and J. Bean, eds., *Beyond Sex-Role Stereotypes: Reading Toward a Psychology of Androgyny* (Totowa, NJ: Rowman and Littlefield, 1976); Andrea Dworkin, *Women Hating* (New York: Dutton, 1974), pt. 4; Carol Gould, "Privacy Rights and Public Virtues: Women, the Family and Democracy," in Carol Gould, *Beyond Domination* (Totowa, NJ: Rowman and Littlefield, 1983), pp. 3–18; Carol Gould, "Women and Freedom," *Journal of Social Philosophy,* vol. 15 (1984), pp. 20–34; Linda Lindsey, *Gender Roles* (Englewood Cliffs, NJ: Prentice-Hall, 1990); Marilyn Friedman, "Does Sommers Like Women?" *Journal of Social Philosophy,* vol. 22 (1991), pp. 75–90. For some feminists who oppose the ideal of androgyny, see Mary Daly, *Gyn-Ecology: The Meta-Ethics of Radical Feminism* (Boston: Beacon Press, 1978);

Kathryn Paula Morgan, "Androgyny: A Conceptual Critique," Social Theory and Practice, vol. 8 (1982); Jean Bethke Elstain, "Against Androgyny," *Telos*, vol. 47 (1981), pp. 5–21; Kari Weil, *Androgyny and the Denial of Difference* (Charlottesville: University of Virginia, 1992), especially part 3.

2   For a discussion of the failure of political philosophers to explore the feminist implications of their ideals, see Susan Okin, "Feminism and Political Philosophy," in *Philosophy in a Different Voice*, ed. by Janet Kourany (Princeton, NJ: Princeton University Press, 1998), pp. 116–44.

3   Joyce Trebilcot, "Two Forms of Androgynism," reprinted in *Feminism and Philosophy*, ed. Mary Vetterling-Braggin, Frederick Ellison, and Jane English (Totowa, NJ: Rowman and Littlefield, 1977), pp. 70–78.

4   Mary Ann Warren, "Is Androgyny the Answer to Sexual Stereotyping?" pp. 178–79.

5   Trebilcot, "Two Forms of Androgynism," pp. 74–77.

6   On this point, see Edmund Pincoffs, *Quandaries and Virtue* (Lawrence: University of Kansas, 1986), chap. 5.

7   Of course, I cannot provide a full account of how these virtues are to be justifiably inculcated, although I will make some specific recommendations later in this chapter.

8   See, for example, Morgan, "Androgyny: A Conceptual Critique," pp. 256–57.

9   See, for example, Mary Daly, *Gyn-Ecology: The Meta-Ethics of Radical Feminism*, p. xi.

10 Margrit Erchler, *The Double Standard* (New York: St. Martin's Press, 1980), pp. 69–71; Elizabeth Lane Beardsley, "On Curing Conceptual Confusion," in *"Femininity," "Masculinity," and "Androgyny,"* ed. Mary Vetterling-Braggin (Totowa, NJ: Littlefield and Adams, 1982), pp. 197–202; Mary Daly, "The Qualitative Leap beyond Patriarchal Religion," *Quest*, vol. 1 (1975), pp. 20–40; Janice Raymond, "The Illusion of Androgyny," *Quest*, vol. 2 (1975), pp. 57–66.

11 For a valuable discussion and critique of these two viewpoints, see Iris Young, "Humanism, Gynocentrism and Feminist Politics," *Women's Studies International Forum*, vol. 8 (1985), pp. 173–83.

12 See Christina Sommers, "Philosophers against the Family," in George Graham and Hugh LaFollette, *Person to Person* (Philadelphia: Temple University Press, 1989), pp. 82–105; "Do These Feminists Like Women?" *Journal of Social Philosophy*, vol. 21 (1990), pp. 66–74; "Argumentum ad Feminam," *Journal of Social Philosophy*, vol. 22 (1991), pp. 5–19; *Who Stole Feminism?* (New York: Simon and Schuster, 1994).

13 Elizabeth Wolgast, *Equality and the Rights of Women* (Ithaca, NY: Cornell University Press, 1980).

14 Moreover, given that the basic rights we have in society, such as a right to equal opportunity and a right to welfare, are equal for all citizens and are not based on our differing natural abilities, these rights are not, even in this derivative sense, based on one's sex.

15 Anne Moir and David Jessel, *Brain Sex* (New York: Dell Publishing Co., 1991).

16 See, for example, Virginia Held, *Rights and Goods* (New York: Free Press, 1984), especially chap. 11, and Gloria Steinem, "What It Would Be Like If Women Win," *Time*, August 31, 1970, pp. 22–23; Mary Jeanne Larrabee, "Feminism and Parental Roles: Possibilities for Changes," *Journal of Social Philosophy*, vol. 14 (1983), p. 18. See also National Organization for Women (NOW) Bill of Rights, and *Statement on the Equal Rights Amendment*, United States Commission on Civil Rights (1978).

17 See Barbara Katz Rothman, "How Science Is Redefining Parenthood," *Ms*, August 1982, pp. 154–58.

18 See, for example, Ann Ferguson, "Androgyny as an Ideal for Human Development," in *Feminism and Philosophy*, pp. 45–69; and Evelyn Reed, "Women: Caste, Class or Oppressed Sex?" in *Morality in Practice*, ed. James P. Sterba, 2d ed. (Belmont, CA: Wadsworth Publishing Co., 1983), pp. 222–28.

19 James P. Sterba, *How to Make People Just* (Totowa, NJ: Rowman and Littlefield, 1988), pp. 125–26.

20 Unfortunately, it is doubtful whether this distinctive aspect of a socialist defense of androgyny can be maintained. See Heidi Hartmann, "The Unhappy Marriage of Marxism and Feminism: Toward a More Progressive Union," in *Feminist Philosophies*, ed. Janet Kourany, James Sterba, and Rosemarie Tong (Englewood Cliffs, NJ: Prentice-Hall, 1992), pp. 343–355.

21 Alison Jaggar, "On Sexual Equality," in *Sexual Equality*, ed. Jane English (Englewood Cliffs, NJ: Prentice-Hall, 1977), p. 97.

22 Ibid., p. 99.

23 Ibid.

24 Ibid., p. 102.

25 Ibid., p. 105.

26 "Sexual Difference and Sexual Equality," in *Theoretical Perspectives on Sexual Difference*, ed. Deborah Rhode (New Haven, CT: Yale University Press, 1990), pp. 239–54.

27 Ibid., p. 242.

28 Ibid., p. 241.

29 Ibid., p. 246.

30 Ibid., pp. 253–54.

31 Sterba, *How to Make People Just*, especially chaps. 2–5, 7–9.

32 Alison Jaggar, "Comments on James P. Sterba," in James P. Sterba, Alison Jaggar, et al., *Social Justice and Morality* (Lanham, MD: Rowman and Littlefield, 1994), pp. 45–52.

33 Ibid., p. 48. Earlier, when Jaggar raised this same objection as a commentator on the symposium paper I presented at the APA Central Division Meeting in 1992, I maintained that there was no tendency in my work to focus on changing people rather than social institutions, noting Jaggar's approval of my discussion of how the ideal of androgyny would require significant changes in family structures.

34 Alison Jaggar, "Toward a Feminist Conception of Moral Reasoning" in Sterba, Jaggar, et al., *Social Justice and Morality*, pp. 115–46.

35 Ibid., p. 116. The omitted words are "that might be called androgynous." Does the omission of these words make a difference? Could it be that

Jaggar is really objecting to merely my use of the word "androgyny" and not the ideal I use the word to stand for?

36 The same account is found in Sterba, *How to Make People Just,* chap. 5; "Feminist Justice and the Family," in *Justice: Alternative Political Perspectives,* 2d ed. (Belmont, CA: Wadsworth Publishing Co., 1992), chap. 24; and *Morality and Social Justice,* chap. 1.

37 The reason for qualifying this claim is that mothers and fathers, unlike children, may legitimately waive their right to equal opportunity when the reasons are compelling enough.

38 Child-care expenses consume about a fifth of the budgets of low-income families that pay for child care. See Cynthia Costello and Anne Stone, *The American Woman 1994–95* (New York: Norton, 1994), p. 306.

39 *New York Times,* November 25, 1987; Ruth Sidel, "Day Care: Do We Really Care?" in *Issues in Feminism,* ed. Sheila Ruth (Mountain View, CA: Mayfield Publishing Co., 1990), p. 342. One explanation of this lack of day care in the United States is that at present 99 percent of private U.S. employers still do not offer it to their employees. See Susan Faludi, *Backlash* (New York: Crown Publishing Co., 1988), p. xiii.

40 *New York Times,* November 25, 1987; Sidel, "Day Care: Do We Really Care?" See also Phyllis Moen, *Woman's Two Roles* (New York: Auburn House, 1992). According to one nationwide study by an agency of the U.S. Department of Labor, 1 percent of day-care facilities were "superior," 15 percent were "good," 35 percent were essential "custodial" or "fair," and nearly half were considered "poor." See Sidel, p. 341; see also Cost, Quality and Child Outcomes Study Team, *Cost, Quality and Child Outcomes in Child Care Centers,* 2d ed. (Denver: University of Colorado, 1995).

41 See Lenore Weitzman, *The Divorce Revolution: The Unexpected Social and Economic Consequences for Women and Children in America* (New York: Free Press, 1985).

42 Dorothy Dinnerstein, *The Mermaid and the Minotaur* (New York: Harper and Row, 1977); Nancy Chodorow, *Mothering: Psychoanalysis and the Sociology of Gender* (Berkeley: University of California Press, 1978); Vivian Gornick, "Here's News: Fathers Matter as Much as Mothers," *Village Voice,* October 13, 1975.

43 *New York Times,* November 27, 1987.

44 Women's Action Coalition, *WAC Stats: The Facts about Women* (New York: The New Press, 1993), p. 60. According to another study, wives employed in the labor force do approximately 29 hours of domestic labor a week in addition to their labor market jobs. Wives not in the labor force do between 32 and 56 hours of domestic labor a week, the differences being largely due to the presence of young children. Overall, husbands spend approximately 11 hours a week in domestic labor, regardless of whether or not their wives are in the labor force. See Shelley Coverman, "Women's Work Is Never Done," in *Women: A Feminist Perspective,* ed. Jo Freeman, 4th ed. (Mountain View, CA: Mayfield Publishing Co., 1989), pp. 356–68. Research on whether men are increasing their contribution has not yet substantiated a significant increase, but one study did find an increase of eleven minutes a day for husband's domestic labor. See also Joni Hersch

and Leslie Stratton, "Housework, Wages, and the Division of Housework Time for Employed Spouses," *AEA Papers and Proceedings,* vol. 84 (1994), pp. 120–125.

45 *Statistical Abstracts of the United States 1996* (Washington, DC: U.S. Governmental Printing Office, 1996), pp. 393, 400.

46 See *Statistical Abstracts of the United States 1996,* p. 469; *New York Times,* October 6, 18, and 19, 1992. See also Moen, *Women's Roles;* Elaine Sorensen, "The Comparable Worth Debate," in *Morality in Practice,* ed. James P. Sterba, 4th ed. (Belmont, CA: Wadsworth Publishing Co., 1994), pp. 293–94.

47 See *Statistical Abstracts of the United States 1996,* p. 426.

48 See Jerry Jacobs and Ronnie Steinberg, "Compensating Differentials and the Male–Female Wage Gap," *Social Forces,* vol. 69 (December 1990), pp. 439–68.

49 Clifford Hackett, "Comparable Worth: Better from a Distance," *Commonweal,* May 31, 1985.

50 *Rapid City Journal,* October 20, 1992. One might think that the lower pay is due to a larger pool of applicants for these positions, but this would only be the case if men were not now less frequently applying for such positions. For a discussion of related issues, see Sue Headlee and Margery Elfin, *The Cost of Being Female* (Westport, CT: Praeger, 1996).

51 Report on the World Conference of the United Nations Decade for Women, Nairobi, Kenya, July 15–24, 1985. See also the *New York Times,* August 18, 1995, and Judith Lorbor, *Paradoxes of Gender* (New Haven, CT: Yale University Press, 1994).

52 *Hunger 1995: Fifth Annual Report on the State of World Hunger* (Silver Springs, MD: Bread for the World Institute, 1994), p. 87.

53 Birgit Brock-Utne, *Educating for Peace* (New York: Pergamon Press, 1985), pp. 100–101.

54 Similarly, Deborah Tannen contends that when men and women get together in groups they are likely to talk in ways more familar and comfortable to men. See Deborah Tannen, *You Just Don't Understand* (New York: Ballantine Books, 1990).

55 Objections to affirmative action and comparable worth will be taken up in the next chapter.

56 Gertrude Ezorsky, *Racism and Justice* (Ithaca, NY: Cornell University Press, 1991).

57 Elaine Sorenson, *Comparable Worth* (Princeton, NJ: Princeton University Press, 1994), pp. 88–89. See also Ellen Paul, *Equity and Gender* (New Brunswick, NJ: Transaction, 1989), and Mary Ann Mason, "Beyond Equal Opportunity: A New Vision for Women Workers," *Notre Dame Journal of Law, Ethics and Public Policy,* vol. 6 (1992), pp. 359–92.

58 *New York Times,* October 17, 1991. See also Elizabeth Schneider, "The Violence of Privacy," *The Connecticut Law Review,* vol. 23 (1991), pp. 973–99.

59 See Mary Koss, *I Never Called It Rape* (New York: Harper and Row, 1988). Originally Koss's study indicated a 25 percent incidence of rape, but responding to criticism of one of her survey questions, Koss revised her

findings and came up with 20 percent. Diana Russell and Nancy Howell, "The Prevalence of Rape in the United States Revisited," *Signs*, vol. 8 (1983), pp. 688–695; Diana Russell, *Rape in Marriage* (Bloomington: Indiana University Press, 1990), p. 57; and Bert Young, "Masculinity and Violence," presented at the Second World Congress on Violence and Human Coexistence, Montreal, July 12–17, 1992. There is considerable disagreement about what is the best way to gather data on the incidence of rape. Russell's and Howell's type of questions and personal interview strategy seem the best to me, but others disagree, and some of those who disagree have conducted studies that show a lower incidence of rape. For a discussion of the alternatives that tends to favor the studies with the lower incidence of rape, see "Rape: The Making of an Epidemic," *The Blade*, special report, October 10–12, 1993. One assumption of this discussion, that a woman has only been raped if she thinks she has, seems far too strong. Positive answers to questions (from Koss's study), such as "Have you had sexual intercourse when you didn't want to because a man threatened or used some degree of physical force (twisting your arm, holding you down, etc.) to make you?" and "Have you had sex acts (anal or oral intercourse or penetration by objects other than the penis) when you didn't want to because a man threatened or used some degree of physical force to make you?" would seem to suffice. Interestingly, when the word "rape" is not used, but instead an account of rape is read to male subjects, twice as many say they are positively inclined to so act as when the subjects are asked whether they would *rape* if they could get away with it. See Diana Russell, *Making Violence Sexy* (New York: Teachers College Press, 1993), p. 121.

60 Committee on the Judiciary, United States Senate, *Violence against Women, A Majority Staff Report* (Washington, DC: U.S. Government Printing Office, 1992); Ron Thorne-Finch, *Ending the Silence: The Origins and Treatment of Male Violence against Women* (Toronto: University of Toronto Press, 1992), chap. 1; Albert Roberts, *Helping Battered Women* (New York: Oxford University Press, 1996), pt. 1.

61 Dierdre English, "Through the Glass Ceiling," *Mother Jones*, November 1992.

62 Diana Russell, *The Secret Trauma* (New York: Basic Books, 1986), p. 61; Diana Russell, "The Incidence and Prevalence of Intrafamilial and Extrafamilial Sexual Abuse of Female Children," *Child Abuse and Neglect: The International Journal*, vol. 7 (1983), pp. 133–46.

63 On this point, see Catharine MacKinnon, *Feminism Unmodified* (Cambridge, MA: Harvard University Press, 1987), pp. 169–71.

64 See S. Opdebeeck, "Determinants of Leaving an Abusing Partner," presented at the Second World Congress on Violence and Human Coexistence, Montreal, July 12–17, 1992. See Young, "Masculinity and Violence."

65 Myriam Miedzian, *Boys Will Be Boys* (New York: Doubleday, 1991), p. 74.

66 *Donald Victor Butler v. Her Majesty The Queen* (1992).

67 Catharine MacKinnon, *Feminism Unmodified*, chap. 14; *Only Words* (Cambridge, MA: Harvard University Press, 1993), chap. 1. According to MacKinnon, the materials used in the practice of hard-core pornography

are sexually explicit, violent, and sexist, and are in contrast with the materials used in the practice of erotica, which are sexually explicit and premised on equality. But, obviously, it is not always easy to properly classify sexually explicit materials.

68   See MacKinnon, *Feminism Unmodified,* chap. 14. See also Andrea Dworkin, *Pornography: Men Possessing Women* (New York: Plume, 1989); Susan Cole, *Pornography and the Sex Crisis* (Toronto: Amanita, 1989), and *Pornography and Sexual Violence: Evidence of the Links* (London: Everywoman Ltd., 1988).

69   MacKinnon, *Feminism Unmodified,* chap. 14, and Cole, *Pornography and Sexual Violence.* See also Gloria Cowan, "Pornography: Conflict among Feminists," in *Women,* ed. Jo Freeman, 15th ed. (Mountain View, CA: Mayfield Publishing Co., 1995), pp. 347–64; and Diana Russell, ed., *Making Violence Sexy* (New York: Teachers College Press, 1993).

70   Franklin Mark Osanka and Sara Lee Johann, *Sourcebook on Pornography* (New York: Lexington Books, 1989).

71   David Phillips, "The Impact of Mass Media Violence on U.S. Homicides,"*American Sociological Review,* vol. 48 (1983), pp. 560–8. See also Ron Thorne-Finch, *Ending the Silence: The Origins and Treatment of Male Violence against Women* (Toronto: University of Toronto Press, 1992).

72   Miedzian, *Boys Will Be Boys,* pp. 203–4. According to a recent survey reported on CNN (November 12, 1994), student athletes, who represent about 10 percent of college students, are involved in 30 percent of sexual assaults. See also Laura Flanders, "The 'Stolen Feminism' Hoax," *Extra* (September/October 1994), p. 7.

73   Christina Sommers has also challenged this claim, but responses to her challenge have, I think, discredited it, unless she is simply objecting to a more particular version of this claim which maintains that there is a *40 percent* increase in batteries by husbands and boyfriends associated with the yearly Superbowl football game. For Sommers's challenge and responses to that challenge, see *Who Stole Feminism,* chap. 9, and the special issue of *Democratic Culture* (vol. 3, no. 2 [1994]) devoted to Sommers's book. See also Laura Flanders, "The 'Stolen Feminism' Hoax," pp. 6–9.

74   WBBM, January 31, 1993. Playing football also impacts negatively on the life expectancies of football players themselves. The average life expectancy of National Football League players in the United States is fifty-four, nearly two decades below the overall male mean. See Don Sabo, "Sport, Patriarchy and Male Identity," *The Arena Review,* vol. 9 (1985), pp. 1–30.

75   Miedzian, *Boys Will Be Boys,* chaps. 6 and 7.

76   Betty Reardon, *Sexism and the War System* (New York: Teachers College Press, 1985), chap. 3.

77   Of course, I am not denying that violence in the international arena also supports overt and structural violence done to women. What I am claiming is simply that they are mutually supporting.

78   Richard Gelles and Murray Straus, *Intimate Violence* (New York: Simon and Schuster, 1988).

79   Of course, it may be possible to rid oneself of violence in the personal

sphere while still endorsing and participating in the unjustified use of violence in the international arena. But this can only be done by putting considerable strain on one's psychic resources, as the phenomenon of doubling certainly attests. On this point, see Robert Jay Lifton, *The Nazi Doctors* (New York: Basic Books, 1986).

80 The unfairness of the hearings was evidenced by the fact that Anita Hill was not able to prevent intensive examination of her private life, whereas Clarence Thomas was able to declare key areas of his private life off-limits, and by the fact that Thomas was able to characterize the attack on him as motivated by the stereotypes of black men as male studs and rapists, whereas Hill became functionally white. See Nancy Fraser, "Reflections on the Confirmation of Clarence Thomas," in James P. Sterba, *Morality in Practice*, 4th ed. (Belmont, CA: Wadsworth Publishing Co., 1993), pp. 369–80.

81 Cherly Gomez-Preston, *When No Means No* (New York: Carol Publishing Co., 1993), pp. 35–36. Ellen Bravo and Ellen Cassedy, *The 9 to 5 Guide to Combating Sexual Harassment* (New York: John Wiley and Sons, 1992), pp. 4–5. The problem is international as well as national. A three-year study of women in Estonia, Finland, Sweden, and the Soviet Union revealed that nearly 50 percent of all working women experience sexual harassment. A survey released in 1991 by the Santama Group to Consider Sexual Harassment at Work showed that about 70 percent of Japanese women say they have experienced some type of sexual harassment on the job. See Susan Webb, *Step Forward* (New York: Master Media, 1991), pp. xiv, xvii.

82 *New York Times*, November 11, 1996, February 4, 1997.

83 Bravo and Cassedy, *The 9 to 5 Guide to Combating Sexual Harassment*, pp. 43ff.

84 Ibid.

85 Ibid, pp. 49–50.

86 "EEOC 1980 Guidelines on Sexual Harassment," in *Fair Employment Practices, Labor Relations Reporter*, The Bureau of National Affairs, Inc.

87 *Meritor Savings Bank V. Vinson*, 477 U.S. 57, 106 S. Ct. 2399, 91 L.Ed. 49 (1983).

88 *Christoforou v. Ryder Truck Rental*, 668 F. Supp. 294 (S.D.N.Y. 1987).

89 *Rabidue v. Osceola Refining Co.*, 805 F.2d 611, 620 (6th Cir. 1986).

90 In a recent study, Barbara A. Getek determined that a number of factors influence whether people tend to classify certain behavior as sexual harassment. They are:

1) How intrusive and persistent the behavior (the more physically intrusive and persistent the behavior is, the more likely that it will be defined as sexual harassment).

2) The nature of relationship between the actors (the better the actors know each other, the less likely the behavior will be labeled sexual harassment).

3) The characteristics of the observer (men and people in authority are less likely to label behavior as sexual harassment).

4) The inequality in the relationship (the greater the inequality, the more

likely the behavior will be labeled sexual harassment). (Barbara Getek, "Understanding Sexual Harassment at Work," *Notre Dame Journal of Law, Ethics and Public Policy*, vol. 6 [1992], pp. 335–58).

91 Obviously, most offers of this sort will be more subtle, but if they are going to serve their purpose their message must still be relatively easy to discern.

92 Even where there is legalized prostitution, such offers may still be objectively unwelcome.

93 There is an an analogous requirement of subjective consent in the law concerning rape that is similarly indefensible. See Susan Estrich, "Sex at Work," *Stanford Law Review*, vol. 43 (1991), pp. 813–61.

94 Nor should one be concerned that this suggestion would undercut an appropriate presumption of innocence, because the presumption of innocence is weaker for civil cases than for criminal cases. Thus, in a civil law sexual harassment case, the making of an objectively unwanted sexual offer and then firing the person who refused that offer should be sufficient grounds for removing that presumption.

95 Or they could simply not fire those to whom they make the offers.

96 Barbara Getek contends that sexual harassment is caused by the fact that women are stereotypically identified as sexual objects in ways that men are not. She notes that women are stereotypically characterized as sexy, affectionate, and attractive, whereas men are stereotypically characterized as competent and active. These stereotypes, Getek claims, spill over into the workplace, making it more difficult for women to be perceived as fellow workers rather than as sex objects, and it is these perceptions that foster sexual harassment (see Getek, "Understanding Sexual Harassment at Work"). It would seem, therefore, that eliminating the problem of sexual harassment from our society will require breaking down these stereotypes. But this, of course, is just what the ideal of a gender-free or androgynous society hopes to do.

97 *Meritor Savings Bank v. Vinson.*

98 *Rabidue v. Osceola Refining Co.*, 805 F.2d 611, 620 (6th Cir. 1986).

99 "EEOC 1980 Guidelines on Sexual Harassment," in *Fair Employment Practices, Labor Relations Reporter*, Bureau of National Affairs, Inc.

100 *Rabidue v. Osceola Refining Co.*, 805 F.2d 611, 620 (6th Cir. 1986).

101 *Henson v. Dundee*, 682 F.2d 897, 904 (11th Cir. 1982).

102 *Ellison v. Brady*, 924 F.2d 872 (9th Cir. 1991).

103 As one of Getek's studies shows, reasonable men and women can disagree over what constitutes sexual harassment in the workplace. In this study, 67.2 percent of the men as compared to 16.8 percent of the women would be flattered if asked to have sex, while 15 percent of the men and 62.8 percent of the women said they would be insulted by such an offer. Getek, "Understanding Sexual Harassment at Work."

104 *Robinson v. Jacksonville Shipyards*, 760 F. supp. 1486 (M.D. Fla. 1991).

105 Nadine Strossen, "Regulating Workplace Sexual Harassment and Upholding the First Amendment – Avoiding a Collision," *Villanova Law Review*, vol. 37 (1992), pp. 211–28

CHAPTER 5. FROM FEMINISM TO MULTICULTURALISM

1   For a discussion of this form of argument, see Karen Warren, "The Power and Promise of EcoFeminism," *Environmental Ethics*, vol. 12 (1990), pp. 121–46.

2   Although I will be focusing on racism directed at African Americans, the argument I will be developing applies to all forms of racism.

3   Denying people equal opportunity on the basis of culture is a way of showing disrespect to them and their culture. Accordingly, it is possible to conceive of multicultural justice as requiring respect for cultural diversity. See my *Contemporary Social and Political Philosophy* (Belmont, CA: Wadsworth Publishing Co., 1995), chap. 7.

4   See Mary Koss, *I Never Called It Rape* (New York: Harper and Row, 1988). Originally Koss's study indicated a 25 percent incidence of rape, but in responding to criticism of one of her survey questions Koss revised her findings and came up with a 20 percent incidence; Committee on the Judiciary, United States Senate, *Violence against Women: A Majority Staff Report* (Washington, DC: U.S. Government Printing Office, 1992); Ron Thorne-Finch, *Ending the Silence: The Origins and Treatment of Male Violence against Women* (Toronto: University of Toronto Press, 1992), chap. 1; Albert Roberts, *Helping Battered Women* (New York: Oxford University Press, 1996), pt. 1; Cherly Gomez-Preston, *When No Means No* (New York: Carol Publishing Co., 1993), pp. 35–36. Ellen Bravo and Ellen Cassedy, *The 9 to 5 Guide to Combating Sexual Harassment* (New York: John Wiley, 1992), pp. 4–5; Diana Russell, *The Secret Trauma* (New York: Basic Books, 1986), p. 61; Diana Russell, "The Incidence and Prevalence of Intrafamilial and Extrafamilial Sexual Abuse of Female Children," *Child Abuse and Neglect: The International Journal*, vol. 7, no. 2 (1983), pp. 133–46.

5   See *Statistical Abstracts of the United States 1996* (Washington, DC: U.S. Government Printing Office, 1996), p. 469.

6   Report on the World Conference of the United Nations Decade for Women, Nairobi, Kenya, July 15–24, 1985. See also *New York Times*, August 18, 1995.

7   *New York Times*, July 12, 1994; Gerald Jaynes and Robin Williams, eds., *A Common Destiny* (Washington, DC: National Academy Press, 1989), p. 23; Andrew Hacker, *Two Nations* (New York: Ballantine Books, 1992), pp. 46, 231; Gertrude Ezorsky, *Racism and Justice* (Ithaca, NY: Cornell University Press, 1991), p. 27. Actually, the homicide rate in poor black communities is 159 per 100,000, compared to 17 per 100,000 in middle-class white communities. See *Hunger 1995: Fifth Annual Report on the State of World Hunger* (Silver Springs, MD: Bread for the World Institute, 1995), p. 43.

8   For a discussion of these studies, see Ezorsky, *Racism and Justice*, pp. 14–18.

9   Ibid., p. 20. See also *New York Times*, October 19, 1994. It also turns out that the I.Q. gap between Protestants and Catholics in Northern Ireland is the same as the gap between whites and blacks in the United States. See *New York Times*, October 26, 1994.

10 Gregory Herek and Kevin Berrill, eds., *Hate Crimes* (London: Sage

Publications, 1992), chap. 1; Henry Lewis Gates, Jr., "Backlash," *New Yorker*, May 17, 1993, vol. 69, pp. 42ff.

11 Gary Comstock, *Violence against Lesbian and Gay Men* (New York: Columbia University Press, 1991), chap. 2.

12 Richard Mohr, *More Perfect Union* (Boston: Beacon Press, 1994), p. 54.

13 Ibid., p. 77.

14 *Bowers v. Hardwick*, 106 S.Ct. 2841 (1986). However, the most recent Supreme Court decision, *Romer v. Evans* (1996), may signal a reversal of judicial opinion on homosexuality.

15 Mohr, *More Perfect Union*, p. 19.

16 John Searle, "The Storm over the University," *New York Review of Books*, December 6, 1990.

17 Dinesh D'Souza, *Illiberal Education* (New York: Vintage Books, 1991), pp. 68–69.

18 Mary Louise Pratt, "Humanities for the Future: Reflections on the Western Culture Debate at Stanford," in *The Politics of Liberal Education*, ed. Darryl Gless and Barbara Herrnstein Smith (Durham, NC: Duke University Press, 1992), p. 25.

19 Ibid.

20 Ibid., p. 15.

21 Richard A. Lanham, "The Extraordinary Convergence: Democracy, Technology, Theory and the University Curriculum," in Gless and Herrnstein Smith, *The Politics of Liberal Education*, p. 35. See also John Searle, "The Storm over the University," and *U.S. Statistical Abstracts for 1996*, p. 181.

22 For a defense of affirmative action which shows that treating people unequally (i.e., giving affirmative action to qualified women and minority candidates but not to qualified white male candidates) is compatible with treating them as equals, see Ronald Dworkin, *Taking Rights Seriously* (New York: Oxford University Press, 1977), chap. 9.

23 Christopher Morris, Existential Limits to the Rectification of Past Wrongs," *American Philosophical Quarterly*, vol. 21 (1984), pp. 175–82; Ellen Frankel Paul, "Set-Asides, Reparations, and Compensatory Justice," in *Compensatory Justice*, ed. John Chapman (New York: New York University Press, 1991), pp. 97–142; Thomas Schwartz, "Welfare Judgments and Future Generations," *Theory & Decisions*, vol. 11 (1979), pp. 181–94.

24 A few African Americans, particularly those who have come, or whose ancestors have come, from the Caribbean, are not the product of American slavery, but almost all African Americans have slavery of some sort in their background.

25 Charles Murray, "Affirmative Racism," *New Republic*, December 31, 1984.

26 In the example cited from Murray, the black woman appears to have lacked the qualifications so that even "a suitably designed educational enhancement program" would not have resulted in her becoming, within a reasonably short time, as qualified as or even more qualified than her peers. For that reason, affirmative action was not justified in this case.

27 James Fishkin, *Justice, Equal Opportunity and the Family* (New Haven, CT: Yale University Press, 1983), pp. 88, 89, 105.

28 Carl Cohen, *Naked Racial Preference* (Lanham, MD: Madison Books, 1995), p. 31.

29 Robert Simon, "Affirmative Action and Faculty Appointments," in *Affirmative Action and the University*, ed. Steven Cahn (Philadelphia: Temple University Press, 1993) pp. 93–121.

30 Cohen also suggests, however, that the inclusiveness of such an affirmative action program might lead to its abandonment. He writes: "If the complications grow excessive we may think it well to avoid the artificial inequalities likely to flow from inadequate data, or flaws in the compensatory calculation by refraining altogether from those calculations and again treating all applicants on the same footing" (p. 31). But if this is Cohen's view, it would have the effect of simply freezing in place the effects of past injustices.

31 For a discussion of this issue, see: Ezorsky, *Racism and Justice*; Michel Rosenfeld, *Affirmative Action and Justice* (New Haven, CT: Yale University Press, 1991); and Jeffrey Rosen, "Is Affirmative Action Doomed?" *New Republic*, October 17, 1994.

32 In order to distribute the burdens of affirmative action programs more fairly, general revenues could be used, where appropriate, to defray the costs of whatever educational or training programs are required for implementing such programs.

33 Paula England, *Comparable Worth* (New York: Aldine De Gruyter, 1992), chap. 1.

34 Ibid. One possible exception would seem to be the "job" of prostitute, but what does that tell us about the justice of the wage gap between women and men?

35 Julianne Malveaux, "Comparable Worth and Its Impact on Black Women," in *Slipping Through the Cracks*, ed. Margarette Simms and Julianne Malveaux (New Brunswick, NJ: Transaction, 1986), p. 56.

36 Clifford Hackett, "Comparable Worth: Better from a Distance," *Commonweal*, May 31, 1985.

37 England, *Comparable Worth*, chap. 2.

38 Elaine Sorenson, "The Comparable Worth Debate," in *Morality in Practice*, 4th ed., ed. James P. Sterba (Belmont, CA: Wadsworth Publishing Co., 1994), pp. 293–99.

39 Robert Williams and Lorence Kessler, *A Closer Look at Comparable Worth* (Washington, DC: National Foundation for the Study of Equal Employment Policy, 1984).

40 Of course, it is far from clear that these roles as they presently exist are not fashioned, at least in part, by discriminatory practices, but for the sake of argument here, let us assume that they are not.

41 Solomon Polachek, "Women in the Economy," in *Comparable Worth: Issues for the 80s* (Washington, DC: U.S. Commission on Civil Rights, 1984), pp. 34–53.

42 For example, see Sorenson, "The Comparable Worth Debate," and English, *Comparable Worth*. Again, let us assume for the sake of argument that these are truly nondiscriminatory factors.

43 Ronnie Steinberg, "The Debate on Comparable Worth," *New Politics*, vol. 1 (1986), pp. 108–26.

44 For example, Ellen Paul, *Equity and Gender* (New Brunswick, NJ: Transaction Books, 1989), pp. 51, 46. See also Steven Rhoads, *Incomparable Worth* (New York: Cambridge University Press, 1993).

45 National Committee on Pay Equity, "The Wage Gap: Myths and Facts," in *Race, Class and Gender*, ed. Paula Rothenberg, 2d ed. (New York: St. Martin's Press, 1992), p. 134.

46 Elaine Sorenson, *Comparable Worth* (Princeton, NJ: Princeton University Press, 1994), p. 12.

47 Ibid., pp. 12–14.

48 Steven Willborn, *A Comparable Worth Primer* (Lexington, MA: Lexington Books, 1986), p. 94. As a consequence of the state of Minnesota's wide-ranging comparable worth policy, however, women in the state now earn 80.5 percent of what men earn. See Sorenson, *Comparable Worth*, p. 114.

49 In one survey, over 60 percent of Americans claim that blacks already have equal opportunity, and presumably an even greater percentage think that women already have equal opportunity. See *New York Times*, July 12, 1994. According to a ABC Nightline poll done in the fall of 1994, 70 percent of whites believe that blacks have achieved equality with whites, while 70 percent of blacks do not believe that they have achieved equality with whites.

50 Brena Sue Thorton, "The New International Jurisprudence on the Right to Privacy: A Head-on Collision with Bowers v. Hardwick," *Albany Law Review*, vol. 58 (1995), pp. 725–74.

51 See *Bowers v. Hardwick*.

52 See Burton Leiser, *Liberty, Justice and Morals*, 2d ed. (New York: Macmillan Publishing Co., 1979), chap. 2.

53 Richard Mohr, *Gays/Justice* (New York: Columbia University Press, 1988).

54 Clearly, if there is to be freedom of religion, a non–theologically based argument is needed here.

55 Notice, however, that under certain circumstances harm is done when people fail to interfere with or frustrate the human procreative process, with the consequence that more children are brought into existence than can be responsibly cared for.

56 Of course, it might not always be necessary to show that someone is harmed for evil to be done. It might simply suffice to show that someone has not benefited. Moreover, it might be claimed that someone would benefit (by coming into existence) if existing people did not refuse to procreate. Yet, as we noted above, gays and lesbians need not refuse to procreate. So this particular objection cannot be directed explicitly at them.

57 J. Bancroft, "Homosexuality: Compatible with Full Health," *British Medical Journal*, vol. 297 (1988), pp. 308–9. Evelyn Hooker's classic study found that psychiatrists, when presented with results of standard psychological diagnostic tests from which indications of sexual orientation were omitted, were able to do no better than if they had guessed randomly in their attempts to distinguish gay files from nongay ones, even

though the psychiatrists believed gays to be crazy and supposed themselves to be experts in detecting craziness. This study done in the 1950s proved a profound embarrassment to the psychiatric establishment and eventually led to the American Psychiatric Association's dropping of homosexuality from the registry of mental illness in 1973. See Evelyn Hooker, "The Adjustment of the Male Overt Homosexual," *Journal of Projective Techniques*, vol. 21 (1957), pp. 18–31.

58 D. J. West, *Homosexuality* (Chicago: Aldine, 1967), pp. 48ff.

59 M. W. Ross, "Societal Relationships and Gender Roles in Homosexuals," *Journal of Sex Research*, vol. 19 (1983), pp. 273–88.

60 Suzanne Pharr, *Homophobia: A Weapon of Sexism* (Little Rock, AR: Chardon Press, 1988), pp. 18–19; B. Harrison, *Making the Connections* (Boston: Beacon Press, 1985), p. 140; Mohr, *A More Perfect Union*, pp. 116–19.

61 *Romer v. Evans* (1996), U.S. LEXIS 3245

62 An appeal to the status/conduct distinction also provides an answer to Justice Scalia's question of why the Court should not also strike down state constitutional provisions prohibiting polygamy. The answer is that these provisions proscribe an action not a status.

63 It is hard to see how any social and political ideal could impose more minimal moral requirements than a libertarian political ideal without collapsing into egoism, which, by definition, is not a moral perspective since it imposes no constraints at all on self-interest narrowly conceived.

64 See Annie Booth and Harvey Jacobs, "Ties That Bind: Native American Beliefs as a Foundation for Environmental Consciousness," *Environmental Ethics*, vol. 12 (1990), pp. 27–43; Baird Callicott, *In Defense of the Land Ethic* (Albany: State University of New York Press, 1989), chaps. 10 and 11; Donald Hughes, "Forest Indians: The Holy Occupation," *Environmental Review*, vol. 2 (1977), pp. 1–13.

65 Quoted in Warren, "The Power and Promise of Ecological Feminism," p. 146.

66 Edward Curtis, *Native American Wisdom* (Philadelphia: Temple University Press, 1993), p. 87.

67 Luther Standing Bear, *Land of the Spotted Eagle* (Boston: Houghton Mifflin, 1933), p. 45.

68 This view is discussed in Lynn White's "The Historical Roots of Our Ecological Crisis," *Science*, vol. 155 (1967), pp. 1203–7.

69 See Lloyd Steffen, "In Defense of Dominion," *Environmental Ethics*, vol. 14 (1992), pp. 63–80; Eileen Flynn, *Cradled in Human Hands* (Kansas City, MO: Sheed and Ward, 1991), chap. 3; Robin Attfield, *The Ethics of Environmental Concern* (New York: Columbia University Press, 1983), chap. 2.

70 The following account of the Green Revolution draws on Vandana Shiva, *The Violence of the Green Revolution* (London: Zed Books, 1991), and Francis Moore Lappe and Joseph Collins, *Food First* (Boston: Houghton Mifflin, 1977), chaps. 15 and 16.

71 Alfred Howard, *The Agricultural Testament* (London: Oxford University Press, 1940).

72 John Augustus Voeleker, *Report on the Improvement of Indian Agriculture* (London: Eyre and Spothswoode, 1893), p. 47

73 This is clearly only a sufficient condition for inclusion in the educational canon, not a necessary condition. Works that do not support rights to welfare and to equal opportunity but have other excellences should also be included.

74 James P. Sterba, *Social and Political Philosophy: Classical Western Texts in Feminist and Multicultural Perspectives*, 2d ed. (Belmont, CA: Wadsworth Publishing Co., 1997).

75 Audre Lorde, "The Master's Tools Will Never Dismantle the Master's House," in *Sister Outsider* (Freedom, CA: The Crossing Press, 1984), pp. 110–14; bell hooks, "Sisterhood: Political Solidarity between Women," in *Feminist Philosophies,* ed. Janet Kourany, James Sterba, and Rosemarie Tong (Englewood Cliffs, NJ: Prentice-Hall, 1992), pp. 391–404; Marie Lugones and Elizabeth Spelman, "Have We Got a Theory for You! Feminist Theory, Cultural Imperialism, and the Demand for 'The Woman's Voice,'" in *Feminist Philosophies*, pp. 378–90; and Gloria Anzaldua, *Borderlands/la Frontera: The New Mestiza* (San Francisco: Spinsters/Aunt Lute Book Company, 1987).

CHAPTER 6. FROM ANTHROPOCENTRISM TO NONANTHROPOCENTRISM

1 See John Passmore, *Man's Responsibility for Nature* (London: Charles Scribner's Sons, 1974), and George Sessions and Bill Devall, *Deep Ecology* (Salt Lake City: Gibbs Smith Publisher, 1985).

2 See Paul Taylor, *Respect for Nature* (Princeton, NJ: Princeton University Press, 1987), and Murray Bookchin, *The Ecology of Freedom* (Montreal: Black Rose Books, 1991). It is also possible to view Passmore as pitted against Taylor and Bookchin as pitted against Sessions, but however one casts the debate, those who defend an anthropocentric ethics are still opposed to those who defend a nonanthropocentric ethics.

3 My reconciliation project contrasts with Bryan Norton's in *Toward Unity among Environmentalists* (Oxford: Oxford University Press, 1991). Whereas Norton's project seeks to achieve a reconciliation at the level of practical policies, mine seeks a reconciliation at the level of general principles as well. Whereas Norton's reconciliation project tends to exclude deep ecologists like George Sessions and biocentric egalitarians like Paul Taylor from the class of environmentalists that he is seeking to reconcile; my reconciliation project explicitly includes them.

4 See Taylor, *Respect for Nature*, pp. 129–35, and R. Routley and V. Routley, "Against the Inevitability of Human Chauvinism," in *Ethics and Problems of the 21st Century*, ed. K. E. Goodpaster and K. M. Sayre (Notre Dame, IN: University of Notre Dame Press, 1979), pp. 36–59.

5 Assuming God exists, humans might also be better off if they could retain their distinctive traits while acquiring one or another of God's qualities, but consideration of this possibility would take us too far afield. Nonhuman animals might also be better off it they could retain their distinctive traits and acquire one or another of the distinctive traits possessed by other nonhuman animals.

6 This assumes there is an environmental niche that cheetahs can fill.

7 I owe this formulation to the prodding of my colleague Alvin Plantinga.

8 The previous argument has established that we do not have any non-question-begging reasons to treat humans as superior overall to other living beings, by showing that the reasons standardly given for human superiority do not meet the standard of non-question-beggingness. What I have not established, of course, is that it would be impossible for us to have any such reasons because no such reasons can be given, but it seems to me that the burden of proof here is not on me to demonstrate the impossibility of there being any reasons of this sort, but rather the burden of proof is on those who would use an appeal to human superiority to justify aggressing against nonhuman nature.

9 Strictly speaking, not to treat humans as superior overall to other living beings is to treat them as either equal overall, *or inferior overall*, to other living beings, but I am using "equal overall" to include both of these possibilities, since neither possibility involves the domination of nonhuman nature and, moreover, the latter possibility is an unlikely course of action for humans to take.

10 For the purposes of this chapter, I will follow the convention of excluding humans from the class denoted by "animals."

11 For an account of what constitutes justifiably held property within human ethics, see Chapter 3.

12 By human ethics, I simply mean those forms of ethics that assume, without argument, that only human beings count morally.

13 Of course, one might contend that no principle of human defense applies in human ethics because either "nonviolent pacifism" or "nonlethal pacifism" is the most morally defensible view. However, I will argue in the next chapter that this is not the case, and that still other forms of pacifism more compatible with just war theory are also more morally defensible than either of these forms of pacifism.

14 The Principle of Human Preservation also imposes a limit on when we can defend nonhuman living beings against human aggression. Defense of nonhumans against human aggression is only justified when the humans who are aggressing are not doing so to meet their basic needs as permitted by the Principle of Human Preservation.

15 The difference between a standard of a decent life and a standard of a healthy life is, however, only one of degree. A standard of a decent life emphasizes the cultural and social dimensions of basic needs, while a standard of a healthy life emphasizes their physical and biological dimensions. For further discussion of basic needs, see James P. Sterba, *How to Make People Just* (Totowa, NJ: Rowman and Littlefield, 1988), pp. 45–50.

16 Moreover, this kind of fuzziness in the application of the distinction between basic and nonbasic needs is characteristic of the application of virtually all our classificatory concepts, and so is not an objection to its usefulness.

17 It should be pointed out that the Principle of Human Preservation must be implemented in a way that causes the least harm possible, which

means that, other things being equal, basic needs should be meet by aggressing against nonsentient rather than sentient living beings, so as to avoid the pain and suffering that would otherwise be inflicted on sentient beings.

18 It is important to recognize here that we also have a strong obligation to prevent lifeboat cases from arising in the first place.

19 It should also be pointed out that the Principle of Human Preservation does not support an unlimited right of procreation. In fact, the theory of justice presupposed here gives priority to the basic needs of existing beings over the basic needs of future possible beings, and this should effectively limit (human) procreation. Nor does the Principle of Human Preservation allow humans to aggress against the basic needs of animals and plants even to meet their own basic needs, when those needs could effectively be met by utilizing available human surplus resources.

20 This principle is clearly acceptable to welfare liberals, socialists, and even libertarians. For arguments to that effect, see Chapter 3. See also Sterba, *How to Make People Just* and the special issue of the *Journal of Social Philosophy*, vol. 22, no. 3, devoted to *How to Make People Just*, including my "Nine Commentators: A Brief Response."

21 Of course, libertarians have claimed that we can recognize that people have equal basic rights while in fact failing to meet, but not aggressing against, the basic needs of other human beings. However, I have argued in Chapter 3 that this claim is mistaken.

22 It should be pointed out that, although the Principle of Disproportionality prohibits aggressing against the basic needs of animals and plants to serve the nonbasic needs of humans, the Principle of Human Defense permits defending oneself and other human beings against harmful aggression of animals and plants, even when this only serves the nonbasic needs of humans. The underlying idea is that we can legitimately serve our nonbasic needs *by defending* our persons and our property against the aggression of nonhuman others but *not by aggressing against* them. In the case of human aggression, a slightly weaker principle of defense holds: We can legitimately serve our nonbasic needs by defending our persons and property *except* when humans are engaged in aggression against our nonbasic needs because it is the only way to meet their basic needs. This exception is grounded in the altruistic forbearance that we can reasonably expect of humans. In addition, in the case of human aggression, even when that aggression is illegitimate, it will sometimes be possible to effectively defend oneself and other human beings by first suffering the aggression and then securing adequate compensation later. Since in the case of nonhuman aggression this is unlikely to obtain, more harmful preventive actions against nonhuman aggression will be justified. There are simply more ways to effectively stop aggressive humans than there are to stop aggressive nonhumans.

23 It might be objected here that this argument is still speciesist, in that it permits humans to aggress against nonhuman nature whenever it is necessary for meeting our own basic needs or the basic needs of humans we happen to care about. But this objection surely loses some of its force

once it is recognized that it is also permissible for us to aggress against the nonbasic needs of humans whenever it is necessary for meeting our own basic needs or the basic needs of humans we happen to care about. Actually, the differences in our moral requirements with respect to humans and nonhumans are grounded in altruistic forbearance that we can reasonably expect of humans but not of nonhumans, and in the additional ways we have of effectively stopping human aggression but not nonhuman aggression.

24 Another way to put the central claim here is to say that species equality rules out domination, where domination is taken to mean aggressing against the basic needs of other living beings for the sake of satisfying nonbasic needs. So understood, species equality does not rule out treating species differently, even preferring one's basic needs, or the basic needs of one's species to the basic needs of nonhuman individuals, species, and whole ecosystems.

25 Aldo Leopold's view is usually interpreted as holistic in this sense. Leopold wrote: "A thing is right when it tends to preserve the integrity, stability and beauty of the biotic community. It is wrong when it tends otherwise." See his *A Sand County Almanac* (Oxford: Oxford University Press, 1949).

26 For a defender of this view, see Taylor, *Respect for Nature*.

27 I am assuming that in these cases of conflict, the good of *other* human beings is not at issue. Otherwise, as we have already noted, other considerations will apply.

28 For example, it is now quite clear that our war with Iraq could have been avoided if early on we had refused to support the military buildup of Saddam Hassein.

29 Moreover, depending on how one assesses the impact of humans upon the whole biotic community, requiring humans to be saints and sacrifice their basic needs whenever they conflict with the greater good of the whole biotic community could be quite demanding; for example, it could demand that humans decimate their numbers for the greater good of the whole biotic community. Actually, one thing that humans are required to do for the good of the whole biotic community is to put into effect a strong population-control policy.

30 Where it is most likely to be morally required is where our negligent actions have caused the environmental problem in the first place.

31 One remains free to sacrifice one's basic needs here, if that is what one wants to do.

32 Actually, in human ethics, taking away the means of survival from people who justly possess them is not morally justified even when it is needed for one's own survival. Again, this is grounded in the altruistic forbearance that we can reasonably expect of humans. This is different from the lifeboat case, discussed earlier, in which the human individuals are all trying to acquire the yet unowned means of survival when there is not enough for all.

33 Peter Singer's *Animal Liberation* (New York: Avon Books, 1975) inspired this view.

34 Baird Callicott, "Animal Liberation: A Triangular Affair," *Environmental Ethics*, vol. 2 (1980), pp. 311–28.

35 Mark Sagoff, "Animal Liberation and Environmental Ethics: Bad Marriage, Quick Divorce," *Osgood Hall Law Journal*, vol. 22 (1984), pp. 297–307.

36 Mary Ann Warren, "The Rights of the Nonhuman World," in *Environmental Philosophy*, ed. Robert Elliot and Arran Gare (University Park: Pennsylvania State University Press, 1983), pp. 109–34, and Baird Callicott, *In Defense of the Land Ethic* (Albany: State University Press of New York, 1989), chap. 3.

37 U.S. Department of Agriculture, Economic Research Service, Beltsville, MD, as quoted in Frances Moore Lappe, *Diet for a Small Planet* (New York: Ballantine Books, 1982), p. 69.

38 Robin Hur, as quoted in Lappe, p. 80.

39 For the grounds for meeting our basic nutritional needs in ways that prevent animal pain and suffering, see note 17 above.

40 Sagoff, "Animal Liberation and Environmental Ethics, pp. 301–5.

41 There is an analogous story to tell here about "domesticated" plants, but there is no analogous story about "extra humans" who could be raised for food, given that the knowledge these "extra humans" would have of their fate would most likely make their lives not worth living. But even assuming that this is not the case, with the consequence that this particular justification for domestication is ruled out because of its implications for a similar use of humans, it still would be the case that domestication is justified in a sustainable agriculture to provide fertilizer for crops to meet basic human needs.

42 Of course, if we permitted farmland and grazing land to return to their natural states, certain wild animals would surely benefit as a result, but why should we be required to favor the interests of these wild animals over the interests of farm animals, especially when favoring the latter serves our own interests as well? For further discussion, see Bart Gruzalski, "The Case against Raising and Killing Animals for Food," in *Ethics and Animals*, ed. H. Miller and W. Williams (Clifton, NJ: Humana Press, 1983), pp. 251–63.

43 I believe I owe this objection to Michael DePaul.

44 It might be objected here that this restriction on killing or taking the basic resources of even innocent humans is not absolute and could be outweighed if, for example, the lives of a sufficient number of humans could be saved. By parity of reasoning, then, why couldn't killing or harming humans be justified as well if the lives of a sufficient number of nonhumans (maybe all the future members of an endangered species) were at stake? The main objection to sanctioning such sacrifices is that they would require the people who are to be sacrificed to be saints, and morality is not normally in the business of *requiring* people to be saints.

45 Holmes Rolston, *Environmental Ethics* (Philadelphia: Temple University Press, 1988), pp. 66–68; Bookchin, *The Ecology of Freedom*, p. xxxvi.

46 See the discussion of possible grounds of human superiority in Taylor,

Respect for Nature, pp. 135–52, and in Bryan Norton, *Why Preserve Natural Variety?* (Princeton, NJ: Princeton University Press, 1987), pp. 135–50.

47 This is clearly true for welfare liberals and socialists, and it can even be shown to be true for libertarians, because most failings to meet the basic needs of others really turn out to be acts of aggressing against the basic needs of others. See note 21 above.

48 The same holds true in human ethics, where most of the ways we have of preferring our own nonbasic needs over the basic needs of other humans actually involve aggressing against those needs to meet our own nonbasic or luxury needs, rather than simply failing to meet them. See note 47.

49 Cockroaches have been known to survive even inside nuclear reactors.

50 Actually, what we are presently doing may be only meeting our short-term and not even our long-term needs, and almost certainly not meeting the long-term needs of future generations of human beings. Accordingly, a policy that took our long-term needs as well as the needs of future generations of human beings into account would most likely be a policy that was more in coincidence with the needs of nonhuman nature. Nevertheless, it would be odd to expect a complete coincidence of interest here any more than we would expect a complete coincidence of interest (pace Adam Smith) among all human beings. In addition, any coincidence of interest between humans and nonhuman nature would only provide further support for the requirements of my principles of environmental justice. (For further discussion of the degree of coincidence of interests between humans and nonhuman nature, see Norton, *Toward Unity among Environmentalists*.)

51 Assuming that God exists, even she would *not* have a right to dominate her creatures. In truth, no one can have such a right, because no one is superior to another living being in such a way that he or she would have a right to dominate it.

52 Of course, considering something valuable and choosing to do it may give something the value of a chosen option, but this value may still be overridden, even from the agent's own standpoint.

53 I am assuming here that part of what is required for reasoning correctly is that the reasoning be done in a non-question-begging way.

54 I am assuming that objective value theorists would want to incorporate a condition of accessibility into their accounts. It is difficult for me to conceive what would be the point of a value theory for humans without such a condition.

55 Subjective and objective theories of value have tended to highlight different features of a defensible theory of value. A subjective theory of value stresses that what is valuable for us must be accessible to us. An objective theory stresses that what is valuable for us depends not just on us but on the qualities of things in the world.

56 One might object here that if humans immediately came back to life, they would not have been "killed." Possibly, but what if they came back to life five minutes later or ten minutes later or fifteen minutes later? In my judgment, a more telling objection is that creatures who came back to life

in this way would no longer be humans. But irrespective of whether they were humans, given their constitution they would favor the new moral rule about killing. And this is my point – that moral rules depend on one's constitution. Of course, nothing hangs on accepting this example. For my purposes, it suffices to recognize that our aesthetic judgments depend on the way we are constituted.

57 Eugene Hargrove, "Weak Anthropocentric Intrinsic Value," in *After Earth Day*, ed. Max Oelschlaeger (Denton: University of North Texas Press, 1992), pp. 147ff.

58 Ibid., p. 151. Notice that there are at least two ways that X might intrinsically value Y. First, X might regard Y as good in itself for X or as an end in itself for X, in contrast to valuing Y instrumentally. Second, X might regard the good of Y as constraining the way that X can use Y. This second way of intrinsically valuing Y is the principal way we value human beings. It is the sense of value that Kantians are referring to when they claim that people should never be used as means only. Another way to put what I have been arguing is that we should extend this second way of intrinsically valuing to animals and plants. I discuss these two interpretations of intrinsic value later in this chapter.

59 This is another analysis of "intrinsic value" that differs somewhat from the analysis set out in the previous note and discussed later in the text.

60 As I indicated in the previous note, to say X has intrinsic value in the relevant sense here is to say that the good of X should constrain the way we treat it. In this context, it implies that we do not kill aliens without very strong moral reasons for doing so (e.g., legitimate self-defense).

61 For example, in "Animal Liberation: A Triangular Affair," Baird Callicott had defended Edward Abbey's assertion that he would sooner shoot a man than a snake.

62 For example, Eugene Hargrove argues that, from a traditional wildlife perspective, the lives of individual specimens of quite plentiful nonhuman species count for almost nothing at all. See chapter 4 of his *Foundations of Environmental Ethics* (Englewood Cliffs, NJ: Prentice-Hall, 1989).

63 *National Law Journal*, September 21, 1992. See also B. J. Goldman, *Not Just Prosperity: Achieving Sustainability with Environmental Justice* (Washington, DC: National Wildlife Federation, 1993).

64 *National Law Journal*, September 21, 1992.

65 Ibid.

66 Ibid.

67 Ibid.

68 Marcia Coyle, "When Movements Coalesce," in ibid.

69 John Bellamy Foster, "Let Them Eat Pollution: Capitalism and the World Environment," *Monthly Review*, vol. 44 (1993), p. 14; Hussein Adam, "Somalia: Environmental Degradation and Environmental Racism," in *Faces of Environmental Racism*, ed. Laura Westra and Peter Wenz (Lanham, MD: Rowman and Littlefield, 1995), pp. 195–96.

70 Carl Anthony, "A Place at the Table," *Sierra*, May/June 1993, p. 57.

71 Similar rules, such as "No taxation without representation," have been proposed at other times and places.

72 Robert Bullard, "Overcoming Racism in Environmental Decisionmaking," *Environment*, vol. 36 (May 1994), p. 15.

73 Brian Steverson, "On the Reconciliation of Anthropocentric and Nonanthropocentric Environmental Ethics," *Environmental Values*, vol. 5 (1996), pp. 349–61.

74 For support here, Steverson cites Singer, *Practical Ethics* (Cambridge: Cambridge University Press, 1979), pp. 68–71. Singer, however, is arguing against an attempt to base *all* of our moral obligations on reciprocity.

75 See Tom Regan, "Does Environmental Ethics Rest on a Mistake?" *The Monist*, vol. 75 (1992), pp. 161–83.

76 Under this interpretation, however, it is possible for something to have both intrinsic value and instrumental value, to be both an end and a means.

77 There is no opposing notion of instrumental value here.

78 The necessity of implementing the Principle of Human Preservation in a way that causes the least possible harm requires that, other things being equal, basic needs should be met by aggressing against nonsentient rather than against sentient living beings so as to avoid the pain and suffering that would otherwise be inflicted on sentient beings. This constitutes a basis for preferring the interests of sentient living beings over those of nonsentient living beings when implementing the Principle of Human Preservation.

79 With respect to humans who lack the capacity for reciprocal altruism, the compassion of fellow humans and the difficulty of distinguishing them from other humans who have that capacity provide sufficient grounds for extending to them the same protections as are given to other humans. I owe this point to Lilly Russo.

80 Given this notion of intrinsic value, I don't see how there is any category mistake in affirming degrees of intrinsic value. In "Does Environmental Ethics Rest on a Mistake?" Tom Regan argues that the various notions of intrinsic value that do not allow for degrees of intrinsic value do not serve the goals of an environmental ethics very well. I think he may be right about this, which may be a good reason in favor of my proposed notion of intrinsic value that does allow for degrees of intrinsic value.

81 Steverson also thinks that John Stuart Mill's claim in *Utilitarianism* that it is better to be Socrates dissatisfied than a pig satisfied also somehow supports a preference for nonbasic needs of humans over basic needs of nonhumans. But it isn't clear just how Mill's claim could provide this support. Mill makes his claim in the context of setting out his test of higher and lower pleasures: "Of two pleasures, if there be one to which all or almost all who have experience of both give a decided preference that is the more desirable pleasure." Yet has any human ever really experienced what it is like to be a pig? Mill considers cases in which humans actually do prefer lower to high pleasures and claims that the reason why they do so is because they have "become incapable of the other." But isn't that just what pigs are – animals that are incapable of our so-called higher pleasures? In order, then, to interpret Mill's claim so that his test of higher and lower pleasures applies to it, we must interpret it as claim-

ing that it is better for people who are capable of both higher and lower pleasures to experience the higher pleasures (the Socrates-like pleasures), even if that leaves them somewhat discontent, than it is for them to experience only lower pleasures (the piglike pleasures), even if that leaves them perfectly content.

Unfortunately, the trade-offs that we are considering in the context of an environmental ethics are quite different. They are between at least two different entities, not one entity that is capable of being in one of two ways. In fact, aggressing against the basic needs of nonhumans to satisfy the nonbasic needs of humans will frequently involve killing off nonhumans to satisfy the nonbasic needs of humans. So we don't have a common entity that is capable of existing in one of two ways as we do in Mill's case. Accordingly, Mill's claim about the preferability of higher to lower pleasures cannot be used to support the satisfaction of nonbasic needs of humans by aggressing against basic needs of nonhumans.

82 See, for example, R. M. Hare, *Moral Thinking* (Oxford: Oxford University Press, 1981).

83 Ibid.

84 It is not my intention here to endorse all the requirements of a utilitarian perspective, but only to note the coincidence here between the requirements of that perspective and those of my own.

85 No one has actually raised this objection to my view yet, but it could be raised as it has been raised against Paul Taylor's work. See, for example, Michael Zimmerman et al., eds., *Environmental Philosophy* (Englewood Cliffs, NJ: Prentice-Hall, 1993), p. 8.

86 Taylor, *Respect for Nature*, pp. 68–71 and 17.

87 Ibid., pp. 68–71.

88 One way to think about species is as ongoing genetic lineages sequentially embodied in different organisms. See Lawrence Johnson, *A Morally Deep World* (New York: Cambridge University Press, 1991), p. 156; Rolston, *Environmental Ethics*, chap. 4.

89 Interestingly, Taylor himself now seems willing to enlarge the class of moral subjects (private correspondence).

90 Ecosystems can be simple or complex, stable or unstable, and they can suffer total collapse.

91 Johnson, *A Morally Deep World,* chap. 6. Happily, this definition distinguishes moral subjects (living systems) from cars, refrigerators, etc. See also Lawrence Johnson, "Toward the Moral Considerability of Species and Ecosystems," *Environmental Ethics*, vol. 14 (1992), pp. 145–51.

92 Aggressing against the basic needs of ecosystems presupposes that it is possible to specify what is for the good of those ecosystems.

93 Moreover, it is by focusing only on the welfare of existing farm animals that animal rights defenders, like Tom Regan, argue that we should stop eating all farm animals and let them live out their natural lives, but limit their reproduction so that their numbers will decline drastically to the point where we would only be maintaining small numbers of them in improved, zoolike environments. But once considerations of the welfare

of flocks and herds, and species and subspecies, are also taken into account, the option discussed in the text seems morally preferable to Regan's depopulation option.

94 In addition, the modified principles do not seem to impose any greater sacrifices on humans than do the unmodified principles.

CHAPTER 7. FROM JUST WAR THEORY TO PACIFISM

1 Some would say with too generous a measure.
2 Jan Narveson, "Pacifism: A Philosophical Analysis," *Ethics*, vol. 75 (1965), pp. 259–71.
3 Cheyney Ryan, "Self-Defense, Pacifism and the Possibility of Killing," in *The Ethics of War and Nuclear Deterrence*, ed. James P. Sterba (Belmont, CA: Wadsworth Publishing Co., 1985), pp. 45–49.
4 Alternatively, one might concede that even in this case killing is morally evil but still contend that it is morally justified because it is the lesser of two evils.
5 For two challenging defenses of this view, see Duane L. Cady, *From Warism to Pacifism* (Philadelphia: Temple University Press, 1989), and Robert L. Holmes, *On War and Morality* (Princeton, NJ: Princeton University Press, 1989). Among the members of Concerned Philosophers for Peace, antiwar pacifism seems to be the most widely endorsed pacifist view.
6 See Cady, *From Warism to Pacifism*, pp. 51, 89ff., and Holmes, *On War and Morality*, p. 278.
7 Douglas P. Lackey, "The Moral Irrelevance of the Counterforce/Countervalue Distinction," *The Monist*, vol. 70 (1987), pp. 255–76. For a similar view, see Susan Levine, "Does the 'Counterfactual Test' Work for Distinguishing a Means from a Foreseen Concomitant?" *Journal of Value Inquiry*, vol. 18 (1984), pp. 155–57.
8 Unfortunately, the Nonexplanation Test does not work for an important set of cases. Consider the following example, first discussed by Philippa Foot in "The Problem of Abortion and the Doctrine of Double Effect," *Oxford Review*, vol. 5 (1967), pp. 5–15: Imagine that a fat person who is leading a party of spelunkers gets herself stuck in the mouth of a cave in which flood waters are rising. The trapped party of spelunkers just happens to have a stick of dynamite with which they can blast the fat person out of the mouth of the cave; either they use the dynamite or they all drown, the fat person with them. Now if we apply the Nonexplanation Test to this example and ask whether bringing about the death of the fat person helps to explain why the party of spelunkers dynamited the fat person out of the mouth of the cave to free themselves, the answer is clearly no. But the reason for this is not that the evil consequences (bringing about the death of the fat person) are merely foreseen, but rather that the intended means logically entails the "evil consequences." Dynamiting the fat person out of the mouth of the cave is just killing the fat person in a particular way. In this case, intending to dynamite the fat person out of the mouth of the cave is intending to bring about the death of the fat person. So while the Nonexplanation Test works for a wide range of

cases, it does not work for cases where the intended means entails the "evil consequences."

9 This is because the just means restrictions protect innocents quite well against the infliction of intentional harm.

10 By an "unjust aggressor" I mean someone who the defender is reasonably certain is wrongfully engaged in an attempt upon her life or the lives of other innocent people.

11 What is relevant in this case is that the foreseen deaths are a relatively small number (one in this case) compared to the number of innocents whose lives are saved (six in this case). The primary reason for using particular numbers in this case and those which follow is to make it clear that at this stage of the argument no attempt is being make to justify the large-scale killing that occurs in warfare.

12 And more severe than some just war theorists have tended to recognize.

13 See Holmes, *On War and Morality*, pp. 208–11.

14 Although there are strong cases for India's military action against Pakistan in Bangladesh and the Tanzanian incursion into Uganda during the rule of Idi Amin, there are questions that can be raised about the behavior of Indian troops in Bangladesh following the defeat of the Pakistani forces and about the regime Tanzania put in power in Uganda.

15 See, for example, William V. O'Brien, *The Conduct of Just and Limited War* (New York: Praeger, 1981), and John Courtney Murray, *Morality and Modern War* (New York: Council on Religion and International Affairs, 1959)

16 The just cause provision was violated because the extremely effective economic sanctions were not given enough time to work. It was estimated at the time that, when compared to past economic blockades, the blockade against Iraq had a nearly 100 percent chance of success if given about a year to work (see *New York Times*, January 14, 1991). The just means provision was also violated because the number of combatant and noncombatant deaths was disproportionate. As many as 120,000 Iraqi soldiers were killed, according to U.S. intelligence sources. Moreover, what we have learned about Iraq's resistance to the less stringent economic blockade that followed the war does not undercut the reasonableness of pursuing a more stringent economic blockade on the basis of the available information we had before the war. Moreover, the humiliating defeat of Iraqi forces in the Gulf War may have contributed to the hardened Iraqi resistance to the less stringent postwar economic blockage.

17 Of course, antiwar pacifists are right to point out that virtually all wars have been fought with less and less discrimination and have led to unforeseen harms. These are considerations that in just war theory must weigh heavily against going to war.

18 For another use of this term, see Kenneth H. Wenker, "Just War Pacifism," *Proceedings of the American Catholic Philosophical Association*, vol. 57 (1983), pp. 135–41. For a defense of a view similar to my own, which is considered by the author to be a defense of pacifism, see Richard Norman, "The Case for Pacifism," *Journal of Applied Philosophy*, vol. 2 (1988), pp. 197–210.

19 Of course, more needs to be done to specify the requirements of just war

pacifism. One fruitful way to specify these requirements further is to appeal to a hypothetical social contract decision procedure, as has been done with respect to other practical problems. Here I have tried to establish the defensibility of just war pacifism without appealing to any such procedure. Yet once the defensibility of just war pacifism has been established, such a decision procedure may prove quite useful in working out its particular requirements.

20 George Mavrodes, "Conventions and the Morality of War," in *Morality in Practice*, ed. James P. Sterba, 1st ed. (Belmont, CA: Wadsworth Publishing Co, 1983), pp. 302–10.

21 Gregory Kavka, "Nuclear Deterrence: Some Moral Perplexities," in *The Ethics of War and Nuclear Deterrence*, pp. 127–38.

22 James Child, *Nuclear War: The Moral Dimension* (New Brunswick, NJ: Transaction, 1986), especially pp. 140–49.

23 Ibid., p. 142.

24 Betty Reardon, *Sexism and the War System* (New York: Teachers College Press, 1985), especially chap. 3.

25 Eric Reitan, "The Irreconciliability of Pacifism and Just War Theory: A Response to Sterba," *Social Theory and Practice*, vol. 20 (1994), pp. 117–34.

26 I at least implicitly endorsed the epistemological interpretation of aggressors in "Reconciling Pacifists and Just War Theorists," *Social Theory and Practice*, vol. 18 (1992), pp. 213–18. I have also more explicitly endorsed the view elsewhere. See "Just War Theory and Nuclear Strategy," *Analyse & Kritik*, special issue, vol. 9 (1987), pp. 155–74.

27 On Reitan's view, soldiers on patrol qualify as persons who are engaged in or preparing to engage in some act that would contribute toward unjust aggression. Thus, they satisfy the second definition of aggressors, which Reitan wants to reject, in this case, on the grounds that failure to do so would lead antiwar pacifists to justify participation in some just wars.

28 Reitan claims that for antiwar pacifism "surrender and flight take moral precedence over standing and fighting," but this is the case only if nonbelligerent correctives are neither hopeless nor too costly. If they are not, and if belligerent correctives are neither hopeless nor too costly, then clearly "standing and fighting" would be at least morally permissible, and maybe even morally required.

29 One troubling objection to my reconciliation thesis was raised by Barbara McKinnon during the term when I was visiting at the University of San Francisco. McKinnon's objection concerned the limit I want to put on when belligerent correctives are too costly to constitute a just cause or are lacking in the proportionality required by just means, especially the limit that I want to derive from a discussion of Case 8. In Case 8, only the intentional or foreseen killing of an unjust aggressor and the foreseen killing of one innocent bystander would prevent serious injuries to the members of a much larger group of innocent people. With regard to that case, I argued that we must not kill innocents, even indirectly, simply to prevent serious injuries to ourselves and others. I allowed, however, that sometimes our lives and well-being are threatened together. Or better, if

we are unwilling to sacrifice our well-being then our lives are threatened as well. Nevertheless, I claimed that if we are justified in our use of lethal force to defend ourselves in cases where we will indirectly kill innocents, it is because our lives are also threatened, not simply our well-being. And I claimed that the same holds for when we are defending others.

McKinnon's objection was that my restriction on just war theory here appears too strong, because it would seem to preclude killing even one innocent bystander in a defensive effort that was designed to save many innocents from serious, but not fatal, injury – say, each was to lose an arm or a leg. The problem with the kind of case that McKinnon is sketching is that it is not sufficiently specified to allow us to make an adequate moral assessment of it. What is the unjust aggressor's plan in inflicting serious harm? Presumably, it is to gain control of the victims' lives in order to dominate them in some fashion. But what if the victims continued to resist that domination, would not the aggressor at some point threaten to end the victims' lives? But then the aggressor's attack upon the victims' bodies is simply preliminary to an attack upon their lives, assuming that they refuse to submit to domination. In that case, the aggressor's attack is ultimately life-threatening, and therefore could be resisted by means that, unfortunately, have the consequence that an innocent bystander is killed. Yet notice that, however this case is resolved, it is not a problem case that separates just war theory from antiwar pacifism. Rather, it is a problem case that they both need to solve; the difficulty of the case is a shared difficulty.

30 As we did in our analysis of the eight cases.

CHAPTER 8. CONCLUSION

1 Hence, the title of the book.

2 This is not to deny, as we noted in Chapter 5, that the application of these basic rights will not vary from societal context to societal context and therefore require a knowledge of the local culture for their proper application.

3 Alan Durning, "Life on the Brink," *World Watch*, vol. 3 (1990), p. 29; Michael Wolff, *Where We Stand* (New York: Bantam Books, 1992), p. 23.

4 Federal Reserve Board, "Financial Characteristics of High Income Families," *Federal Reserve Bulletin* (Washington, DC: Government Printing Office, December 1986), pp. 164–71; Richard Parker, *The Myth of the Middle Class* (New York: Harper and Row, 1972), p. 212.

5 John Cassidy, "Who Killed the Middle Class?" *New Yorker*, October 16, 1995, p. 114; *New York Times*, March 5, 1992.

6 See Durning, "Life on the Brink," p. 24; Peter Singer, "The Famine Relief Argument," in *Morality in Practice*, 5th ed. (Belmont, CA, 1996), pp. 85–95.

7 Lester Brown et al., *Vital Signs 1995* (New York: Norton, 1995), p. 144. In 1960, the richest 20 percent of the world's people received 70 percent of the global income, the poorest 20 percent only 2.3 percent.

8 Ibid.

9   Randy Albelda et al., *The War on the Poor* (New York: The New Press, 1996), p. 90.

10 For further argument, see James P. Sterba, "The Constitution: A Fundamentally Flawed Document" and "A Brief Reply to Three Commentators," in *Philosophical Reflections on the United States Constitution*, ed. Christopher Gray (Lewiston, NY: Edwin Mellen Press, 1989), pp. 134–61, 196–200.

11 Kim Willenson, *The Bad War* (New York: New American Library, 1987), p. 250.

12 See Charles De Benedetti, *An American Ordeal: The Antiwar Movement of the Vietnam Era* (Syracuse, NY: Syracuse University Press, 1990).

13 For the importance of solidarity in the civil rights movement, see Aldon Morris, *The Origins of the Civil Rights Movement* (New York: Free Press, 1984); Doug McAdam, *Political Process and the Development of Black Insurgency* (Chicago: University of Chicago Press, 1982); Richard King, *Civil Rights and the Idea of Freedom* (Oxford: Oxford University Press, 1992).

14 For an account of the boycott, see Rhoda Lois Blumberg, *Civil Rights* (Boston: Twayne Publishers, 1984), chap. 3.

15 Of course, this is not to blame feminists for the failure to ratify the ERA. That blame rests squarely on the shoulders of those who opposed or failed to support the amendment. Rather, it is just to suggest that still more challenging tactics might have succeeded in overcoming that opposition. For a related discussion, see Jane Mansbridge, *Why We Lost the ERA* (Chicago: University of Chicago Press, 1986), chap. 10.

16 See Chapter 4.

17 James P. Sterba, "A Rational Choice Theory of Punishment," *Philosophical Topics*, vol. 18 (1990), pp. 171–82.

Bibliography

Adam, Hussein. "Somalia: Environmental Degradation and Environmental Racism." In *Faces of Environmental Racism*, ed. Laura Westra and Peter Wenz, pp. 195–96. Lanham, MD: Rowman and Littlefield, 1995.

Albelda, Randy, et al. *The War on the Poor*. New York: The New Press, 1996.

Anthony, Carl. "A Place at the Table." *Sierra*, May/June 1993, pp. 51–58, 90–91.

Anzaldua, Gloria. *Borderlands/la Frontera: The New Mestiza*. San Francisco: Spinsters/Aunt Lute Book Company, 1987.

Attfield, Robin. *The Ethics of Environmental Concern*. New York: Columbia University Press, 1983.

Baier, Kurt. *The Moral Point of View*. Ithaca, NY: Cornell University Press, 1958.

———. "Moral Reasons and Reasons to Be Moral." In *Values and Morals*, ed. A. I. Goldman and J. Kim, pp. 231–56. Dordrecht: Reidel Publishing Co., 1978.

———. "The Social Source of Reason." *Proceedings and Addresses of the American Philosophical Association*, vol. 51 (1978), pp. 707–33.

———. "Moral Reasons." In *Midwest Studies in Philosophy*, ed. Peter French et al., vol. 3 (1982), pp. 62–74.

———. "Justification in Ethics." *Nomos*, ed. J. R. Pennock and J. W. Chapman, vol. 28 (1986), pp. 3–27.

———. *The Rational and the Moral Order*. La Salle, IL: Open Court 1995.

Bancroft, J. "Homosexuality: Compatible with Full Health." *British Medical Journal*, vol. 297 (1988), pp. 308–9.

Beardsley, Elizabeth Lane. "On Curing Conceptual Confusion." In *"Femininity," "Masculinity," and "Androgyny,"* ed. Mary Vetterling-Braggin, pp. 197–202. Totowa, NJ: Littlefield and Adams, 1982.

Benhabib, Seyla. *Situating the Self*. New York: Routledge, 1992.

Bergland, Bob. "Attacking the Problem of World Hunger." *National Forum*, vol. 69 (1979), pp. 3–6.

Besecker, Janet, and Phil Elder. "Lifeboat Ethics: A Reply to Hardin." In *Readings in Ecology, Energy and Human Society*, ed. William Burch. New York: Harper and Row, 1977.

Blumberg, Rhoda Lois. *Civil Rights*. Boston: Twayne Publishers, 1984.

Bookchin, Murray. *The Ecology of Freedom*. Montreal: Black Rose Books, 1991.

Booth, Annie, and Harvey Jacobs. "Ties That Bind: Native American Beliefs as a Foundation for Environmental Consciousness." *Environmental Ethics*, vol. 12 (1990), pp. 27–43.

Bravo, Ellen, and Ellen Cassedy. *The 9 to 5 Guide to Combating Sexual Harassment*. New York: John Wiley and Sons, 1992.

Broadie, Sarah. *Ethics with Aristotle*. (New York: Oxford University Press, 1991).

Brock-Utne, Birgit. *Educating for Peace*. New York: Pergamon Press, 1985.

Brown, Lester, et al. *Vital Signs 1995*. New York: Norton, 1995.

Brown, Lester, ed. *The World Watch Reader*. New York: Nelson, 1991.

———. *State of the World 1992*. New York: Norton, 1992.

———. *State of the World 1995*. New York: Norton, 1995.

———. *Who Will Feed China?* New York: Norton, 1995.

———. *State of the World 1996*. New York: Norton, 1996.

Brownmiller, Susan. *Femininity*. New York: Ballantine Books, 1984.

Bullard, Robert. "Overcoming Racism in Environmental Decisionmaking." *Environment*, vol. 36 (May 1994), pp. 10–20, 39–44.

Cady, Duane L. *From Warism to Pacifism*. Philadelphia: Temple University Press, 1989.

Callicott, Baird. "Animal Liberation: A Triangular Affair." *Environmental Ethics*, vol. 2 (1980), pp. 311–28.

———. *In Defense of the Land Ethic*. Albany: State University Press of New York, 1989.

Carville, James. *We're Right They're Wrong*. New York: Random House, 1996.

Cassidy, John. "Who Killed the Middle Class?" *New Yorker*, October 16, 1995, pp. 113–24.

Child, James. *Nuclear War: The Moral Dimension*. New Brunswick, NJ: Transaction, 1986.

Chodorow, Nancy. *Mothering: Psychoanalysis and the Sociology of Gender*. Berkeley: University of California Press, 1978.

Cohen, Carl. *Naked Racial Preference*. Lanham, MD: Madison Books, 1995.

Cole, Susan. *Pornography and the Sex Crisis*. Toronto: Amanita, 1989.

Committee on the Judiciary, United States Senate. *Violence against Women, A Majority Staff Report*. Washington, DC: U.S. Government Printing Office, 1992.

Comstock, Gary. *Violence against Lesbian and Gay Men*. New York: Columbia University Press, 1991.

Cost, Quality and Child Outcomes Study Team. *Cost, Quality and Child Outcomes in Child Care Centers*. 2d ed. Denver: University of Colorado, 1995.

Costello, Cynthia, and Anne Stone. *The American Woman, 1994–95*. New York: Norton, 1994.

Coverman, Shelley. "Women's Work Is Never Done." In *Women: A Feminist Perspective*, ed. Jo Freeman, 4th ed., pp. 356–68. Mountain View, CA: Mayfield Publishing Co., 1989.

Cowan, Gloria. "Pornography: Conflict among Feminists." In *Women*, ed. Jo

Freeman, 5th ed., pp. 347–64. Mountain View, CA: Mayfield Publishing Co., 1995.

Coyle, Marcia. "When Movements Coalesce." *National Law Journal*, September 21, 1992.

Curtis, Edward. *Native American Wisdom*. Philadelphia: Temple University Press, 1993.

Daly, Mary. *Gyn-Ecology: The Meta-Ethics of Radical Feminism*. Boston: Beacon Press, 1978.

———. "The Qualitative Leap beyond Patriarchal Religion." *Quest*, vol. 1 (1975), pp. 20–40.

Darwall, Stephen. *Impartial Reason*. Ithaca, NY: Cornell University Press, 1983.

De Benedetti, Charles. *An American Ordeal: The Antiwar Movement of the Vietnam Era*. Syracuse, NY: Syracuse University Press, 1990.

DeGeorge, Richard. "Do We Owe the Future Anything?" *Law and the Ecological Challenge*, vol. 2 (1978), pp. 180–90.

Dinnerstein, Dorothy. *The Mermaid and the Minotaur*. New York: Harper and Row, 1977.

Doyle, James. *The Male Experience*. Dubuque, IA: W. C. Brown & Co., 1983.

D'Souza, Dinesh. *Illiberal Education*. New York: Vintage Books, 1991.

Durning, Alan. "Life on the Brink." *World Watch*, vol. 3 (1990), pp. 22–30.

Dworkin, Andrea. *Women Hating*. New York: Dutton, 1974.

———. *Pornography: Men Possessing Women*. New York: Plume, 1989.

Dworkin, Ronald. *Taking Rights Seriously*. New York: Oxford University Press, 1977.

Ehrlich, Paul, Anne Ehrlich, and Gretchen Daily. *The Stork and the Plow*. New York: Grosset/Putnam, 1995.

Elstain, Jean Bethke. "Against Androgyny." *Telos*, vol. 47 (1981), pp. 5–21.

England, Paula. *Comparable Worth*. New York: Aldine De Gruyter, 1992.

English, Dierdre. "Through the Glass Ceiling." *Mother Jones*, November 1992.

Erchler, Margrit. *The Double Standard*. New York: St. Martin's Press, 1980.

Estrich, Susan. "Sex at Work." *Stanford Law Review*, vol. 43 (1991), pp. 813–61.

Ezorsky, Gertrude. *Racism and Justice*. Ithaca, NY: Cornell University Press, 1991.

Faludi, Susan. *Backlash*. New York: Crown Publishing Co., 1988.

Ferguson, Ann. "Androgyny as an Ideal for Human Development." In *Feminism and Philosophy*, ed. Mary Vetterling-Braggin et al., pp. 45–69. Totowa, NJ: Rowman and Littlefield, 1977.

Fifth Annual Report on the State of World Hunger: Hunger 1995. Silver Springs, MD: Bread for the World Institute, 1994.

Fishkin, James. *Justice, Equal Opportunity and the Family*. New Haven, CT: Yale University Press, 1983.

Flanders, Laura. "The 'Stolen Feminism' Hoax." *Extra* (September/October 1994), pp. 6–9.

Flynn, Eileen. *Cradled in Human Hands*. Kansas City, MO: Sheed and Ward, 1991.

Foot, Philippa. "The Problem of Abortion and the Doctrine of Double Effect." *Oxford Review*, vol. 5 (1967), pp. 5–15.

Foster, John Bellamy. " 'Let Them Eat Pollution: Capitalism and the World Environment." *Monthly Review*, vol. 44 (1993), pp. 10–20.

Fraser, Nancy. "Reflections on the Confirmation of Clarence Thomas." In *Morality in Practice*, ed. James P. Sterba, 4th ed., pp. 369–80. Belmont: Wadsworth Publishing Co., 1993.

Friedman, Marilyn. "Does Sommers Like Women?" *Journal of Social Philosophy*, vol. 22 (1991), pp. 75–90.

Friedman, Milton. *Capitalism and Freedom*. Chicago: University of Chicago Press, 1962.

Gates, Henry Lewis, Jr. "Backlash." *New Yorker*, May 17, 1993, pp. 42ff.

Gauthier, David. *Moral by Agreement*. Cambridge: Cambridge University Press, 1986.

———. "Morality, Rational Choice, and Semantic Representation: A Reply to My Critics." *Social Philosophy and Policy*, vol. 5 (1988), pp. 173–221.

Gauthier, David, and Robert Sugden, eds. *Rationality, Justice and the Social Contract: Themes from Morals by Agreement*. Ann Arbor: University of Michigan Press, 1993.

Gelles, Richard, and Murray Straus. *Intimate Violence*. New York: Simon and Schuster, 1988.

Getek, Barbara. "Understanding Sexual Harassment at Work." *Notre Dame Journal of Law, Ethics and Public Policy*, vol. 6 (1992), pp. 335–58.

Gewirth, Alan. *Reason and Morality*. Chicago: University of Chicago Press, 1978.

Gomez-Preston, Cherly. *When No Means No*. New York: Carol Publishing Co., 1993.

Gordon, Anita, and David Suzuki. *It's a Matter of Survival*. Cambridge, MA: Harvard University Press, 1990.

Gornick, Vivian. "Here's News: Fathers Matter as Much as Mothers." *Village Voice*, October 13, 1975.

Gould, Carol. "Privacy Rights and Public Virtues: Women, the Family and Democracy." In Carol Gould, *Beyond Domination*, pp. 3–18. Totowa, NJ: Rowman and Littlefield, 1983.

———. "Women and Freedom." *Journal of Social Philosophy*, vol. 15 (1984), pp. 20–34.

Gruzalski, Bart. "The Case against Raising and Killing Animals for Food." In *Ethics and Animals*, ed. H. Miller and W. Williams, pp. 251–63. Clifton, NJ: Humana Press, 1983.

Habermas, Jurgen. *Moral Consciousness and Communicative Action*. Cambridge, MA: MIT Press, 1984.

———. *Justification and Application*. Trans. Ciaron Cronin. Cambridge, MA: MIT Press, 1993.

Hacker, Andrew. *Two Nations*. New York: Ballantine Books, 1992.

Hackett, Clifford. "Comparable Worth: Better from a Distance." *Commonweal*, May 31, 1985.

Hare, R. M. *Moral Thinking*. Oxford: Oxford University Press, 1981.

Hargrove, Eugene. *Foundations of Environmental Ethics*. Englewood Cliffs, NJ: Prentice-Hall, 1989.

————. "Weak Anthropocentric Intrinsic Value." In *After Earth Day*, ed. Max Oelschlaeger, pp. 147ff. Denton: University of North Texas Press, 1992.

Harrison, B. *Making the Connections*. Boston: Beacon Press, 1985.

Hartmann, Heidi. "The Unhappy Marriage of Marxism and Feminism: Toward a More Progressive Union." In *Feminist Philosophies*, ed. Janet Kourany, James Sterba, and Rosemarie Tong, pp. 343–55. Englewood Cliffs, NJ: Prentice-Hall, 1992.

Hayek, F. A. *The Constitution of Liberty*. Chicago: University of Chicago Press, 1960.

Headlee, Sue, and Margery Elfin. *The Cost of Being Female*. Westport, CT: Praeger, 1996.

Held, Virginia. *Rights and Goods*. New York: Free Press, 1984.

Herek, Gregory, and Kevin Berrill, eds. *Hate Crimes*. London: Sage Publications, 1992.

Hersch, Joni, and Leslie Stratton. "Housework, Wages, and the Division of Housework Time for Employed Spouses." *AEA Papers and Proceedings*, vol. 84 (1994), pp. 120–125.

Holmes, Robert L. *On War and Morality*. Princeton, NJ: Princeton University Press, 1989.

Hooker, Evelyn. "The Adjustment of the Male Overt Homosexual." *Journal of Projective Techniques*, vol. 21 (1957), pp. 18–31.

hooks, bell. "Sisterhood: Political Solidarity between Women." In *Feminist Philosophies*, ed. Janet Kourany, James Sterba, and Rosemarie Tong, pp. 391–404. Englewood Cliffs, NJ: Prentice-Hall, 1992.

Hospers, John. *Libertarianism*. Los Angeles: Nash Publishing, 1971.

————. "Some Unquestioned Assumptions." *Journal of Social Philosophy* (1991), pp. 42–51.

————. "The Libertarian Manifesto." In *Morality in Practice*, ed. James P. Sterba, 5th ed., pp. 21–30. Belmont, CA: Wadsworth Publishing Co., 1997.

Howard, Alfred. *The Agricultural Testament*. London: Oxford University Press, 1940.

Hughes, Donald. "Forest Indians: The Holy Occupation." *Environmental Review*, vol. 2 (1977), pp. 1–13.

Jacobs, Jerry, and Ronnie Steinberg. "Compensating Differentials and the Male–Female Wage Gap." *Social Forces*, vol. 69 (December 1990), pp. 439–68.

Jaggar, Alison. "On Sexual Equality." In *Sexual Equality*, ed. Jane English, pp. 93–109. Englewood Cliffs, NJ: Prentice-Hall, 1977.

————. "Sexual Difference and Sexual Equality." In *Theoretical Perspectives on Sexual Difference*, ed. Deborah Rhode, pp. 239–54. New Haven, CT: Yale University Press, 1990.

————. "Comments on James P. Sterba." In James P. Sterba, Alison Jaggar, et al., *Social Justice and Morality*, pp. 45–52. Lanham, MD: Rowman and Littlefield, 1994.

————. "Toward a Feminist Conception of Moral Reasoning." In James P. Sterba, Alison Jaggar, et al., *Social Justice and Morality*, pp. 115–46. Lanham, MD: Rowman and Littlefield, 1994.

Jaynes, Gerald, and Robin Williams, eds. *A Common Destiny*, p. 23. Washington, DC: National Academy Press, 1989.

Johnson, Lawrence. *A Morally Deep World*. New York: Cambridge University Press, 1991.

———. "Toward the Moral Considerability of Species and Ecosystems." *Environmental Ethics*, vol. 14 (1992), pp. 145–51.

Kaplan, A. G., and J. Bean, eds. *Beyond Sex-Role Stereotypes: Reading Toward a Psychology of Androgyny*. Totowa, NJ: Rowman and Littlefield, 1976.

Kavka, Gregory. "Nuclear Deterrence: Some Moral Perplexities." In *The Ethics of War and Nuclear Deterrence*, ed. James P. Sterba, pp. 127–38. Belmont, CA: Wadsworth Publishing Co., 1985.

King, Richard. *Civil Rights and the Idea of Freedom*. Oxford: Oxford University Press, 1992.

Koss, Mary. *I Never Called It Rape*. New York: Harper and Row, 1988.

Kraut, Richard. *Aristotle on the Human Good*. Princeton, NJ: Princeton University Press, 1989.

Kymlicka, Will. *Contemporary Political Philosophy*. New York: Oxford University Press, 1990.

Lackey, Douglas P. "The Moral Irrelevance of the Counterforce/Countervalue Distinction." *The Monist*, vol. 70 (1987), pp. 255–76.

Lanham, Richard A. "The Extraordinary Convergence: Democracy, Technology, Theory and the University Curriculum." In *The Politics of Liberal Education*, ed. Darryll Gless and Barbara Herrnstein Smith, pp. 33–56. Durham, NC: Duke University Press, 1992.

Lappe, Frances Moore. *World Hunger*. New York: Grove Press, 1986.

Lappe, Frances Moore, and Joseph Collins. *Food First*. Boston: Houghton Mifflin, 1977.

Larrabee, Mary Jeanne. "Feminism and Parental Roles: Possibilities for Changes." *Journal of Social Philosophy*, vol. 14 (1983), pp. 16–22.

Leggett, Jeremy, ed. *Global Warming*. New York: Oxford University Press, 1990.

Leiser, Burton. *Liberty, Justice and Morals*. 2d ed. New York: Macmillan Publishing Co., 1979.

Leopold, Aldo. *A Sand County Almanac* Oxford: Oxford University Press, 1949.

Levine, Susan. "Does the 'Counterfactual Test' Work for Distinguishing a Means from a Foreseen Concomitant?" *Journal of Value Inquiry*, vol. 18 (1984), pp. 155–57.

Lifton, Robert Jay. *The Nazi Doctors*. New York: Basic Books, 1986.

Lindsey, Linda. *Gender Roles*. Englewood Cliffs, NJ: Prentice-Hall, 1990.

Lorbor, Judith. *Paradoxes of Gender*. New Haven, CT: Yale University Press, 1994.

Lorde, Audre. "The Master's Tools Will Never Dismantle the Master's House." In *Sister Outsider*, 110–14. Freedom, CA: The Crossing Press, 1984.

Lugones, Marie, and Elizabeth Spelman. "Have We Got a Theory For You! Feminist Theory, Cultural Imperialism, and the Demand for 'The Woman's Voice.'" In *Feminist Philosophies*, ed. Janet Kourany, James

Sterba, and Rosemarie Tong, pp. 378–90. Englewood Cliffs, NJ: Prentice-Hall, 1992.

Machan, Tibor. *Human Rights and Human Liberties*. Chicago: Nelson-Hall, 1975.

———. *Individuals and their Rights*. (La Salle, IL: Open Court, 1989).

———. "The Nonexistence of Welfare Rights" (new expanded version). In *Liberty for the 21st Century*, ed. Tibor Machan and Douglas Rasmussen, pp. 218–20. Social, Political, and Legal Philosophy Series, ed. James P. Sterba. Lanham, MD: Rowman and Littlefield, 1995.

MacIntyre, Alasdair. *After Virtue*. Notre Dame, IN: University of Notre Dame Press, 1981.

Mack, Eric. "Individualism, Rights and the Open Society." In *The Libertarian Alternative*, ed. Tibor Machan, pp. 21–37. Chicago: Nelson-Hall, 1974.

———. "Libertarianism Untamed." *Journal of Social Philosophy*, special issue (1991).

MacKinnon, Catharine. *Feminism Unmodified*. Cambridge, MA: Harvard University Press, 1987.

Malveaux, Julianne. "Comparable Worth and Its Impact on Black Women." In *Slipping through the Cracks*, ed. Margarette Simms and Julianne Malveaux, pp. 47–62. New Brunswick, NJ: Transaction, 1986.

Mansbridge, Jane. *Why We Lost the ERA*. Chicago: University of Chicago Press, 1986.

Martin, Rex. *Rawls and Rights*. Lawrence: University of Kansas Press, 1984.

Mason, Mary Ann. "Beyond Equal Opportunity: A New Vision for Women Workers." *Notre Dame Journal of Law, Ethics and Public Policy*, vol. 6 (1992), pp. 359–92.

Mavrodes, George. "Conventions and the Morality of War." In *Morality in Practice*, ed. James P. Sterba, 1st ed., pp. 302–10. (Belmont, CA: Wadsworth Publishing Co, 1983.

May, Larry, and Robert Strikwerda. *Rethinking Masculinity*. Lanham, MD: Rowman and Littlefield, 1992.

McAdam, Doug. *Political Process and the Development of Black Insurgency*. Chicago: University of Chicago Press, 1982.

McKibben, Bill. *The End of Nature*. New York: Anchor Books, 1989.

Miedzian, Myriam. *Boys Will Be Boys*. New York: Doubleday, 1991.

Miller, G. Tyler, Jr. *Living with the Environment*. Belmont, CA: Wadsworth Publishing Co., 1990.

Moen, Phyllis. *Woman's Two Roles*. New York: Auburn House, 1992.

Mohr, Richard. *Gays/Justice*. New York: Columbia University Press, 1988.

———. *More Perfect Union*. Boston: Beacon Press, 1994.

Moir, Anne, and David Jessel. *Brain Sex*. New York: Dell Publishing Co., 1991.

Morgan, Kathryn Paula. "Androgyny: A Conceptual Critique." *Social Theory and Practice*, vol. 8 (1982).

Morris, Aldon. *The Origins of the Civil Rights Movement*. New York: Free Press, 1984.

Morris, Christopher. "Existential Limits to the Rectification of Past Wrongs." *American Philosophical Quarterly*, vol. 21 (1984), pp. 175–82.

Moulton, Janice. "A Paradigm of Philosophy: The Adversary Method." In

Discovering Reality, ed. Sandra Harding and Merrill B. Hintikka, pp. 149–64. Dordrecht: Reidel Publishing Co., 1983.

Murray, Charles. "Affirmative Racism." *New Republic*, December 31, 1984.

Murray, John Courtney. *Morality and Modern War*. New York: Council on Religion and International Affairs, 1959.

Nagel, Thomas. *Equality and Partiality*. Oxford: Oxford University Press, 1991.

Narveson, Jan. "Pacifism: A Philosophical Analysis." *Ethics*, vol. 75 (1965), pp. 259–71.

———. *The Libertarian Idea*. Philadelphia: Temple University Press, 1988.

———. "Liberty, Equality and Distributive Justice." In *The Liberty–Equality Debate*, ed. Larry May. Lawrence: University of Kansas, forthcoming.

National Committee on Pay Equity. "The Wage Gap: Myths and Facts." In *Race, Class and Gender*, ed. Paula Rothenberg, 2d ed., pp. 129–35. New York: St. Martin's Press, 1992.

Nielson, Kai. "Why Should I Be Moral? Revisited." *American Philosophical Quarterly*, vol. 21 (1984), p. 90.

Nodding, Nell. *Caring: A Feminine Approach to Ethics and Moral Education*. Berkeley: University of California Press, 1984.

Norman, Richard. 'The Case for Pacifism." *Journal of Applied Philosophy*, vol. 2 (1988), pp. 197–210.

Norton, Bryan. *Why Preserve Natural Variety?* (Princeton: Princeton University Press, 1987).

———. *Toward Unity among Environmentalists*. Oxford: Oxford University Press, 1991.

Nozick, Robert. *Anarchy, State, and Utopia*. New York: Basic Books, 1974.

O'Brien, William V. *The Conduct of Just and Limited War*. New York: Praeger, 1981.

Okin, Susan. "Feminism and Political Philosophy." In *Philosophy in a Different Voice*, ed. Janet Kourany, pp. 116–44. Princeton, NJ: Princeton University Press, 1998.

Opdebeeck, S. "Determinants of Leaving an Abusing Partner." Paper presented at the Second World Congress on Violence and Human Coexistence, Montreal, July 12–17, 1992.

Osanka, Franklin Mark, and Sara Lee Johann. *Sourcebook on Pornography*. New York: Lexington Books, 1989.

Parfit, Derek. *Persons and Reasons*. Oxford: Clarendon Press, 1984.

———. "A Reply to Sterba." *Philosophy and Public Affairs*, vol. 16 (1987), pp. 193–94.

Park, Charles, Jr., ed. *Earth Resources*. Washington, DC: Voice of America, 1980.

Parker, Richard. *The Myth of the Middle Class*. New York: Harper and Row, 1972.

Passmore, John. *Man's Responsibility for Nature*. London: Charles Scribner's Sons, 1974.

Paul, Ellen. *Equity and Gender*. New Brunswick, NJ: Transaction, 1989.

———. "Set-Asides, Reparations, and Compensatory Justice." In *Compensatory Justice*, ed. John Chapman, pp. 97–142. New York: New York University Press, 1991.

Pharr, Suzanne. *Homophobia: A Weapon of Sexism*. Little Rock, AR: Chardon Press, 1988.

Phillips, David. "The Impact of Mass Media Violence on U.S. Homicides." *American Sociological Review*, vol. 48 (1983), pp. 560–68.

Pincoffs, Edmund. *Quandaries and Virtue*. Lawrence: University of Kansas, 1986.

Polachek, Solomon. "Women in the Economy." In *Comparable Worth: Issues for the 80's*, pp. 34–53. Washington, DC: U.S. Commission on Civil Rights, 1984.

Pratt, Mary Louise. "Humanities for the Future: Reflections on the Western Culture Debate at Stanford." In *The Politics of Liberal Education*, ed. Darryl Gless and Barbara Herrnstein Smith, pp. 13–31. Durham, NC: Duke University Press, 1992.

Rasmussen, Douglas. "Individual Rights and Human Flourishing." *Public Affairs Quarterly*, vol. 3 (1989), pp. 89–103.

Rasmussen, Douglas, and Douglas Den Uyl. *Liberty and Nature*. La Salle, IL: Open Court, 1991.

Rawls, John. *A Theory of Justice*. Cambridge, MA: Harvard University Press, 1971.

———. *Political Liberalism*. New York: Columbia University Press, 1993.

Raymond, Janice. "The Illusion of Androgyny." *Quest*, vol. 2 (1975), pp. 57–66.

Reardon, Betty. *Sexism and the War System*. New York: Teachers College Press, 1985.

Reed, Evelyn. "Women: Caste, Class or Oppressed Sex?" In *Morality in Practice*, ed. James P. Sterba, 2d ed., pp. 222–28. Belmont, CA: Wadsworth Publishing Co., 1983.

Regan, Tom. "Does Environmental Ethics Rest on a Mistake?" *The Monist*, vol. 75 (1992), pp. 161–83.

Regis, Edward, ed. *Gewirth's Ethical Rationalism*. Chicago: University of Chicago Press, 1984.

Reiman, Jeffrey. *Justice and Modern Moral Philosophy*, pp. 97–112. New Haven, CT: Yale University Press, 1990.

———. "What Ought 'Ought' Implies 'Can' Imply? Comments on James Sterba's *How to Make People Just*." *Journal of Social Philosophy*, special issue (1991).

Reitan, Eric. "The Irreconciliability of Pacifism and Just War Theory: A Response to Sterba." *Social Theory and Practice*, vol. 20 (1994), pp. 117–34.

Report on the World Conference of the United Nations Decade for Women, Nairobi, Kenya, July, 15–24, 1985.

Rhoads, Steven. *Incomparable Worth*. New York: Cambridge University Press, 1993.

Richmond-Abbot, Marie, ed. *Masculine and Feminine*. 2d ed. New York: Random House, 1991.

Roberts, Albert. *Helping Battered Women*. New York: Oxford University Press, 1996.

Rolston, Holmes. *Environmental Ethics*. Philadelphia: Temple University Press, 1988.

————. "Feeding People versus Saving Nature?" *Hunger and Morality*, pp. 259–60. 2d ed. Englewood Cliffs, NJ: Prentice-Hall, 1996.

Rose, Richard, and Rei Shiratori, eds. *The Welfare State East and West*. Oxford: Oxford University Press, 1986.

Rosen, Jeffrey. "Is Affirmative Action Doomed?" *New Republic*, October 17, 1994.

Rosenfeld, Michel. *Affirmative Action and Justice*. New Haven, CT: Yale University Press, 1991.

Ross, M. W. "Societal Relationships and Gender Roles in Homosexuals." *Journal of Sex Research*, vol. 19 (1983), pp. 273–88.

Rothman, Barbara Katz. "How Science Is Redefining Parenthood," *Ms*, August 1982, pp. 154–58.

Routley, R., and V. Routley. "Against the Inevitability of Human Chauvinism." In *Ethics and Problems of the 21st Century*, ed. K. E. Goodpaster and K. M. Sayre, pp. 36–59. Notre Dame, IN: University of Notre Dame Press, 1979.

Russell, Diana. "The Incidence and Prevalence of Intrafamilial and Extrafamilial Sexual Abuse of Female Children." *Child Abuse and Neglect: The International Journal*, vol. 7 (1983), pp. 133–46.

————. *The Secret Trauma*. New York: Basic Books, 1986.

————. *Rape in Marriage*. Bloomington: Indiana University Press, 1990.

————. *Making Violence Sexy*. New York: Teachers College Press, 1993.

Russell, Diana, and Nancy Howell. "The Prevalence of Rape in the United States Revisited." *Signs*, vol. 8 (1983), pp. 688–95.

Ryan, Cheyney. "Self-Defense, Pacifism and the Possibility of Killing." In *The Ethics of War and Nuclear Deterrence*, ed. James P. Sterba, pp. 45–49. Belmont, CA: Wadsworth Publishing Co. 1985.

Sabo, Don. "Sport, Patriarchy and Male Identity." *Arena Review*, vol. 9 (1985), pp. 1–30.

Sagoff, Mark. "Animal Liberation and Environmental Ethics: Bad Marriage, Quick Divorce." *Osgood Hall Law Journal*, vol. 22 (1984), pp. 297–307.

Schneider, Elizabeth. "The Violence of Privacy." *Connecticut Law Review*, vol. 23 (1991), pp. 973–99.

Schwartz, Thomas. "Welfare Judgments and Future Generations." *Theory & Decisions*, vol. 11 (1979), pp. 181–94.

Searle, John. "The Storm over the University." *New York Review of Books*, December 6, 1990.

Seidler, Victor. *Rediscovering Masculinity*. New York: Routledge, 1989.

Sessions, George, and Bill Devall. *Deep Ecology*. Salt Lake City: Gibbs Smith Publisher, 1985.

Shiva, Vandana. *The Violence of the Green Revolution*. London: Zed Books, 1991.

Shue, Henry. *Basic Rights*. Princeton, NJ: Princeton University Press, 1980.

Sidel, Ruth. "Day Care: Do We Really Care?" In *Issues in Feminism*, ed. Sheila Ruth, pp. 336–45. Mountain View, CA: Mayfield Publishing Co., 1990.

Silver, Cheryl. *One Earth, One Future*. Washington, DC: National Academy Press, 1990.

Simon, Robert. "Affirmative Action and Faculty Appointments." In Steven

Cahn, ed., *Affirmative Action and the University*, pp. 93–121. Philadelphia: Temple University Press, 1993.

Singer, Peter. *Animal Liberation*. New York: Avon Books, 1975.

———. *Practical Ethics*. Cambridge: Cambridge University Press, 1979.

———. "The Famine Relief Argument." In *Morality in Practice*, 5th ed., pp. 85–95. (Belmont, CA: Wadsworth Publishing Co., 1996).

Sivard, Ruth. *World Military and Social Expenditures*. Washington, DC: World Priorities, 1993.

Sommers, Christina. "Philosophers against the Family." In *Person to Person*, ed. George Graham and Hugh LaFollette, pp. 82–105. Philadelphia: Temple University Press, 1989.

———. "Do These Feminists Like Women?" *Journal of Social Philosophy*, vol. 21 (1990), pp. 66–74.

———. "Argumentum ad Feminam." *Journal of Social Philosophy*, vol. 22 (1991), pp. 5–19.

———. *Who Stole Feminism?* New York: Simon and Schuster, 1994.

Sorenson, Elaine. *Comparable Worth*. Princeton, NJ: Princeton University Press, 1994.

———. "The Comparable Worth Debate." In *Morality in Practice*, ed. James P. Sterba, 4th ed., pp. 293–99. Belmont, CA: Wadsworth Publishing Co., 1994.

Stace, W. T. *The Concept of Morals*. New York: MacMillan, 1937.

Standing Bear, Luther. *Land of the Spotted Eagle*, p. 45. Boston: Houghton Mifflin, 1933.

Steffen, Lloyd. "In Defense of Dominion." *Environmental Ethics*, vol. 14 (1992), pp. 63–80.

Steinberg, Ronnie. "The Debate on Comparable Worth." *New Politics*, vol. 1 (1986), pp. 108–26.

Steinem, Gloria. "What It Would Be Like If Women Won." *Time*, August 31, 1970, pp. 22–23.

Sterba, James P. "Abortion and the Rights of Distant Peoples and Future Generations." *Journal of Philosophy*, vol. 77 (1980), pp. 424–40.

———. *The Demands of Justice*. Notre Dame, IN: University of Notre Dame Press, 1980.

———. "Is There a Rationale for Punishment?" *American Journal of Jurisprudence*, vol. 29 (1984), pp. 29–43.

———. "Just War Theory and Nuclear Strategy." *Analyse & Kritik*, special issue, vol. 9 (1987), pp. 155–74.

———. *How to Make People Just*. Totowa, NJ: Rowman and Littlefield, 1988.

———. "The Constitution: A Fundamentally Flawed Document," and "A Brief Reply to Three Commentators." In *Philosophical Reflections on the United States Constitution*, ed. Christopher Gray, pp. 134–61, 196–200. Lewiston, NY: Edwin Mellen Press, 1989.

———. "A Rational Choice Theory of Punishment." *Philosophical Topics*, vol. 18 (1990), pp. 171–82.

———. "Response to Nine Commentators." *Journal of Social Philosophy*, vol. 22 (1991), pp. 100–18.

————. "Reconciling Pacifists and Just War Theorists." *Social Theory and Practice*, vol. 18 (1992), pp. 213–18.

————. "Reconciling Conceptions of Justice." In James P. Sterba et al., *Morality and Social Justice*, pp. 1–38. Lanham, MD: Rowman and Littlefield, 1994.

————. *Contemporary Social and Political Philosophy*. Belmont, CA: Wadsworth Publishing Co., 1995.

————. *Social and Political Philosophy: Classical Western Texts in Feminist and Multicultural Perspectives*. 2d ed. Belmont, CA: Wadsworth Publishing Co., 1997.

Steverson, Brian. "On the Reconciliation of Anthropocentric and Nonanthropocentric Environmental Ethics." *Environmental Values*, vol. 5 (1996), pp. 349–61.

Strossen, Nadine. "Regulating Workplace Sexual Harassment and Upholding the First Amendment – Avoiding a Collision." *Villanova Law Review*, vol. 37 (1992), pp. 211–28.

Tannen, Dehorah. *You Just Don't Understand*. New York: Ballantine Books, 1990.

Taylor, Paul. *Respect for Nature*. Princeton, NJ: Princeton University Press, 1987.

Thorne-Finch, Ron. *Ending the Silence: The Origins and Treatment of Male Violence against Women*. Toronto: University of Toronto Press, 1992.

Thorton, Brenda Sue. "The New International Jurisprudence on the Right to Privacy: A Head-on Collision with Bowers v. Hardwick." *Albany Law Review*, vol. 58 (1995), pp. 725–74.

Trebilcot, Joyce. "Two Forms of Androgynism." In *Feminism and Philosophy*, ed. Mary Vetterling-Braggin, Frederick Ellison, and Jane English, pp. 70–78. Totowa, NJ: Rowman and Littlefield, 1977.

————, ed. *Mothering*. Totowa, NJ: Rowman and Littlefield, 1983.

Voeleker, John Augustus. *Report on the Improvement of Indian Agriculture*. London: Eyre and Spothswoode, 1893.

Warren, Karen. "The Power and Promise of EcoFeminism." *Environmental Ethics*, vol. 12 (1990), pp. 121–46.

Warren, Mary Ann. "Is Androgyny the Answer to Sexual Stereotyping?" In *"Femininity," "Masculinity," and "Androgyny,"* ed. Mary Vetterling-Braggin, pp. 170–86. Totowa, NJ: Rowman and Littlefield, 1982.

————. "The Rights of the Nonhuman World." In *Environmental Philosophy*, ed. Robert Elliot and Arran Gare, pp. 109–34. University Park: Pennsylvania State University Press, 1983.

Webb, Susan. *Step Forward*. New York: Master Media, 1991.

Weitzman, Lenore. *The Divorce Revolution: The Unexpected Social and Economic Consequences for Women and Children in America*. New York: Free Press, 1985.

Wenker, Kenneth H. "Just War Pacifism." *Proceedings of the American Catholic Philosophical Association*, vol. 57 (1983), pp. 135–41.

West, D. J. *Homosexuality*. Chicago: Aldine, 1967.

White, Lynn. "The Historical Roots of our Ecological Crisis." *Science*, vol. 155 (1967), pp. 1203–7.

Bibliography

Willborn, Steven. *A Comparable Worth Primer*. Lexington, MA: Lexington Books, 1986.

Willenson, Kim. *The Bad War*. New York: New American Library, 1987.

Williams, Robert, and Lorence Kessler. *A Closer Look at Comparable Worth*. Washington, DC: National Foundation for the Study of Equal Employment Policy, 1984.

Wolff, Michael. *Where We Stand*. New York: Bantam Books, 1992.

Wolgast, Elizabeth. *Equality and the Rights of Women*. Ithaca, NY: Cornell University Press, 1980.

Women's Action Coalition. *WAC Stats: The Facts about Women*. New York: The New Press, 1993.

Young, Bert. "Masculinity and Violence." Paper presented at the Second World Congress on Violence and Human Coexistence, Montreal, July 12–17, 1992.

Young, Iris. "Humanism, Gynocentrism and Feminist Politics. *Women's Studies International Forum*, vol. 8 (1985), pp. 173–83.

Zimmerman, Michael, et al., eds. *Environmental Philosophy*. Englewood Cliffs, NJ: Prentice-Hall, 1993.

Index

Index